Richard Pococke's Irish Tours

Portrait of Richard Pococke

Richard Pococke's
Irish Tours

edited by
John McVeagh

IRISH ACADEMIC PRESS

This book was typeset
in 10.5 on 12 Times New Roman for
IRISH ACADEMIC PRESS
Kill Lane, Blackrock, Co. Dublin
and in North America for
IRISH ACADEMIC PRESS
c/o ISBS, 5804 NE Hassalo St, Portland, OR 97213

A catalogue record for this book
is available from the British Library.

ISBN 0-7165-2539-9

Printed in Great Britain by
Cambridge University Press, Cambridge

Preface

For permission to reproduce illustrative material I am indebted to the National Library of Ireland and the Library of Trinity College, Dublin.

In preparing this book I received valuable help on detailed points from Seamus MacMathúna, John Roberts, Dave Wilcock, Kieran McDaid, and Alan Peacock, and from Kathleen Ferguson throughout.

I am grateful to the University of Ulster for releasing me from one term's teaching duties to enable me to concentrate on this edition in its early stages.

The Esme Mitchell Trust, Belfast and the University of Ulster have granted financial aid to offset some of the publication costs of this edition. I am grateful to both sponsors and record my thanks for their generosity.

Contents

Maps

List of Illustrations

Introduction

Richard Pococke was born in 1704 into a minor but well established Church of England family in the county of Hampshire. His paternal grandfather was rector of Colmer from 1660 to 1719 and his maternal grandfather, Isaac Milles, rector of Highclere. His father was headmaster of All Saints' Grammar School and also curate of All Saints' Church in Southampton. Dr Thomas Milles, his uncle, held the grander post of bishop of Waterford and Lismore in Ireland. Given this background it was natural, perhaps, that Pococke himself should eventually enter the clerical profession.

Since his father died when Pococke was young, he and his mother spent ten years living with his maternal grandfather Isaac Milles, the rector of All Saints. This grandfather also kept a school, at which the young Pococke received his early education. When Isaac Milles himself died in 1720 mother and son moved house once again, this time to Newtown near Newbury. Two years later in 1722 Pococke entered Corpus Christi College, Oxford, as an exhibitioner. He attained his first degree in 1725, and received further degrees in 1731 and 1733.

Both early and late in adult life, as in childhood, Pococke felt the benefits of being surrounded by influential relations and friends. Michael Quane remarks that he was little more than twenty years old when his uncle Thomas Milles, then bishop of Waterford, offered him the precentorship of Lismore in Ireland.[1] It was the first of a number of Irish ecclesiastical appointments which placed Pococke in the prosperous, unharassed worldly condition in which he was able to indulge his passion for scientific and antiquarian travel. His subsequent advancement in the church hierarchy was unspectacular but steady. When he was thirty he became vicar general of Waterford and Lismore, and subsequently proctor for the local chapter to Convocation. Ten years later in 1744, he was made precentor of Waterford. In 1745 he dedicated to the earl of Chesterfield, then lord lieutenant of Ireland, the second volume of his eastern travels, and as a reward was made archdeacon of Dublin. The duke of Devonshire, Chesterfield's successor, also liked Pococke, and made him bishop of Ossory in 1756. Nine years later came further promotion to the bishopric of Elphin. Finally, and in the last year of his life, Pococke was offered and accepted the bishopric of Meath, but enjoyed it for only a few months. He died on 15 September 1765 and is buried at Ardbraccan near Navan.[2]

Richard Pococke was a man obsessed with travel. No less compulsive was his habit of writing every journey down. As already indicated, he published between 1743 and 1745 a substantial record (whose erudition Gibbon praised[3]) of his travels in Egypt and the Middle East; this book was translated later in the eighteenth century into German, French, and Dutch.[4] The journals of his Scottish travels, which were considerable, were published by Daniel William Kemp in

Pococke School, County Kilkenny

1887, and the journals of his various tours through England by J.J. Cartwright in the following year, 1888; both form substantial volumes. So it was, slightly later in his life, with Ireland. As the journals contained in the present volume show, once established in his profession he used his means and his friends, and the friends of friends, to penetrate into all parts of the country of Ireland in a series of explorations rather than tours whose findings he documented fully and carefully as he went along.

But actually Irish travel was a late feature in Pococke's life. As has been suggested, before concentrating on the country of his adopted residence he had travelled through both the wilder and the more familiar parts of Europe as well as the almost unvisited Middle East and had also undertaken extensive journeys through England and Scotland. For example, no sooner had he received his Oxford doctorate in 1733 than he and his cousin, Jeremiah Milles, undertook a three-year journey through France, Switzerland, Italy, Belgium, Holland, Hanover, Prussia, Austria and Greece. In one sense this journey might be seen as the normal grand tour of the day, according to the theory of which young men of leisure and means completed their university education by observing at first hand the politics, art and manners of the leading countries of Europe. But in fact Pococke's tour was by no means conventional. Hanover and Prussia were not on the usual route of young Englishmen at that time. Greece too only became a common destination for English tourists later in the century. In Pococke's time

Stuart and Revett, the influential popularisers of Greek art, were only beginning their rediscoveries of ancient culture. Their work initiated the change in outlook which helped Greece to displace Italy during the Romantic period as the imaginative centre of Europe. Pococke and Milles visited Greece before this change took place. Their interest in the region was in advance of its time.[5]

Returning to Ireland in 1736, Pococke instantly set off travelling again, this time leaving Dublin, where he was now based, for Holyhead and Oxford, and then proceeding on a tour of Old Sarum, Salisbury, Andover, and Stonehenge.[6] While doing this he was preparing a bolder enterprise which again underscores his adventurous spirit; a trip to the near East which would include an expedition to Egypt and a river journey up the Nile. This expedition took Pococke five years to complete. He sailed for Alexandria in 1737 and returned to England in 1742; and once returned, he sat down to work up his notes into that scholarly, two-volume travel book which has been already mentioned, and which come out in separate volumes in 1743 and 1745. Again, the thing to note about this travel is Pococke's disregard of accepted itineraries and accepted limits, of which a good example occurred—never mind the Nile journey—when he was halfway back from Egypt to England. Arriving at the Savoy Alps, he and his companions in defiance of their guides fought their way into the Vale of Chamounix, and marked their arrival on the glacier by toasting Admiral Vernon and success to British arms.[7] All then returned to their guides, who had given them up for lost. The matter-of-fact audacity of this gesture seems typical of Richard Pococke the individual as well as a typically Augustan flourish. In Pococke's time the Savoy Alps were a virtually unknown region, not the fashionable (and safe) tourist centre they had become seventy years later, when Shelley and Byron were celebrating their wonders in poetry.

These eastern and European travels formed the base experience for Pococke's later journeys around Ireland. Summarizing some contemporary reactions to Pococke's scientific writing, Kemp comments on the traveller's habit of illuminating his descriptions of the British Isles with his knowledge of Mediterranean and Middle Eastern geography. It is indeed a feature. Cape Wrath reminds Pococke of the statues of Memnon, Ben Vheir of Mount Tabor, Dingwall and a nearby hill of Jerusalem and Calvary.[8]

In 1745 Pococke began planning a month's tour of Scotland, corresponding in advance, says Kemp, with the archaeologist Stukeley, and making the journey in the autumn of 1747. He visited Penrith, Carlisle, Berwick, Edinburgh, Stirling and Glasgow and then returned to Ireland via Portpatrick, probably deterred from penetrating the more northern parts of Scotland at that time by the late season and by the aftermath of the 1745 rebellion. In 1746 there followed another short tour of the Scottish border country and of northern England, but it was not till another fifteen years had passed that Pococke managed to undertake a tour of the whole of Scotland. Meanwhile, in 1752 he published with Dean Milles his *Inscriptionum Antiquarum Graec. et Latin liber. Accidit numismatum . . . in*

Aegypto cusorum . . . catalogus, initiating a scholarly correspondence which he kept up for years concerning the antiquities of different regions. The interest in Scotland was resumed in 1760, when Pococke began a six-months' tour with a second visit to the border country and, then pressed on into the unvisited north. He first went to Glasgow, then up Scotland's western side past Loch Lomond and Inverary, I-Colm-Kill and Lochaber, and followed General Wade's road to Loch Ness, Culloden and Easter Ross and on to the very far north: Sutherland, Cape Wrath, Thurso and the Orkneys. Returning, he chose the eastern route and visited Elgin, Aberdeen, Dundee, Dunkeld, Blair in Athole, Perth, St Andrews, Dunfermline, Dunblane, Stirling, Edinburgh and Dunbar. He left Scotland and made for London, where he spent some time.

In 1764 Pococke undertook a lengthy tour through England; two volumes of manuscripts are filled with his account of it. In July 1765, promoted to the bishopric of Meath, he spent some weeks improving the grounds round his palace prior to his death on 15 September.

Pococke's Irish travel was, in its terms, equally adventurous. The few parts of the country which he did not reach or describe make up the central plain between Enniskillen, Athlone, Nenagh and Armagh which is, ironically, Ireland's most accessible region. In October 1747, when he arrived in Donaghadee, County Down, after a Scottish tour, he paid a quick visit to the Giant's Causeway. The journal of this trip, hitherto unnoticed among Pococke's Scottish writings, is reprinted here; and something more can be recaptured of his response to the Causeway from the descriptive notes he sent to the editor of the Royal Society's *Philosophical Transactions*, who published them in 1748 and 1753. These notes too are reprinted in the present edition. (See below, pp. 197–205). In 1749 Pococke travelled through parts of Connaught and Munster, and although no record of this journey seems to survive we know from later hints that Gort and Killmallock formed part of the itinerary, as did Kilfinane and Charleville.[9] In 1752 Pococke undertook his most extensive Irish tour, a circuit of the Irish coastline. He set off in an anti-clockwise direction from Dublin, going first northwards to Belfast, then west and south to Donegal, Galway and Limerick, eastwards to Cork and Wexford and at last northwards again to Dublin, where he arrived after four months of continuous travel. From this circuit of Ireland, Pococke omitted only the south-western parts of the country beyond Adare, County Limerick, at which point he turned eastwards to Cork, no doubt because of the late season. Included though were some brief inland journeys—explorations might be a better term—through Inishowen and other parts of Donegal, and also around Cork and Wexford. In 1753 Pococke toured the Dublin area in a number of short journeys; among the places visited were Ballinglass, Athy, Stradbally, Timohoe, Durrow, Roscree, Thurles, Tara, Trim and Navan. In 1758 he travelled through the south-western areas which had been left out in 1752, this time starting from his home town of Kilkenny and travelling to Cork, Bantry, Dingle, Tralee, Killarney, Mallow and back to Kilkenny. In 1760, setting out on a tour through northern England and Scotland, he recorded his route from Dublin to Donaghadee.

Of Pococke's written record of these tours, as has been said, only parts remain. Apparently nothing has come down to us of the journal he probably kept during 1749; if it existed, it has vanished from sight. For the general reader, even the published accounts are now anything but readily accessible. Pococke's 1752 journal and his 1753 letters (which break off in mid-sentence) were edited by George Stokes in 1891; they have long been out of print. Padráig Ó Maidín in 1958–60 edited Pococke's journal of his 1758 tour of Cork and Kerry, and in 1985 C.J. Woods edited his brief journal of a 1760 journey from Dublin to Donaghadee. Both editors chose to reproduce Pococke's text in the pages of learned journals not easily available outside the research library. The appearance of the present volume means that for the first time all that is known to survive of Pococke's descriptions of mid-eighteenth-century Ireland is now available to the general reader.

Pococke travelled in a compact and well organized little party. D.W. Kemp notes that two servants, a valet and a groom, formed his regular companions; and he quotes a slightly comical picture of Pococke drawn by a chance traveller who encountered him journeying through Scotland. Pococke, he writes, was on his own in the lead, sitting astride a horse, with his companions following with the baggage at a respectful distance. One sees too from the odd remark Pococke makes in his journal that he carried along a number of topographical reference books, and he seems to have regularly stopped to compare the Ireland they described with the real country he observed around him. More than once he corrects misrepresentations in the maps and topographical literature. Petty, for example, and other mapmakers had failed, he finds, unsurprisingly, to show the true conformation of the coastline in north-western Donegal,[10] with its large bays and strands. Muckish Abbey, he commented in another place, which existed in the maps, he could not find in reality.[11] Achill Island was misrepresented as split in two by a creek of the sea; the supposed creek, he found, was only a deep inlet.[12] Charles Smith's speculations about Abbey Stowrey or Abbeystrewry in County Cork, he dismisses as inaccurate.[13] From these and other incidental comments, we may infer that William Petty's map of Ireland was one of the reference books Pococke carried with him; others may have included Smith and Harris on County Down, and Smith on County Cork.[14]

One thing that makes Pococke interesting on Ireland is the attention he pays to unusual places—not the city of Dublin, whose presence can weigh down the journals of some eighteenth-century English visitors, but such provincial centres as Kilkenny and Belfast, the remoter parts of Donegal, the Mullet and the Dingle peninsula, and the offshore Islands Achill, Valentia and Cape Clear. This Ireland of the regions with its prehistoric remains and its bloodily mauled historical relics, its still strange ways of life, its beautiful or bare landscapes continually impressing themselves upon the traveller's gaze, finds in Pococke a detailed observer keen to look, enquire, describe, and record. Secondly, he nurtured an interest in many subjects. Archaeology, geology and botany interested him, so that many a time he pauses to note the rock formations of the area he is travelling through, or analyse its soil, or summarise the life forms it supports. Ecclesiastical and architectural history formed another of his specialities. And on the economic side he particularly noted in his travels from region to region the extractive industries, if they existed, like mining and fishing, and examined the development of agricultural techniques and the planting of new towns, new roads, and new manufactures. Because they reveal so persistently curious a mind, Pococke's travel journals, though unrevised and unpolished, thus offer us a richer account of mid-century Ireland than we might find, for example, in Wesley's voluminous Irish journals, in spite of the latter's twenty-one separate tours. Furthermore Pococke ranged beyond the Ireland of Arthur Young, his more famous successor. And since Wesley, Pococke and Young travelled more extensively through Ireland than any other English man or woman of the age, one could claim that in Pococke's Irish writings we may discover a rarer documentation of the country at mid-century then in any other first-hand source. Although no one would claim that Pococke was free from the cultural preconceptions of his class or age, a striking feature of his writing is its interest in the manifestations of Ireland's religious and cultural life coupled with the avoidance of any racial judgement. And it may be that to recognise the significance of this feature, as well as of his contribution to the topography of Ireland, and to the delineation of Ireland by English writers, we should go back a little in time, and ask the questions: What tradition did Pococke inherit as a topographical writer? What character is given to Ireland by earlier English visitors?

Most English contact with Ireland before Pococke's century had been undertaken for military reasons and was directed towards a colonial objective. The Elizabethan campaigns, the plantations under James 1, the Cromwellian reconquest followed by confiscations, the further expropriations after King William's war all sprang (on the English side) from a mixture of the pragmatic urgencies of the moment with a generalized fear of the danger posed to England by an independent Catholic Ireland left to its own devices on the western flank. English attitudes, that is to say, sprang from a fundamental hostility. The topographical literature this relationship produced is very often, therefore, highly partisan, though sometimes sufficiently complex and contrary to achieve a rich irony. Perhaps the main theme of seventeenth-century writing about life in Ireland produced by English visitors had been, unsurprisingly, its chaotically dangerous nature. We may see examples of this from both sides in the conflict in the autobiographies of the Jacobite Anne Fanshawe and of the Quaker William Edmundson. Fanshawe is vivid on the horrors of plague-ridden Galway during the 1650s.[15] Edmundson describes being mugged and tortured by rapparees or dispossessed Irish-guerilla fighters of the Williamite period.[16] These convey something of the disturbance of individual life; a military slant is offered by the journal of John Stevens, who fought on the losing side of the battle of the Boyne and helped in the unavailing defence of Limerick.[17] Like the Ulster news broadcasts of recent history, such representations highlighted for their English readers, sitting safe at home, an exaggerated sense of the barbarity of Irish

William Petty, Map of Ireland, 1683

life. They proved, it must have seemed, how Ireland's endemic violence menaced all the structures of civilized life. Thus seventeenth-century England perceived Ireland as a land of 'troubles'. (It is interesting that Pococke in 1752, looking backwards, uses the word in its modern sense.)[18] The idea drew conviction from the authority of earlier pronouncements. English suggestions, going back through Sir John Davies in 1612[19] and Spenser in 1596[20] to the twelfth-century Giraldus,[21] had often stressed that the Irish character was innately uncivil. Such was the predominant view of Ireland among English writers up to the time of Pococke, and it continued to hold currency after his time. For example, it reappears in the writings of Wesley,[22] Wordsworth,[23] Carlyle,[24] and others.[25] Pococke's Irish descriptions are interesting in that they lack any overt sign of this contempt, partly because he is more interested in describing than in passing judgement.

A parallel theme was the praise of physical Ireland—its beauty, its fertility, its economic potential. This too had been a traditional topic since Giraldus, but it was given extra emphasis by seventeenth-century writers when plantation and colonization were on the increase and it was the writer's purpose, in setting pen to paper in the first place, to persuade his reader to invest effort, life and money in making the Irish colonization work. Examples are Laurence,[26] Gookin[27] and Petty.[28] In fact, the two themes—admirable land, unadmirable people—are not so much parallel topics which never meet as elements of a single attitude, opposite sides of the same coin. Both arise from the perception of Ireland as a desirable country waiting (in the language of the time) to be improved, but strangely neglected by the Irish themselves, who for that reason could be judged unworthy to be its true owners. Hence the English tendency to write up the land of Ireland goes along with their tendency to write down the inhabitants of Ireland as an uncivilized people; a tendency, however, sometimes challenged by the colonizers themselves. For example, William Petty, who mapped Ireland after Cromwell in order to systematize the Anglo-Scottish take-over, and powerfully advocated the policy of planting English families in Ireland, also advised planting Irish families in England, and disputed the truth of the racial stereotype.[29] Nor should one assume that, even in the seventeenth century, only motives of war and dispossession brought the English to Ireland, or spurred them on to write down their impressions on paper. War-torn Ireland still attracted the attention of private individuals like Thomas Dineley or John Dunton, the eccentric London bookseller, who visited town and country in Ireland for antiquarian or business reasons, or out of curiosity. Dineley's journal contains valuable details about some Irish provincial centres.[30] Dunton, as the century closed, wrote a curious account, both highly derivative and highly original in different ways, of a way of life in western Connaught which had existed for centuries but was shortly to disappear for good.[31]

By the 1740s, when Pococke began to travel, Ireland had been subdued and planted, and was outwardly at peace—finally, as it must have seemed. Over half a century earlier, at Aughrim, the last battle had been fought on Irish soil.[32] Even before that date, and possibly no less significant than the battle itself, one of the first Irish country houses not to be fortified, Beaulieu in County Louth, had been built by Sir William Tichborne.[33] Although, once or twice, Pococke notes what would now be called no-go areas in western Kerry,[34] his emphasis falls less upon the danger of Irish roads or the need to spread English dominion further into the Irish countryside than upon the unimproved nature of much of the country itself. For if Pococke is silent on the shortcomings of the Irish race, he is, by contrast, emphatic about the desirability of realising Ireland's economic potential. A motive behind his journeys, indeed, was to note the variety of livelihoods in the country. His writings reflect a sense of satisfaction at Ireland secured. He accepted the rightness of the establishment of English Protestantism in Catholic Ireland, and wherever he could promote it, he did so. He subscribed to the 'Incorporated Society' set up in Dublin to establish English Protestant 'Working Schools' throughout Ireland.[35] When appointed bishop of Ossory in March 1756 he restored the cathedral church of St Canice in Kilkenny—much damaged by Cromwell and never properly repaired in a hundred years, He encouraged the rebuilding of several other churches in his diocese.[36] Side by side with this commitment, in Pococke's writings, to the established power of church and state goes a keen interest in the other realities of Irish life: the religious culture of certain centres of pilgrimage, the meaning of Irish place names and Irish speech, and so on. Yet he seems unperturbed by the evidence which he also notes—for instance, alcoholism—of the demoralization which dispossession and impoverishment had brought upon many of the Irish people; and although, as a writer, Pococke always remains conscious of another Ireland surviving as best it could beside Anglo-Ireland, his most continuous reminder, the more telling for being unasserted, is of the strength and confidence of the new ruling class in which he himself occupied a prominent place. The reader of his travels is led round a chain of mansions, castles and palaces surrounded by extensive walled estates and linked by new-built roads, their firm ownership of the country underpinned by the presence of frequent barracks dotted around the towns and villages of Ireland. To read Pococke is to encounter this power structure at a time when to those inside it and outside it alike it must have appeared unbreakable.

Thus although Pococke may offer his descriptions as an objective record of the condition of Ireland at mid-century they are, of course, highly subjective accounts. As a favoured son of the English clerical caste which ruled Irish life after the Williamite wars, he reflects the ideology of domination. But he also found Ireland deeply interesting for other reasons, and in a number of different ways. Along with his appreciation of English power goes the occasional glimpse, not lacking in sympathy, of the old religion and the old proprietors. Scientifically, he details the geology, archaeology and animal and vegetable life of Ireland, both of the landscape and of the coastal regions. Aesthetically, as we may see from his comments on Killarney, Donegal, parts of Kerry and elsewhere, Pococke can be alert to changes in imaginative perception. The anthropological, the economic, the aesthetic and the imperialist sentiments merge in his single response, whose attractiveness may be said to be in its curiosity untinged by any overt moralistic judgement. (Compare Wesley.) Thus Pococke enthuses over the attractions of wild landscape, praises new cultivation, records the benefits of experimental manufactures, applauds new schools built and endowed to make Protestant adults out of Catholic children, approves the infant tourism of the lakeland regions of Killarney and Fermanagh. He notices Irish people attending mass on a Donegal hillside, or shifting from winter to summer quarters, or running brandy and rum off the coast of Cork, or sharing drams in an eggshell in a cabin on the road. He also observes the ancient places of pilgrimage, noting something of their lore and culture, such as St Patrick's Well near Downpatrick, St Terence Marialia's shrine at Malin Head, St Patrick's Purgatory in Lough Derg, St Declan's devotions at Ardmore,[37] and others.

Their variety of subject matter plus the adventurous itineraries he followed help to make Pococke's Irish tours, for their time, especially interesting. It is hard to find in the writings of any other early eighteenth-century English visitor to Ireland the energetic and intelligent curiosity which fired him. Addison, by comparison, is uninterested in Ireland[38] Luckombe and Twiss are less adventurous.[39] Wesley journeyed through many Irish towns and a great deal of the Irish countryside, but his other-worldly priorities prevented him from taking much pleasure in the country's fine sights, like the glen of the Dargle which he visited in 1765; he himself notes this fact.[40] Only from the second half of the century onwards do English observers such as Young begin to pay close attention to the geography, agriculture, sociology or economy of Ireland.[41] Such interest rose sharply, it is true, as the eighteenth century yielded place to the nineteenth. From the 1770s onwards, Taylor and Skinner's maps, the tourists' handbooks and directories to which they gave rise,[42] the statistical surveys which multiplied after 1800 all show how system and method were beginning to make their way into the representation of Ireland. Pococke's last journey through Ireland took place in 1760, but he was already anticipating this scientific spirit.

Pococke does not try to be a stylish writer. Even if we disregard the problems of an unrevised text—the omissions, solecisms and awkward expressions—his prose achieves, at best, a concise, unemotional clarity. This, it is true, does constitute a style, and one which suits a document intended as a record and description rather than as an exhibition of literary skill. Perhaps we should connect Pococke's Augustan plainness or scientific simplicity with the referential language preferred before literary art by Thomas Sprat, historian of the Royal Society, nearly a century earlier.[43] Pococke was an active member of the Royal Society of his day. Among its other values, he shared, no doubt, its preference for a restrained, laconic language concentrating on the unadorned representation of facts and free of any surrender to deep feeling.

Taylor and Skinner, Map of Ireland, 1783

Note on the Text

Pococke's Irish tours do not survive in his own manuscript version but in fair copies written out by an amanuensis and corrected in come places, but not in others, as if for a publication which never materialized. The corrections may be Pococke's own. The copies have become dispersed. Those of the 1752 tour (circuit of Ireland) and of the 1753 tour (Dublin and some eastern counties), both forming part of the same bundle, are held in Trinity College Library, Dublin. The copy of the 1758 tour of Cork and Kerry is held in the Bodleian Library, Oxford, The copy of Pococke's very brief record of his 1760 journey from Dublin to Donaghadee (when on his way to Scotland) is held in the British Library, On the whole these copies are readable enough, but there are occasional problems: repetitions and gaps occur, and dates get confused—for example, in September 1752, when the old style calendar gave way to the new. It seems that the copyists had trouble with some of the Irish names, which appear in a variety of forms. The copy also includes abbreviations and different spellings of the same word. These anomalies, no doubt, were intended to be regularized when the manuscripts saw print; but they remain uncorrected in the archives. These irregularities mean that the editor has to decide whether to correct, modernize and regularize Pococke's text, or print it as he wrote it.

The present edition reproduces Pococke's orthography as closely as possible. Unlike Stokes, Ó Maidín and Woods, Pococke's previous editors, who all chose to modernize his text to a greater or lesser degree, I have preferred to publish it exactly as it stands in the manuscript. Names, titles and spellings are not modernized but appear in the present edition in their eighteenth-century form: rivlet, litle, tyde, north ward, begining, Dun luce, Arch bishop, under ground, Bally Castle, Fair head, Cause way, Donnegall, Letter kenny, Beer haven, Kilarney, Shanon, Mitchels town, Tiperary, and so on. Or a name may appear in a variety of forms—Bally Castle, Baley Castle, Baleycastle—just as Pococke wrote it. Out of the same preference for authenticity, I have also chosen to reproduce examples of doubtful grammar and unrevised punctuation, and to keep the initial capitalization which was such a characteristic feature in eight-eenth-century writing, By minimising editorial interference between reader and text, I hope that the present edition will allow Pococke's idiosyncratic expression to register on a modern reader, and thus convey something of the immediacy of his impressions of Ireland in the 1750s. Ironing out creases in the text not only removes this flavour but may also remove meaning: examples can be found in the notes. Where a substantial difference arises between my reading and that of an earlier editor, I have noted the difference at the foot of the page. Some of these, I have judged, are cases of misreading. In others, when the manuscript is not quite clear, the reader may choose between interpretations.

Tour the first: to the Giant's Causeway, 1747

Returning from Scotland in October 1747, Pococke landed at Donaghadee, and then detoured to Antrim, Coleraine and the Giant's Causeway. He returned to Dublin by way of Armagh, Newry, Dundalk and Drogheda, arriving home on 4 November.

Pococke's account of his Ulster journey of 1747 is printed here for the first time. The text is taken from the manuscript copy of Pococke's journal of his 1747 Scottish tour, held in the British Library (Add. Mss 23,001). The Scottish descriptions (omitted here) may be read in Tours in Scotland, 1747, 1750, 1760, *by* Richard Pococke, *ed., by Daniel William Kemp (Edinburgh: Publications of the Scottish History Society. Vol. I, 1887).*

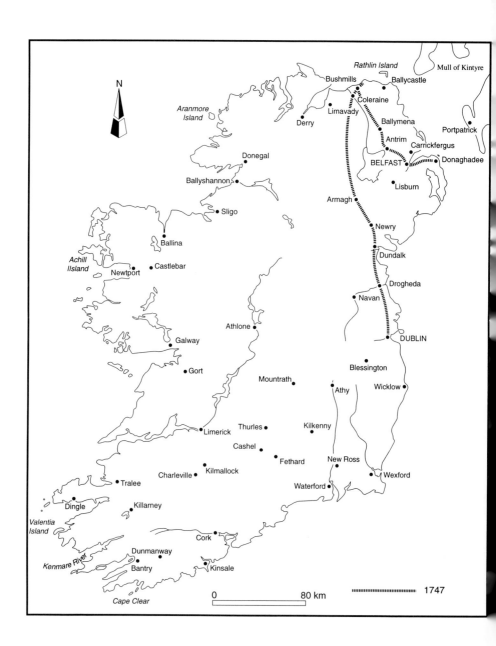

Map of the 1747 tour

23ᵈ Rid to Air, dined, sold my 3 guinea horse for one guinea, he had performed well. I baited at Garvey, lay at Balinfrey.

24. Rid to Lord Stairs improvements, at Castle Kennedy—went by the rout to Port Patrick.

25. sent my things aboard, but being windy would not go, they had a terrible wet passage. Mr. Hamilton Collector of [   ] who was going over & the Controller Spent the Even with me.

26. We sailed in 5 hours to Donaghadee, a fine passage but I was very sick—they go in open Hoys, which have no deck. I took over my excellent mare. Mr Nevin the Minister came & took me to his house.

27. I went with Mr Hamilton to Belfast; Mr. Saurin an acquaintance the minister dined with me. I lay at Temple Patrick.

28. Went through Antrim, dined at Ma ho hill, lay at Ballimona.¹

29. Rid to Bush mills—went to Mr Clenes a clergyman dined with [?] & he went with me to see that most Stupendous work of nature, the Giants Causeway—I lay at Colerain.

30. I went through Carvock. Mr. St. Paul a young man of very good Character Son of your disciple spent the even here, his father had this Living, & he is Curate.

31st. Breakfasted with Mr. St. Paul & mother, she is in the widows house at Armagh. I rid eight miles to Lord Orery's, rid out with my Lord in his Coach & six to see a Building. dined;—Spent the Even in discourse, drinking tea & Cards.

Novr. 1st. I preached, first calling on Archdeacon Congreve;—went with Lord & Lady Orrery in their Coach & 6—to see the Site of an house they intend to build. dined—&c:

2. Lord & Lady Orrery & Lord Boyle, the eldest Son a fine youth & Lady Betty —went in their Coach & 6—8 miles to Ardmagh. we Saw the Cathedral, & Dean D'relincourt's monument by Rysbrach. We went 3 miles to Sr Capel Molineaux's pretty house & improvements;2—where we dined on the cold meat we brought. I took leave & rid fourteen miles to Newry.

3. I rid thorough Dundalk; dined at Dunleer, rid through Drogheda, lay at the man of War.

4. My Coach met me, & Dr. Thomas in it at Drumcondra, I came to Dublin;—called at the Bishop of Waterfords door—on Mr Fletcher, Mrs Hyde, at Mr Colemans & Mrs Travers door. Visited Mr Bristow;—Came home Dr Barber came to see me, He & Dr Thomas dined with me. I went out incog. to a gallery to see the new Ball room & company. The Lord Mayor Sr George Riblon came to see me,—the Alderman Knighted by the Ld. Lieutenant.

5. I visited the Archbishop of Dublin, the Primate; the Speaker & Mrs Chinevix,—went to Christ church where the Bishop of Fernes preach'd before the House of Lords. I dined with the Lord Mayor a Grand Entertainment:— visited Mrs Reynell:

Pray my very kind Love to my Sister
I am Dear Madam
Your Most dutiful son
Richard Pococke

Tour the second: Circuit of Ireland, 1752

Beginning in late June, 1762, Pococke spent four months in travel. He journeyed northwards from Dublin to Belfast and Ballycastle, where he spent time examining the Giant's Causeway. From there he proceeded to Derry, toured round the Inishowen peninsula, made his way to the western edge of County Donegal and then followed the coast to Donegal, Ballyshannon and Sligo. He journeyed to and fro across the Mullet before travelling on to Galway and Limerick. From Limerick and Adair he turned south and west, and briefly inland again, to Cork and Kilkenny, Waterford and Wexford, then went northwards up Ireland's eastern coast to Dublin. He arrived in the capital city in the middle of October.

The source text is the manuscript copy of Pococke's journal in Trinity College Library, Dublin entitled 'Dr. Pococke's Irish Tour 1752' (MS 887). I have counterchecked this manuscript copy with George Stokes's 1891 edition, and list in the notes all textually significant departures made by Stokes from the original. I have not noted his changes in spelling, capitalization, and punctuation.

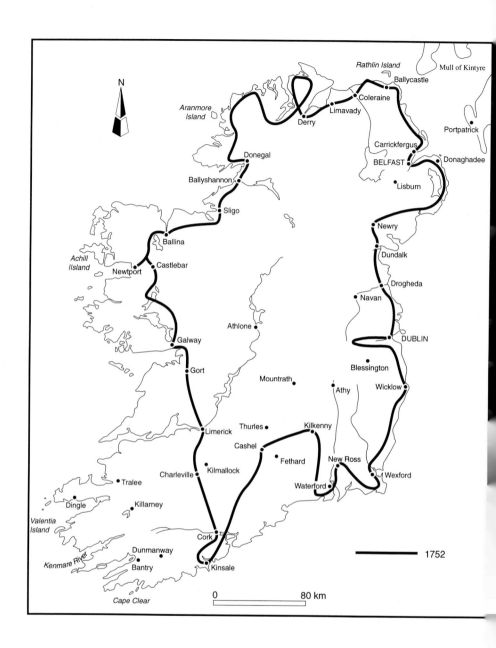

Map of the 1752 tour

Monday June 22^d 1752.   I went to Swords, dined there with the Chapter of Christ Church;—Set out at five northwards, found the country extremely pleasant. At Gormanstown I crossed a rivlet from the County of Dublin into the County of Meath. Near this is Lord Gormanstown's seat,[1] a Roman Catholic married to Lord Tremlestown's sister;—I went on & came to a fine deep rivlet, called the Nany water, which passes by Duleck, on the south side of an eminence towards the sea is [   ] the seat of Mr. Pepper,[2] a charming situation with the fields well laid out round about it, & on each side of the river are beautiful meadows on the rising ground, as well as in the narrow vale; we cross'd this water at Da[   ][3] town & come to Drogheda which is finely situated on two eminencies on each side of the river Boyne & about three miles from the mouth of it: A mile below it is Beaulieu,[4] a place much noted for its beautiful situation, & was the country seat of General Bowles. There are many ruined Churches & Abbies at Drogheda, & they have lately built a beautiful Church with Gothick windows in the body of it, & a handsom Palladian front of Ardbraccan Stone.[5]

Tuesday 23^d.   I set out Northward: When I cross'd the Boyne to Drogheda I came into the County of Louth, which is a good Country of Arable & pasture, but does not abound in trees. Drogheda is near twenty three miles from Dublin. A litle beyond the 24th stone I came to a stream at a place called Kaneagh in Sr. Wm. Petty's map[6] Killineer & soon came up to a small hill called Cullestan, & a litle beyond the 24th stone passed the road which leads to Aherdee; on the top of the hill to the left, I saw a Church called Bemister Boyn[7] with a round tower near it, & I observed on the sea about 3 miles to the north of the Boyn, Tutochen & the high mountains of Slewgullin towards Newry: on the other side of the hill we come to a Stream at Clogh vaddagh or Long Stones, to the right of which is the Church of Mullarah; at the 28th stone we passed by the Castle of A—lair,[8] & a litle further by a river of the same name & soon arrived at Dunleer situated on a rivlet which according to Sr. Wm Petty falls into the river that rises out of Atherdee bog; going on we saw Drumcorlagh on the river to the right, beyond it Dillings Town Lord Antrims a fine Situation which came to the family of his wife a Pluckenet.[9] We went half a mile to Cappogh bridge over the river which runs by Atherdee; & half a mile further to Green Mount a small village at the foot of a mount on the brow of a rising ground fortified with a fossee, & there is a heigth in it at the north west corner, the whole of irregular figure is about 50 paces each way. We came in a mile to Castle Bellingham formerly called Grenan's tower or Garlands town, where Mr, Bellingham has a very good house which he does not inhabit, the river, Hanging ground, & wood between it & the sea is very fine: before I came to this place I saw a ruined Church to the west where I observed a monument to the honour of John Stanler[10] of the holy Order of St. Dominick; erected by John Stanley Apothecary in Drogheda to the memory of this person & some other relations. From Castle Bellingham we soon came to Lurgan Green well inhabited for a mile by weavers & labourers, who live very much on the Cockles, which they get out of the Strand. Three miles further we came to Dundalk, situated towards the mouth of a river on Dundalk bay. This is a Town chiefly consisting of one Street about half a mile long, it was in the time of Edward 2^d a royality & the last where a monarch of all Ireland was crowned and resided, & did chiefly consist of Castles, some traces of which they say are still to be seen. Lord Limerick lives here, & has made some fine plantations & walks behind a very bad house which is in the Street of the town: as walks with Elm hedges on each side, an artificial Serpentine river, a Chinese bridge, a thatch'd open house supported by the bodies of fir trees &c. & a fine Kitchen garden with Closets for fruit.

At the entrance of the town from the South is a Charter School of 30 girls, founded at first as a Charity School for twenty boys & twenty girls by Mrs. Ann Hamilton & erected into a Charter School in 1738 by her son the present Ld. Limerick. They are employed in spinning for the Camerick Manufacture here, which I went to see,[11] this manufacture is carried on by a Company who subscribe, & is about half a mile from the town towards the Bay; the design of the building is to be round a Court, with a large opening at every corner to give air; two sides of it are entirely built, having ten houses on each side, a third side has only six houses built & on the fourth side is the Cashiers house with the yarn house on one side of it & the [   ] House on the other, in which they wind off the yarn on quills for weaving; the flax is brought ready scutched & hackled from France, they then stove or bake it to make it come finer by brushing it which is peculiar to the Cambrick manufacture; the houses are contiguous & consist of two rooms of a floor & of three floors, one of which is underground & vaulted with good lights in front, which are kept shut, for they must work under ground & shut out the fresh air in order to keep the yarn damp, otherwise they cannot weave it: the two rooms hold eight looms, these rooms the Company give rent free, one to each master who may employ eight, either apprentices or journey men, & the Company paies 'em for what they weave, according to the quality[12] of it, the finest is what they call 2600 that is so many quills, to each of which are two threads; so that there are in the breadth 5200 threads, & this is worth about fourteen shillings a yard. The market abroad is not high enough for the export, so that most of the consumption is at home; & tho' the Ladies say they cannot afford to wear it because it does not last so long as the French, yet the most discerning cannot distinguish the best from the French. They make fine Lawns also, & this is all bleached in yards that are near: Working in this Close manner under ground is unwholsom, & occasions the Itch & Scurvy.—They told me they had forty of our Charter boys. I saw such of them as could be got together & gave them a small present & a word of exhortation. There is also a house for dressing flax for Linnen near the town where they did also weave & it is filled with men brought from Holland.[13] They are now building a Sugar house near the town & they have a handsome Court-house & free School.

From Dundalk I went in a Chaise for Carlingford, sending my horses round by Newry to meet me on the other side of the River at Restrevor. Being

Midsummer Eve there were Bonfires all over the Country, & asking the young man who drove me, what the meaning of it was, he said in these words, it is the Eve of St. John Baptist they make a light, it is the light, He came to testify of the light: we met many going to pilgrimage to St. John's Well at NewCastle near Dundalk x.[14]

I went near two miles in the Newry road, & saw to the north on the hill, the old Church of Facart & a mount; we turned out of this road to the east & in half a mile come to a rivlet at Ballimaskanlen, & in two & a half more to Rock Marshal where there is a rivlet runs by a house pleasantly situated on the side of the hill for Lodgers to drink goats Whey; for this road has all along to the north the mountains of Carlingford; we passed in the way to this place by Mr. Tipping's Park,[15] which commands a fine view of the Bay; travelling two miles further we saw on the side of the hill a seat of Mr. Fortescues, called Piemont,[16] now inhabited by one of the Hamiltons, & is a very fine Situation; near it we crossed three mile river, on which is a small village called Rivers town. We turned to the north & descended[17] to Carlingford, a poor town of one long Street of Cabins, at the foot of the high Craggy mountains, from which several litle streams descend & pass through the town; at the west end of the town is an old Castle, said to be built by K. John, & remains of Several Old Towers to the sea, which were built to the walls,[18] that are now destroyed & seem to have been ancient habitations. This is properly the port of Newry from which the vessels go up four miles higher to narrow walls & unload in to Gabbots,[19] they say 400 vessels commonly come into this harbor every year: this & the oyster fishery for Dublin, is the chief support of the Town, & a great number of boats are constantly carrying lime stone from the quarries on each side of the mouth of the harbour to Newry, to be burnt for their buildings. There was a tolerable Inn here, but the Bedchamber being within the kitchen, as soon as I rose, the pigs made my Levee.

On the 24th I crossed over to Restrevor, where Alderman Ross late Lord Mayor of Dublin has a small house pleasantly situated under the hills, which are covered with wood near an old Mansion house in which his Father liv'd: I went to pay him a visit, but being early in the morning he was not risen, I went on to the West for near two miles & then turned to the North East along the side of the hills over a rivlet, which joyns another & falls in at Newry; before I came to eight mile bridge a fine view presented of the Country to the North of beautiful hills under corn, mostly oats in fine verdure, & on one of them saw a Mount, called the White Mote. Asking here about the road, if it was hilly,? they told me it was, but that the hills were all level, by which I suppose they meant that they were not high. I came over the hills to Briansford, on the side of Tullamore park,[20] which belongs to Lord Limerick; this park is a very fine situation, being divided into two parts by a rivlet which runs in a deep rocky bed covered with trees, & affords a most Romantic prospect, to this rivlet there is a gentle descent; on the other side the Park takes in for a mile the foot of the high mountains of Moran

& particularly of the highest call'd Slieve Donard, which is 1060 yards high from the surface of the sea to which it extends:[21] the park is all finely wooded[22] & cut into Visto's up the side of the steep hill; there is a handsom bridge over the rivlet, where the rocky cliffs on each side may be twenty feet deep, & so cover'd with trees that you can hardly see the water at the bottom in some places. Here just over the rivlet Lord Limerick has built a thatch'd open place to dine in, which is very Romantick, with a stove near to prepare the Entertainment: above on the North side of this He has begun to build a pretty Lodge, two rooms of which are finished, designing to spend the Summer months here: between this part & the sea, are houses for those who come to drink Goats Whey in May & June, when the milk on account of the flowers on which the Goats feed is in greatest perfection. I here met Ld John Murray brother & Heir apparent to the Duke of Athol, a Colonel of the High-land Regiment in this kingdom, a most accomplished fine bred Gentleman, & when I went away I found I had been as in his house; & he gave me a letter to the Commanding officer at Carrickfergus, hearing me say that I proposed to stay there on Sunday, that he might show me the civilities of the place.

On the 25th I went a mile to Maghera, after having been at Newcastle a mile to the South east on the sea; it is a good house lately purchased with some land by Mr. Annesley & I went to Tullamore park I have described. In Maghera Church yard is part of a round tower about twelve feet high, & it may be fifteen feet in diameter, 'tis said, the top was blown down & remained on the ground without breaking in pieces, but I could not be well informed, that it was really so;[23] here is an ancient burial place of the Magennis's. I ascended two miles up to the Castle of Dundrum,[24] which commands a fine view of all the country; it is of an irregular multangular form, with a fine round tower in it, which in the inside is about thirty feet in diameter; it is sd. to be built by Sr. John De Curcey for the Knights Templars. From this place I saw plainly the Isle of Man. As the Northern & Southern tydes meet here, it occasions a great sea & a most extraordinary suction into the bay, which makes it extremely dangerous to come near the Coast, where there are frequent Shipwrecks. I descended a mile to Mount Panther, with a design to pay a visit to Dr. Delany, but he was not arrived; so passing under the village of Clough finely situated on a rising ground, & the residence of Mr. Annesley,[25] third son of the famous Francis Annesley of the inner Temple, I came to Mr. Bayley's on the bay of Dundrum, to whom I had sent that I would come & dine with him; this Gentleman is brother to Sr. Nicholas Bayley & has a family Living of 800 a year. Soon after I came in Dr. Delany sent his servant, to borrow something for that they were on the road, & being invited to dine, they soon came in, He & his Lady; & being all agreably surprised, I dined, & rid seven miles East to Kilogh, between the sandy banks on the sea, which sometimes move so, as not only to bury rabbit warrens, but as it is supposed whole villages, as has happened in Cornwall. Kilogh is most pleasantly situated in a small bay which is about a mile deep & not half a mile over, it consists of one Street, but is in a declining way, no soldiers being sent to the Barrack of late years; the linnen manufactory also has failed, & the boiling of rock salt from Liverpool, & the fishery likewise is very small, tho' there is a good pier built to shelter the boats from the South East wind; but there is notwithstanding one of the best Inns here in the whole road. Just out of the town is a Charter School founded by Judge Ward to whom the town belongs, it is for twenty boys & twenty girls, & I went to see it. Near the town is a stream running from a rock, it is the lightest water in Ireland; & comes out of the cliffs, which are a cement of pebbles; the rock below being of a slaty kind: at some distance beyond it there is a hole or cave, where the tide comes in, & when it retires, makes a great noise & bubbles up in a very extraordinary manner.

On the 26th I went two miles north east to Ardglass, where when the tide is quite out, by crossing the strand, the road is about half a mile nearer, it is said, to have been the next town for trade in Ulster after Carrickfergus before the time of Queen Elizabeth. The customs of this place & Kilogh were granted by Hen. 8th to the Earl of Kildare, who sold 'em to K. Charles 1st. This place seems to have been fortyfied by a long building & some towers, the former seems to have been the habitation & Store houses of ten Merchant families, consisting of a ground floor & one story over it; what is remarkable from the upper rooms there is a communication something like what they call the murdering holes,[26] but going quite down to the ground so as not to be observed on[27] the outside, which might serve as shoars to the upper apartmts. & it may be for other purposes; a square tower joyns to this, which is cover'd by another to the South, & there is a third to the east of that, to the north west of them there is a large tower, over the gate way of which was an inscription relating to the Lords of it, the Kildare family; & on the height to the west are remains of a gate way to what they call the King's Castle. This is a good harbour for small boats, & a ship may ride in 15 feet water at the west part of it, but it is a very small harbour. From this place I crossed the Country seven miles to Down Patrick, & came to St. Patrick's Well under Strud hill, a famous place for pilgrimages;[28] the water rises from a spring cover'd over, & runs into two baths, one public the other private; at the spring they wash their eyes, & in the baths the people as a part of their religion, go in naked & dip themselves: Near the well they go round a sort of an Altar, probably the side of an old Chapel by way of Penance, sometimes on their knees; & near it a Chapel was lately built, but 'twas not thought proper to permit them to cover it: on the side of this hill, to the south is a rock something in form of a seat which they call St. Patrick's Chair, with a way round it over the broken rock, & to go in this way, sometimes even on their knees, is also a part of the penance; & on Midsummer day when they are performing their pilgrimages there are a great number of priests near who give them Absolution. A mile farther is Down Patrick where the hills form a beautiful Amphitheatre; on two of these hills the town is built, & the third side is covered with the wood & gardens that are about a house, which if I mistake not belongs to Mr. Southwell, who is Lord of the town: & on the western hill are the walls of the ancient Cathedral, called the Abby, which is not large but has a very venerable aspect; near it are the remains of a round tower. This spot commands a view of the lake beneath, now indeed almost drained, & of all the country to the south & west, the small hills being cover'd with corn. From this hill also is a view of the Abby of Inch in an Island of the Lough, & of Mr. Maxwell's large house of Finnibrothy near it.[29] Below the Abbey is a very handsom brick building, in the middle part an apartment for six men & six women, & at each end a School for ten girls, at the other for as many boys, who are to be fed & lodged as well as cloth'd & taught; all the foundation of Mr. Southwell of Kings Weston. At the lower end of the town is the Town house, & above it a handsom portico of twenty-four Arches for the linnen Market; which is very considerable at this place, & adjoining to that is a School, to teach the poor children of the town, who are not in the other Schools; near this is a good new built Church, & beyond that a free School house for teaching Latin, which seemed to be in a ruinous way. The chief support of this place is a market & Fairs for linnen. This is the proper place of Residence for the Bishop & Dean of Down, but neither of them have houses here. I had almost forgot to mention four Apartments for Clergymens widows, which are maintained as well as I could be informed by subscription. On a hill to the North of the town is an ancient fortification, called the Rath of Down patrick, encompassed with three fossees, it is about 700 yards over, as I have been inform'd; it measures by the ascent sixty feet from the bottom, & it may be questioned, whether this is not the ancient dunum of Ptolemy.[30] Near Down Patrick is a famous horse course for races, here two or three plates are run for, which are given by the Corporation of Horse Brass in the County of Down, erected by King James II, under a charter into a Corporation, with liberty to purchase £200 a year in lands; & a power to have a treasurer, Register & other officers, & that a fair should be held for six days at the time of the races, Customs to be paid belonging to the Corporation, during which fairs, they have power to hold a Court for certain purposes. I crossed over the communication between this Lough & that of Strangford, & turning to the left come to Inch Abby, removed from Carrig near Erynach; the church appears to have been a grand building, there are three windows to the East, & two on each side near it, all narrow & turned with Gothick arches; on the south side are seen the tops of the seats for the administering Priest & those who assisted him, as cut in the wall & beautified with Gothick sculpture.

I saw a number of women in an adjacent Cabbin, & my curiosity led me to go in, it was a Wake over the body of an old man, who was stretched on the floor & covered over with a sheet. About 3 feet above the Corpse was a board covered with a white cloth, on which they place candles, & the women sit round the Corpse, they are entertained with a Spirit of Barley, call'd Whiskey, with Tobacco & sometimes with bread, cakes, &c & frequently drink to excess with such instances of mortality before their eyes, & this they look upon as an act of

Devotion. I returned back over the bridge, & saw the Sluices to let out the fresh water & keep out the tide, but as there are not sluices enough to carry off the former the draining of the land is not compleated. A litle beyond this is the port of Down Patrick from the bay of Strangford, to which vessels can come of about fifty Tons. About a mile farther & over this arm of the sea, which they call the Lough, are ruins of the Abbey of Saul, founded by St. Patrick for Canons Regular, & rebuilt by Malachy O-Morgair Bishop of Down, it is now entirely ruined, but very near it, are some of the walls of an Old Castle. They have lately built a small Church on the site of the Monastery, having according to the Style of this Country, only windows on the South side & one at the East end. Two or three miles farther we came to the plantation of Castle Ward[31] belonging to Judge Ward, situated very beautifully on the bay of Strangford; they are very fine not only in Groves & clumps of trees, but in quick fences to the road, adorned with flowering shrubs as well as rows of trees. Here is a Contrivance for a Mill by a flood gate to let in the tyde, & another to let it out when they please, by which means they can keep the mill almost always going. On a point of land over the bay to the North of this, is a lofty old fabrick called Castle Audley, supposed to be built by one of the Audley family, who settled in Ireland under John de Curcey, about the time of Henry 2$^{d.}$ which family has not been long extinct. I went from Castle Ward to the Charter School of Strangford, which is very near it, for the founding of which the late Earl of Kildare left £500 & his Dowager gave two acres for ever, & 20 acres at half rent;—it is for twenty boys & twenty girls. Strangford is very pleasantly situated on the hanging ground over the bay,[32] but it is a very poor town without trade, consisting of litle more than one small Street, the buildings of which are mostly on the upper side. The Parish Church is a mile off, if I mistake not at Baley cuther, & the chapel in the town repaired by the late Earl of Kildare is going to ruin. About two miles south of Strangford is the Castle of Kilclief in which about the middle of the last century a Bishop of Down resided.

On the 27th I crossed from Strangford in the ferry a mile to the Country call'd Ardes, which is a peninsula & to the town called Porta ferry, which tho' small is a much better place then Strangford; it is built up the side of the hill & has some export of Corn & Kelp. This Living is the corps of the Chancellorship of Down. In all these parts are Meeting houses, & here is one Mass house, the only one in all Ardes, the bulk of the people in the County of Down being Presbyterians. This Country of Ardes is very beautiful being a rising ground, something like the Isle of Wight, except that there is no flat on each side, & it is all cover'd with corn; they manure with Marle, which they have in most of the grounds from the North of Strangford Lough to the bay of Dundrum, there is a great mixture of Shells in it: Those about Down Patrick I observed were a small beautiful turbinated Shell, in Ardes a larger kind, scollops, oysters, cockles & others, it is a mixture of Clay & Sand; the land will bear a Crop of Barley & two of oates,

& sometimes they sow it four years, but then it hurts the Land; & it produces hardly any herbage the first year after it is laid down: if they plough it seven years as some do it ruines the land for several years; but after three years tillage it will bring tolerable grass the first year & very good for three years, & then they plough it again, but must not put on more marle, it has been found out about 80 years & probably in a course of years they may find it proper to try whether more marle may not do the land good. This Country chiefly belongs to the Savages, Echlins, Baylies & Montgomeries: There is one road on the West side of this Country to Newtown & another on the East to Donaghadee; I took the western road, in two miles I came to Abbacy or Ardquine (a Bishop's estate lease) to the Echlins, descendants to a Bishop of Down in 1635. It is thought by some from the name to be the site of the Priory of Eynes, which is not known. About two miles further is a seat of the Savages call'd Ardchin pleasantly situated on the Lake; but not much improved—the sea has covered most of the low land there is in this country which is not much, & made it Morassy, but they have now drained a good part of it. Two miles further is Echlins Ville, so called from the owner, & as much farther Inishargy the seat of Mr. Bayley; & two miles further is Rosemount,[33] the seat of the Montgomeries, so call'd from a mount on the hill over it, & on the sea there is a small Danish fort. This estate is a purchase of a Collateral branch of the family of Sr. James Montgomery, second son of Lord Montgomery, at the time of King Charles the first, who was bred to the Law, had travelled, & by the Epitaph in the Church, appears to have been a linguist & a lover of Poetry. The Mansion house is built near the Old Gray Abbey, which is in the style of the Church of Inch, & part of it is repaired for divine service. A Bell metal jug was found in 1722 in the bog of Baylays Murphey near this place, about eight inches high, with a Spout & Handle, & was presented to the University of Dublin. And in 1728 an earthen Urn with burnt bones in was found on the Abbey lands.[34] The Old Town is near the Abbey, & the New-town a furlong from it on the sea. They have two or three quarries of very good slate in this Neighbourhood. This part of the Country is call'd great Ardes & also Clan bois, from an antient clan as supposed; The southern part is litle Ardes. As we approached towards the North end of the Lough, the road was more pleasant, as it commanded a better view of the opposite country, from which they cross over the Strand when the tyde is out, having a pillar built on each side as a mark to direct the passengers. I arrived at Newtown most pleasantly situated on the North end of this bay, something like St. Maries near Southampton, the Lough & the lands to the south having much the appearance of Southampton bay & the Isle of Wight: It is a burrough town, & they have a considerable trade in Linnen, especially Diapers. There are remains here of a Dominican Convent, in which Chapters of the order have been held. I omitted to see the beautiful family Chapel of the Colviles, who have as I was informed sold this estate to one Mr. Stewart. This town is seven miles from Donaghadee, at which place I landed from Scotland in 1747.[35] A mile in that road is Movilee a monastery of Canons of the order of St. Austin, founded by St. Finian in 550. To the south west of Newtown about a mile is a hill called Scraba or Strabo, where there is a quarry of Free Stone; the buildings I saw of it in this Country stand very well, tho' it burns black, but I was informed that the Stone of the College Library which scales is of this quarry which possibly might be owing to some mismanagement in the quarrying or carriage, & it may be by reason that it might have taken salt water.

I ascended a long hill north ward to Bangor; on the top of it they were finishing a thatch'd meeting house; I came to this place in order to Cross above two leagues to Carrickfergus, but the wind being high I went round by Belfast.

Bangor is pleasantly situated on a high ground over the Bay of Carrickfergus,[36] it is a poor Burrough town consisting of a long broad street down the side of the hill to the sea; the houses are about 200 in number. Tho' they have a slate quarry near the town, yet the houses are all thatch'd. The chief support of the inhabitants is spinning, there being but two fishing boats, tho' it is finely situated for a fishery; it was the estate of the Hamiltons Lords of Claneborg, one of which was Earl of Clanbrazil, & has been divided between two Coheiresses; the Mother of Lord Ikerrin, now Earl of Carrick, & Judge Ward's Lady; the Mansion house here is very indifferent, but the spruce firr, the Ilex, Bays, Hollies & other ever greens, planted at first chiefly in the Flower garden are grown to be very fine forest trees: the church is on the side of the old Abbey, in it is a monument to Beatrix Hamilton, with a remarkable copy of English verses, through which there runs a very great Strain of piety. There is also a monument to John Gibson the first Protestant Dean of Down in 1623, in which it is mentioned that when he came there, he had only forty communicants, & when he dyed he left 1200. There was here a famous Abbey of Canons, founded by St. Congall about 555, which he himself governed by a particular rule, but afterwards it took the order of St. Austin. It is thought that the History of this Abbey is confounded with that of Bangor in England: in the relation that is given of the great number of monks, & of many of them that were killed at one time. There are remains of one part of it, with the ancient narrow Gothick windows. Mr. Winder the Minister of this place came to see me, & showed me all these things with great Civility. On the high ground here, we saw very plainly that part of Scotland, which is called the Mull of Galway. A litle to the East of Bangor is Groom Port bay where Duke Schomberg with 1000 men came to anchor in 1689 & soon took Carrickfergus & was created Earl of Bangor:[37] In great Copland Island at the mouth of the Bay is a slate quarry. I had a very pleasant ride near the Bay for ten miles to Belfast in the Country of Antrim, the direct road being but eight, & there are several gentlemens houses very finely situated over the bay. Belfast stands on the west side of the bay, just at the end of it & is a considerable town of trade, especially in the linnen manufacture, in which they are all concern'd, buying the yarn & giving it to be wove, they also send several ships to the West Indies. It is the Estate of the Earl of Donnegal; & the town are very uneasy that they cannot get new leases to build, all of them being near expiring, for the estate is entailed on the sons of Mr. Chichester, who are minors, whose Mother is sister to Sr. Roger Newdigate; This Lord is, as in a state of infancy & in the hands of relations who agree to divide all between them, & have not taken out a Commission of Lunacy: & the guardians of the Minors, oppose the procuring an Act of Parliament to enable him to lett the Lands.

The river Lagan runs through a very fine country, & falls into the sea at Belfast, where there is a bridge over it, of about 20 arches 840 feet in width, with a Causeway at both ends which make up 1722 feet, it is 22 feet broad. The Country on this river, & all the way to Ardmagh is look'd upon as the finest spot in Ireland, & being well watered & between the Lough of Strangford & Lough Neagh & Carrickfergus bay, these situations give it a very great advantage. The town of Belfast consists of one long broad Street, & of several lanes in which the inferior people live; the church seems to be an old tower or Castle, to which they have built so as to make it a a greek Cross, & is a very mean fabrick for such a considerable place; indeed the congregation is but small, & most of them of the lower rank, for of 400 houses, there are but about sixty families that go to Church; The richer people with a number of others are of the new light Presbyterians, the rest of the old light & papists. The new light are look'd on as Arians; & these two lights have a greater aversion to each other, than they have to the Church.[38] The Earl of Donnegals house at the end of the town was burnt down about the begining of this century & two daughters were burn'd in it; the garden, groves, meadows & fields on the river belonging to it are very delightful.

On the 29th it being a wet morning I did not set out till noon for Carrickfergus eight miles distant, it is a pleasant road near the bay. This is a poor town tho' well situated; the Castle is built on a rock, which is washed on three sides by the sea, it is a strong place & is kept in pretty good order; & no one being permitted to go to it in time of war, the orders have not been taken off in time of peace. Lord Donnegal has a very large house here, built about the time of Queen Elizabeth, when his Ancestor Sir [   ] Chichester was Lord Deputy of Ireland, & obtained the grants of his great Estate, which in this Country as I was inform'd is £8,000 a year, that he has 5 or £6,000 a year in other parts, & that if the whole were out of Lease it would let for £30,000 a year. There are great plenty of small Scollops in this sea: The Mayor has the admiralty from Fair point to the North to Beer looms near Strangford, the Creeks of Bangor & Belfast excepted, they had also in the same extent all Customs, which Ld. Strafford purchased for the King for £2000, after which the Custom house was removed to Belfast & this town began to decline. I dined here. The Mayoralty here is worth disputing, & has caused a division in the town, for it is about £100 a year, chiefly arising out of lands given for forage for the Kings troops, who have not of late years been sent to the Barracks[39] here. I set forward on the sea Coast & passed by Castle Dobbs,[40] the seat of that Gentleman who is member for Carrickfergus,[41] & has so strenuously pushed the affair of a passage through Hudson's bay, but without success. The Castle is a low situation behind the hill, but he is building on a very fine spot on the rising ground. A litle further is a very pleasant Mansion house

J.N. Brewer, Carrickfergus Castle, 1825

of Mr. Brice: I ascended a litle height, at the top of which a new & most beautiful scene appear'd of the delightful harbour of Larne, which comes in between the land, & makes what they call Magee Island a Peninsula; but I could not learn that there was any rivlet or opening from the South end of this bay into the Sea, as the Maps represent it, which would make it an Island. It is about 6 miles in length & a mile & a half broad, & much resembles the high ground that runs the length of the Isle of Wight, but it is not so high, & there is no level ground on each side but it is all cover'd with corn & rich pasturage. I saw two roads one along the top of it, another on the west with many houses on each side of it, & if I mistake not there is a third on the east side; It is without trees the most beautiful & extraordinary spot that can be imagined: this & the Country to Larne is the Estate of the Ld. Donnegal, as all to the north belongs to the Earl of Antrim. I travelled near this fine harbour, & came to a new kind of soil a white limestone, which having flint in it, as chalk always has, I do much suspect that it was formerly in that State, for it will now almost mark white; the flint in it is chiefly of a pale blew & whitish: above this is what they call rotten rock, a sort of Crumbling stone, which makes excellent roads, soon dissolving & is easy to the horses feet, but it does not last so long as the lime stone, which tho' much harder yet it soon makes a smooth road, but when Narrow & raised in the middle, as is the Case here, it is slippery & dangerous at least for horses not accustomed to it. Over the rotten rock is a blackish firestone, called a white stone, it most of it appears to me, to be of the granite kind, but with very small grains. I passed by a pleasant village in a litle vale, from which it has the name of Glyn, & come to a spring on the shoar, in which there is a very small fresh water shell-fish, of the Wilk or turbinated kind, & a small limpet, no bigger than a vetch, sticking to[42] the Stones, which I never saw before in fresh water: but what is most remarkable about this well, on the Shoar, they find the Asteriae & Astroitae, some of them smaller than ever I met with before, but they are difficult to be found.

Larne is pleasantly situated at the north end of this bay, a point of land running out to the South east; directly south of which is the harbour for large vessels, where they are well defended against the weather; & that point is a most pleasant rising ground, on which there is an old Castle. Larne tho' a poor town, consists of a street not much less than half a mile in length, & a rivlet falling from the hills at one end, a race of it is brought along behind the houses, which is a great conveniency as well as beauty. They have a litle linnen trade, a few fishing boats & Salt works (as along the coast) of Salt rock of Cheshire boiled with sea water. They have also some litle traffick in sending out lime Stone & furnishing the Neighbouring parts with lime: Near the ancient church there is a Mount, which I take to be of the Monumental kind, & beyond that is a field, called the Chapel field, where they say are some marks of the foundation of an old Chapel.

On the 30th I set out north ward & ascending the hill, saw a beautifull Country between the low hills to the sea & the mountains to the west, it is almost all covered with oats, with houses very thick all over it, & litle plantations about them in their gardens, so that they appear like little groves or clumps of trees all over the Country, which strikes the more, as there is not any other tree to be seen in the Country: it is entirely an open Country like Common fields. From this ground I saw the rocks, called by the sailors the maidens, & by the Country people the Whilkins. I turn'd out of the way to go to the sea Cliffs, which are of the black-Stone, in order to see what they call the black cove, but found it to be nothing but a passage worn through the rock; beyond this is a fine head called Baley gelly[43] the seat of Mr. [   ]. I travelled through this fine Country, which makes up the great Living of larne Castle: They are notwithstanding very indifferent husbandmen, their common method being to plough one year & lay down one year, nor have they the method I saw in the County of Down of making folds with green sod, to fold their sheep in order to manure the land. I ascended a high hill which is the point that makes the bay of Glenarme, & struck out of the road to the East, to go through Lord Antrim's litle park, which is the most beautiful & romantick ground I ever beheld; it is the very point which makes the bay to the north, & is a hanging ground over the sea, from which there is a wood, then there is an uneven lawn with some wood in several parts & rocks rising up so as that at a distance, some of them appear like ruins of Castle's, then there is a very steep ascent, not less than 80 or 90 yards high cover'd with wood, this leads to a lawn, & going on towards the north the point of ground rises higher & terminates in a beautifull mount which Commands a fine prospect, where My Lord often dines: further to the North is another heighth, all the hanging ground from them beautifully cover'd with wood: above this lawn which is within these heights is the perpendicular rock, at least an hundred yards in height, out of which Shrubs & trees grow in a most beautifull manner; the ascent up to the door of the park at a lower part of the hill is difficult; above this height is the high road from Larne to Glenarme & they tell many extraordinary Stories of men & cattle that have fallen down these precipices & have not been much hurt. I descended a long hill to Glenarme, a village situated on each side of a river in a Narrow vale, between the hills on the bay of Glenarme, where Lord Antrim has resided in an ordinary house, since his habitation at Ballimagarry near Dun luce was burnt; but there is an old house with good room in it, without a roof which he is about to repair.[44] There are some remains of an old Abbey on the bay, & a sort of rampart on the north of it, as for a place of defence to retire to in a time of danger. Over the town to the north is a hill with an easy ascent, on which there is an horse course, which Commands a fine View, especially of the great park, & here my Lord has a Stable for his race horses; this Nobleman's Chief amusement being the fine horses which he breeds every year. Mr. Broome a relation to the late Bishop of Down Dr. Rider, now Archbishop of Tuam, is minister of this parish; he paid me a visit, & carried me to see Lady Antrims grotto, in which there are a great number of fine & curious Shells, & many of the pinna, which are found off the north east point of Ireland. He brought me compliments from My Lord Antrim that he would be glad to see me. Mr. Broome rid with me to the great park, which is as curious & beautiful as the other, but in a different way: two rivers rise in the hills meet below & make the river of Glenarme, which flows in the narrow valley; the park wall runs along the top of the hills & almost encloses these three rivers, being about nine miles in circumference: the entrance to the park is about half a mile to the west of Glenarme, & on both sides of the river both below & on the sides of the hills, is an agreeable variety of Lawn & Wood for a mile; further on it is all woody on both[45] sides, & just at the entrance of this wood on an eminence, is a banqueting house in a very romantick Situation; When one has enter'd the wood, the bed of the river is deeper, having perpendicular rocks on each side from twenty to forty feet high & trees grow out of them, & one sees between them many beautifull Cascades, particularly one near 30 feet high; about ten feet below the top, is a Shelf, & at top the rock overhangs so as no salmon can get up but they frequently leap & fall on that shelf, & often bruise themselves so that they dye. Above it is another very beautifull Cascade in two or three falls in the breadth of the river, but the finest is in the middle; I went up the eastern river to see the most beautifull of all; which tumbles down in a sheet near 30 feet; from this we ascended up the hill to the east through the wood & come to a lawn, & had a view to the west of the round high top of the [   ] sleamish (I am the hill) [*sic*] by way of eminence, near which St. Patrick when he first came from Scotland, fed hogs.[46] & on the hill Skerries not far from it, are remains of a church, which is said to be the first in Ireland. We returned down by the hill to the gate of the park we came in at. I waited on Lord & Lady Antrim, & lay at My Lds. house.

On the first of July, I walk'd up to the Course, & set out; My Lord sent a man five miles with me, & Mr. Brougham & Mr. O'Neale accompanied me there. We passed the end of Kle Glyn & ascended towards a high point called Mount Gerran point, in the Map Ardclinnie point,[47] over which there is a very steep road, & at the bottom of it, is a rock, which, before part of it fell down, was thought to be the figure of a fish. From this point the mountains are very fine, quite perpendicular towards the top with trees growing out of them as in the litle park, from which large white lime stone rocks have roll'd down, in many of which I saw Belemnites which are frequently found on the shoars, as well as echini; but it is very difficult to separate them from the rock: the lower part of this opening call'd Red bay is much admired,[48] having the same kind of ground on each side of the valley, but no wood below, so that I think it is not near so beautifull as the ground of the great park; but it is said that the late Lord had thought of making a park there, which he might have done, only by building a wall at the sea & at the west angle. In this road we observed several Streams running from the hill, which flow'd under ground into the sea, on the north side of this vale a river falls into the sea, near the mouth of it are Cliffs of a sandy red stone in which there are four or five coves, & some families live in them: & just over the point are remains of an old Castle call'd Red bay Castle. On the southside of the bay I observed an old Church, which answers to the situation of Galbally in Sr. Wm. Petty's map.[49] When I passed this point turning round I was surpriz'd at the sight of the end of the mountain to the north east of the valley, which appeared with a most beautifull Square top—& in some situations like a Lozenge this is call'd Clockay-Brackeen. I came to another litle valley call'd Cushendale where I dined; Going two miles to Cushenden bay; I was directed about half a mile from the road to see some caves, which are not so curious altogether as the sea cliff, which is the most beautifull I ever saw, it consists of pebbles of a middling size of different colours all cemented together; so that it has the appearance of variegated marble, & is exactly like the Hertfordshire stone which is used for the top of Snuff boxes, except that the Stones are much larger, that is from about four or five to 8 or 9 inches in diameter. The Sheep take Shelter in these caves in the winter, & there is in some part of the grotts a cake of their dung near a foot thick, which the people have not as yet taken away for manure. Over the north side of this bay is an old tower, which is I suppose what is called in the map Caries Castle. This head of Land is the most North eastern point of Ireland. We returned to the road on the other side of the river & up a very long hill, to a heathy[50] Country, which affords good turf with a gravel under it, & the white lime stone is found in many parts through the Country: The soil being alter'd from Red bay to this place, in which space there is no lime stone: Very fine roads are made here all the way to Bally Castle in which coming near the northern shoar of Ireland we turn'd to the west & passed by Caravadount, below which is a Danish fort, & a litle further to the south is a fine flat hill called Drumnikilliah which much resembles the situation of Jerusalem: & so we arrived at Bally Castle: From the eastern shore I saw the Isle of Sanda to the east of which a Mc Doñel is Laird: & the Mul of Cantyr in Scotland seemed surprisingly near in the bay of Cushendon; tho' it is almost thirty miles distant, but it is a very high land; They often go over to that land for game; where there is great plenty of what is called the black game, which Lord Antrim has brought over more than once, but could never get them to breed or keep them long, so that probably they return back. Bally Castle is situated in a sort of a Creek, at the mouth of the small river Glenshesk in the large open bay which is made by Fair head & the point at Balin toy, near which Sheep Island is seen, having the Isle of Rathling stretching to the north of it from east to west. The tyde comes in from the north, & probably the tides meeting off Fair head & the Mull of Cantire cause such an Eddy current that in the bay the flow lasts nine hours & the ebb only three, the tide rises here from 2 ft. to 3 feet excepting that high winds raise it still higher. Bally Castle is a strong instance of the assiduity & judgement of one person Mr. Boyd to whom the place belongs,[51] who holds it as a fee farm under Lord Antrim, who has made most of his tenants happy in such a tenure; for all this Country as I mention'd before belongs to Ld. Antrim; His ancestors from Scotland, the McDonalds, conquer'd it, & Queen Elizabeth granted it to them by patent; The family are now distinguished by the title of Antrim; it extends from near Larne to Coleraine: from Larme to Glenarme the people are mostly Presbyterian, as well as from

Bally Castle to Coleraine; but from Glenarme to Bally Castle they are for the most part Papists.

Mr. Boyds great work was to make a safe harbour for Shipping, which he had done most effectually, having received £10,000 from the publick for that purpose: It was effected by a pier to the north & east made of piles of oak, fixed together with iron, & all fill'd within with large Stones, so that it makes three very good Quays: But unfortunately last winter, some of the piles to the north gave way in a violent Storm, & about the same time some of the inner piles of the eastern pier fail'd, occasioned by fastening their cables to them: But when they came to examine the foot of the piles, they found they had been eaten by a small worm, of a different kind from those of the Indies or Holland, or from those I saw at Shoreham, being very small about a quarter of an inch long, & as big as a midling pin; Looking on them in a microscope, on the back they appear like a smooth grub, on the belly a litle like a shrimp, with seven legs on each side, & I think a smaller pair behind, it has large black eyes & the snout seems to be pointed, & probably has on it such a pair of Shells to bore as the larger have, but I could not discern it: They make holes in the length of the part of the wood which is always under the salt water, for the air or fresh water kills them: this mole is on the west side of the litle bay: To the east along the shoar which faces to the north it is sandy, & piles are droven in to keep the sea from gaining on the bank, & when it does gain, they fill it again with great expence, & they are now making a strong pier built of Stone & mortar, where the piles have fail'd, on one side are Store houses, on another Smiths forges & all sorts of trades, for building boats & for carrying on the work of the piers. Besides this Mr. Boyd has built a very good Inn, a Brewery, Tan-yard, houses for boyling Soap, & Salt, making Candies, & a very fine bleach-yard; all which he farms out. He has also built a handsome house for himself[52] & a brick wall on two sides of a garden of seven acres; & at the same time has carried on the works of a very Considerable Colliery, which is to the east towards Fair head on the sea side; The first is about a mile from the town, where there is a fine box-wheel for raising the water out of the coalpits, turned by a Stream brought from the river by a channel cut along the side of the hill & through some high ground for above a mile; about half a mile further is a Shaft near the top of the Cliff, & as much further another, to which there is an entrance from the Shoar by a passage, the top & side of which are supported by wood work: At the colliery are quays for Shipping them on small vessels made at great expence with large stones. From the first pit there is a way made with wood, as at White haven & Newcastle for two Carts to be drawn on. This sea cliff is very curious, but appears most beautifull at Fairhead. There is first a stratum of fire Stone, which is in pillars of one Stone, some of them being near twenty feet long, & this seems to be some tendency towards the naturall production of the Giants Causeway; This in Fair head has something of the appearance of a Gothick work: then there is what they call Till, which I take it, is a ragged broken Stone, then free Stone, next a vein of Coal followed by Till, & then two layers of free Stone of different qualities; for there they have grinding Stones & whet Stones out of different quarries. They have a vitriol Spring in one part, & one sees several perpendicular veins in the Cliffs which they call faults in the work—they extend into the sea, & one of them being about fifteen or twenty feet broad, appears like a large Causeway.

This Gentleman in the Colliery & all the manufactures he supports, has about 300 people employed every day, & in the years of scarcity he took care to buy corn & have it sold at a reasonable price. All these things undertaken & carried on by one man, are a very uncommon & extraordinary instance in a practical way of human understanding & prudence. The Old Town of Ballycastle is a quarter of a mile from the port, which consists of a short Street, & here they hold their markets; & just below it is an old mansion house in ruins of the Antrim family. When I came to Bally castle Mr. Boyd soon found out, I had compliments to him from the Arch bishop of Dublin, he obliged me to make his house my home; where I met my acquaintance his daughter Mrs. Macaulay, married to Dr. Macaulay Vicar General of the Diocese of Dublin.

On the 2^d he showed me all these things. To the east of the town is a building they call the Abbey, which I suppose was a Convent, in it is a Chapel, on the side of which is the following inscription.

In Dei Deiparaeque virginis honorem illustrissimus ac Nobilissimus Dominus Randolphus M'Donnel Comes de Antrim hoc Sacellum fieri curavit. An. Dom. 1612.[53]

On the 3^d I set out with Mr. Harrison Minister of the place & another gentleman to see the Charter School, about half a mile beyond the town & founded by Mr. Boyd for [   ] & [   ] girls, & taking leave of them I travelled to the west near the sea cliffs, which are of lime Stone from a litle beyond Baley Castle to the end of Balintoy bay, where the Cliffs are of that sort of rock which is in the Cliffs of the Giants Causeway. About two miles from Ballycastle I observ'd on the left a long low hill called Cregeny, where I saw pillars like those in the Giants Causeway of a large size I measured some of them which were pentagons, one was thirty one inches over, the other twenty; so this is to be reckoned the beginning of this extraordinary natural production. I descended the hill & going along the plain came near the west side of the Bay of Balintoy, passing by the church & village of that name, & came to the estate of Mr. McNeal, where following a rivlet I come to a small bay, where the Stones had some litle resemblance of the Cause way at a distance, but I found them in large pieces as in quarries; I dined here by the stream. Going on westward I soon came to a litle bay, in which there is a small high peninsula with ruins of a Castle on it, called Dunseverick; from which I walk'd along the top of the sea Cliffs, & coming to a litle bay, to which there is a tolerable descent, the Cliff being all covered with grass, I descended as I suppose between two & three hundred yards; on the east side of this bay is a curious high rock, & as there are shelves in the Steep Cliffs, so the goats go along these shelves to feed: Here we found people

Susannah Drury, East Prospect of the Giant's Causeway, 1752

Susannah Drury, West Prospect of the Giant's Causway, 1752

a' fishing: Returning up we came to Port Mahr, for they give all those litle creeks or bays the name of ports; I saw the tops of pillars at the bottom of this bay, next we came to Port Forts Frid, where there are pillars in the Cliffs, & some of them stand single & in a litle port beyond it called Beneagore, are two or three litle risings in the manner of the Giants Causeway. The next is port Loganeny, where there is a good way down the Cliff & there are pillars towards the top & bottom. The next is Portnabrok, where two eagles flew out of the rocks, which were of a lighter colour then any I have seen, & possibly may be of the Vulture kind, but I am inform'd since that they are the rock Eagle, & are larger than the mountain eagle; here are pillars at the bottom of the Shoar, but the two rows above are extremely fine & regular; as well as I could conjecture, there was ten feet of rock, then a tier of pillars forty feet, rock 40 feet, pillars 40 feet, rock 20 ft. & then a Steep descent with grass growing on it at least forty feet high: Turning the small end of the glass it had a most beautiful effect, they appeared like a landscape of Portico's at a distance, & not unlike the view we have engraved of Palmyra. The next is Port Noffer & then is Portnespagna, which is formed to the west by the point on which are those pillars call'd the chimneys. This litle bay has its name from a tradition that a Spanish man of war came near in hazy weather & thought the rocks & pillars were a fort & fired at them, but the rocks made a melancholy reprizal, when as they say she was soon after dash'd against them. I then walked on & looked dawn on what they call the Giants Causeway, which I viewed in 1747, having walked about four miles along the see Cliffs with equal pleasure & astonishment, viewing this wonderful work of Nature. From the Cliffs I struck down through Bush Mills, Danluce, & Ballimagarry to Port Rush, where not meeting with accommodation, I was forced at ten a'clook at night to return three miles to Ballimagarry, where I took up my quarters.

I walk'd along on the top of the sea cliffs half a mile to Dunluce & it was very curious to see the Gulls in their nests, which they have made of clay & sand in the sides of the perpendicular rocks, so as that the nests overhang from the rock, & great numbers of birds flying about make a very great noise, the eagles come often & take their young which are a delicious morsel for them. The Cormorants build with sea weed on litle shelves on the sides of the rocks & one sees the hen in the nest & her litle ones sitting round her & the Cock near; which is a very pretty Sight. At Dunluce I went to see the Castle which is on a rock joyn'd to the land by an Istmus that is about thirty feet lower than the top of the rock; & they cross to it by a draw bridge, it is now joyned by a wall about two feet thick & 30 feet over, on which some people go to it: I walk'd over it; it is an old irregular Castle that may be the 8th of a mile in circumference, & under it is a broad Cave with an opening to the south & another to the north to the sea.[54] The Earls of Antrim did live in this Castle, & one of their Ladies not likeing the noise of the waves, had a house built for her just at the entrance of it, where she liv'd; which house is now standing without a roof: This if I mistake not was the Dutchess of Buckingham widow of the Duke who was stab'd at Portsmouth & was married to the head of this family, who had the title of Marquise of Antrim.[55]

George Petrie, Port Coon Cave, the Giant's Causeway, 1835

I went by sea to the Giants Cause way, & taking it as near as I could in a triangle, I measured the three sides & took the bearings & measured an Octagon with all the pillars round it; & return'd, landing in the Port of Balintray, at the mouth of the river Bush; here they say was formerly a port of trade which had priviledges granted to it. Ascending to the right are two Raths, very near to each other with a double fossee; they call 'em Danish forts, & say that to this day, some family in Denmark settles these lands on any marriage. A litle further but on the Cliff is a litle Cape which is defended by a fossee drawn across the neck of it:—There is a tradition that the Danes went off from this place.

On the 5th I walked two miles to Baly willy church of which Mr. Cuppaige is Curate whom I had met at Bally Castle, I preach'd for him, & Mr. Stewart near invited me to dine with him, but I excused my self; & a person who showed me some civility by accompanying me home dined with me; I saw in the way a low rocky hill called Cregahullen-Craig where there are pillars as in the Giants Causeway, some sides of which I measured & found them to be large; There is another a mile further, & I observed even near as far as Solomons porch, six miles beyond Colerain that the rocks have some litle resemblance of the Causeway, but not in true pillars. In the afternoon I went down to the Strand to see grottoes & caves in the Lime Stone white Cliffs, which begin from Dunluce & extend to the strand of Port rush, & they are the most extraordinary & beautifull I ever saw, some in open grottoes, others in large narrow Caves going in a great way, having beautifull Stalactites in them; one of them exceeds the rest in beauty, being about thirty paces wide & 70 long, with three pillars of rock on the east side, the white colour of the rock & the flints intermixt, & in many parts Belemnites add to the beauty & curiosity of the sight.

Port rush is a litle creek encompassed with sandy banks, which gain on the land as the sands do in Cornwall: tho' it is well sheltered yet there runs such a sea, that it is not safe for the boats in winter; at some distance from this Creek is an Island called Skerries, & in the Map Port rush Island, which makes the sea to the south a pretty good road to ride in during the summer-season; but it is only a shelter to the north, the lands on each side being some litle covering to the East & West. This litle town is of so litle consequence that there is not a publick house in it for the accommodation of travellers, they have but one Merchant in the town, who deals chiefly in shipping off corn & kelp. I took a walk also to Ld. Antrims house close to Baley Magarry, which was burnt down about two years ago; it is a fine situation commanding a view of the sea of Enishowen to the north west & of the sea Coast to the east. The house was built of the pillar stones of the quarry I have mentioned near; & I saw one there of nine sides. Lord Antrim had thoughts of building an house on a spot near but it is said has altered his purpose. From the high lands there is a view of the Island of Ila, where it is sd. is the famous Abbey called Colum Kil, in which the ancient Kings of Scotland are buryed; & to the north of this one sees the Island of Jura, appearing like three remarkable hills. There is an ancient kern at Ballimagarry consisting of ground raised five or six feet, it may be 100 feet in diameter, there are some large stones in the middle, they have the name of the person to whose honour, as tradition saies it was made. They have a method in the north of weeding their corn with what they call a Clip, it is a pair of pinchers made of two pieces of wood & handles standing like those of a pair of sheers, & they pull up the strongest docks with it.

On the 7th I rid to the Giants Causeway, & attended the raising the most curious stones I could find, & in the even on my return waited on Mr. Duncane who lives in the way, with a letter I had to him & came home.

On the 8th I went to the Causeway late, & Mr. Duncane came & dined with me, & sent a fresh salmon which was roasted before a turf fire, it was cut in pieces & stuck on five or six sticks set in the ground round the fire & sometimes taken up & turn'd. He left Mr. Bromhall with me, his childrens Tutor, & I came with him to his house, drank tea & came home.

On the 9th I staid within all day & writ letters, Mr. Duncan & Mr. Bromhall came to see me.

On the 10th I went to the Causeway, had many more stones raised in the morning, & in the afternoon put aboard a Sloop I freighted for Dublin, to be filled with coals at Bally castle; came off very late called at Mr. Duncan after ten & lay there. Having viewd & examined this wonderfull work of nature the Giants Cause way, with as much exactness as I could, & made on it some observations: which I sent to the Royal Society & they did me the honour to print them in the Philosophical transactions of the year 1753.[56]

On the 10th I returned to Ballimagarry & set out for Coleraine, & observed the pillars of stone at Cross Reagh within 2 miles of Colrain: I came to that town which is pleasantly situated on a rising ground to the east of the river Bann, which here divides the County of Antrim from the County of Londonderry. This town has large liberties: being an Estate with other lands especially Derry that was forfeited by the rebellion of the O Kanes in the time of Queen Elizabeth, & was granted by King James the First to the twelve Companies of London, who divided most of the lands between 'em, but some are in common & particularly the Salmon fishery. Out of each of ye Twelve Companies two persons are chose, which make what they call in London the Irish Society, for the management of these estates; & most of them are lett at a low rent, & purchased according to the improved value: There is a litle town on the other side, which is the parish of Killowen. There is a handsome town house in Colerain built by the Society; & they have a great market every Saturday for Linnen & yarn which is the chief Support of the place. I rid a mile below Colerain to see the Salmon fishery which is very great; they catch 'em with what I think is called a seine-Net, that goes across the river, & so they draw in the net. They have caught sometimes, tho' very rarely 2500 in a day; sell 'em here for a penny a pound fresh; but most of 'em are salted The fish go up in June & July, Spawn in August, & those fish are called fry at first; they come down into the sea about March & April, & return from between 5 to ten[57] pounds in weight, & then they are call'd Grants,[58] & are of a lighter colour than what they call Salmon, & rather better for present use, not so strong as salmon, but do very well for salting; Afterwards they are call'd salmon & sometimes grow to fifty pounds weight, & that as it is imagined in 3 or 4 years: The white salmon trout besides the colour, differs from them in having a double raw of teeth. I returned to Colarain & went a mile up the river to see the salmon-leap, the river falls down about ten feet in two or three falls, divided by the rocks: They leap up, & very handsome apartments are made for them above with grates to let the water in, & so they can go no further, & are taken up by a hand net; this diversion I saw.

Over this is a pleasant situation, the house of Mr. Richardson a member of Parliament, who married Sr. John Eyles daughter & purchased of the Society that estate; opposite to it is a pretty Mount call'd Mount Sandal, which seemed to be monumental.

On the 11th I set out with Mr. Fitzgerald a Surveyor of the Revenue, who had accompanied me yesterday, & with whom I had been acquainted formerly in Munster. We rid four miles to a village pleasantly situated called Ardeau, & a mile further came on the Strand from a Glyn between the high Cliffs through which a rivlet falls into the sea. Even about this part at a distance the rocks appear a litle like the Causeway, but they consist only of large Stones of the rocks in Strata Something in that manner. The Cliffs are very high, at top is a Stratum of Stone; then of rotten rock & then fine white lime Stone. From the height I saw the barr of Sand at Coleraine harbour which crosses the mouth of the river in such a manner as that no vessel of any burthern can come over it, & this appears by the sea breaking against it. At these Cliffs which extend from near Colerain to Magilligan four or five miles, that chain of mountains & which run through the County of Londonderry, Tyrone & Monaghan & as I take it, end to the south in low hills in the County of Cavan. I came to these Cliffs to see a grotto much talk'd of, call'd Solomon's porch, but it is nothing compared to those beautifull grottoes I saw at Ballimagarry: It is only a long narrow cave, the entrance of which without doubt was handsomer before it was very much choak'd up with Sand as it is at present. I observed here that the flint lay more in Strata than in other parts, near this grotto is a fine cold Spring up the Cliff, they come & take a hearty draft of the sea water & then when it purges drink of this water plentifully. We came to the west end of the Cliff, & I was sufficiently recompenced for my disappointment by the pleasure I had in the ride afterwards first for two miles along the Strand; & afterwards when I turned to the south through a plain having high Cliffy hills to the east with a gentle ascent for some way from the bottom, the rich hay country of Magiligan to the west makeing out in that point to the North west towards Greencastle in Innishohowen & makes the entrance about two miles broad into that bay which is called the Lough of Derry, then the high hills of Innishowen cover'd with corn almost to the top: We had a very good road, & passed by the house for Lodging of such people resort[59] to this place in order to drink goats whey, & came into a plain which extends further to the east; & came to the direct road from Coleraine & arrived at Newtown Limne Vaddy pleasantly situated on the river Roe, near which are some seats with good plantations very finely situated. This town consists of one broad Street, & tho' it has a mean appearance, yet it has a great trade in linnen & linnen yarn, insomuch that there are many in the town who can at any time give considerable bills of Exchange on London. This is also an estate of the Society in the hands of [   ]. Stopping here to dine, my acquaintance Dr. Bacon Minister of Ballykeley whom I did design to visit, was passing through & came & dined with me, & then accompanied me to Limna-vaddy. We passed by the river Roe; on each side of which are high rocky cliffs with trees growing out of them, & a wood on each side & some beautifull Cascades of water rush through the rocks; we came to the site of the old Castle of Limne Vaddy, the fortress of the O Kanes, the ancient Lords of this Country: It has the name of Limne Vaddy (the dogs leap) from a narrow passage of the river beneath[60] the rocks a litle higher up, over which a dog may leap, & young men divert themselves by vaulting over it. This estate was in the possession of that Philips & his descendants who was sent over to divide the land between the Companies; & they tell a comical Story, that he represented that he could no way make the division so as to take in this estate, & that on this they gave it to him for his trouble: But I was informed that he having a grant of the lands of the Convent of Colerain exchanged them for these. However that may be, it is an exceeding fine Spot of ground: & the Philips's I have had the pleasure to be long acquainted with, are a younger branch of that family, a cousin of Captn. Philips being the person who sold the estate. There are several Danish forts about this place, some of which the gentlemen have planted with clumps of firrs which have a beautifull effect. There is a lime Stone here which is of a Slaty kind or runs in thin strata, & I was inform'd that when polished, it is of the dove colour of the Ardbraccon Marble. I then went two miles farther to Dr. Bacons parsonage house, a good brick edifice with large gardens & a well improved glebe; the house & part of the improvements were built & made by my worthy friend Dr. Owen Dean of Clonmac noise. This parish of Bally kelly consists of about 700 houses, 30 or 40 acres being a great farm, which gives the Country a very rich look all being under Corn & good pasturage, for they have a Shell bank in the Lough of Derry which affords fine manure, ten quarters of Shells, each of them two barrels being excellent manure for four years, & will produce two Crops of Barley & two of oates. From this I went to the Charter school, very lately open'd for twenty boys & twenty girls founded by the encouragement of the Earl of Tyrone, who gave 64 acres at twenty shillings a year. I went on to the mansion house of this estate, which came to the Earl from General Hamilton & belongs to the Society: The house has been lately burnt & is to be rebuilt; Ld. Tyrone designing to give this estate to his second son: The estate is finely planted, mostly with firrs & delightfully situated on the Lough. I took leave of Dr. Bacon & went on towards Kerry [*sic*], a most pleasant ride: For the Lough growing narrower, the country on the other side appeared in much greater beauty. I observed some very Romantick Situations on the rising ground to the South: To the north I saw a small Lough or large pond, with an Island in it, & over it in a most pleasant situation an old Church; This is called Anack, & is I suppose the same that Sr. Wm. Petty calls Ardnenoynak. I came to the river Fin over which I crossed to London derry; this river rises out of Lough fin which is very near the western coast: The towns of Lifford & Strabane are situated on it, opposite to each other, & it is an exceeding fine Country all up the river. London derry is situated on a height over the river which runs on the east & north sides of it; it is something like the Situation of Guilford, commands a view of a well improved hilly country, of the river & the narrow part of the Lough or rather the mouth of the river: From the Situation of two or three Churchyards, where there were old Churches, I concluded that the old town of Derry was situated on the side of the windmill hill to the North west & perhaps extended down to the Valley below, as I was informed it did. When this estate was granted to the Companies, it was on Condition that they should fortifie it, which they did as it now remains in the modern way, but without any subterraneous works, so that on that account & being encompassed with hills it is by no means a strong place, nor can it possibly be made strong: The walk round the ramparts is very pleasant. The Society also built a handsome Townhouse, & a church at the first Settlement, which is an handsom parish Church; something like many Churches in large country towns in England with an organ & Gallery at the west end. The Bishops & Deans seats are pointing to the west, on each side of the opening to the Chancel; & the stalls of the Prebend are to be in a line with them. There is a monument in the church of Mr. Elvinope of the first inhabitants who died in 1676—102 years old. The bass of the pillars are of oxes heads, which I take to have been an old Roman altar cut in two pieces, brought probably from Scotland or the north of England—The present Primate gave a new organ to the church, who was first Dean & then Bishop of this church. There is a foot Barrack in the town for a Regiment, & a Magazine for powder, & an arsenal for their old Canon. They bombarded & played ye Canon on the town from the windmill hill & from another height to the South west; & it is said that when they began to batter the town, the besieged sent to 'em not to hurt the town which would be their own, & that they need not batter, as the gates were open for them to come in; & it is said that a Colonel of a Regiment offering his service to try if he could enter the gates which were actually left open; they having notice of it, planted Canon one over another, gave them a terrible fire, sallyed out & cut the whole Regiment to pieces. Below the town about three miles is Culmore fort at the mouth of the river, across which a chain was drawn to prevent any relief coming to them; but a Ship went against it under full sail, broke the Chain, & brought them provisions when they were in great distress. In the church are two of the Standards which the besieged took from the enemy. The Governor is styled Governor of Culmore & Londonderry & has a sallary of £600 a year. The Commanding Officer is Deputy Governor, & when no troops are in it the Mayor, who is the returning Officer of Members both for this town & the County, as I was informed. They have here a great market every Wednesday for linnen & flaxen yarn; Colerain, Newtown Limne Vaddy & Strabane having linnen markets on the other days of the week for the same purpose, to which the Merchants go round & buy up the linnens & yarn, the latter is sent to Manchester.

On the 12th I spent the day with the Bishop, who on visiting him, insisted on my coming to his house, & sending my horses to his Stables; I walked round the ramparts with Mr. Bernard, preached, & in the even walked round the town & to Windmill Hill.

On the 13th it rained very hard all the morning, & I set out in the afternoon towards Lough Swiley to spend the evening with Dr. Ledwiche, I met him & he went back with me: This Gentleman is married to a niece of the Bishop: About two miles out of the town I saw on a hill Eloch Castle with a tower close to it, which appeared to me to be a round tower. This side of the river Finn is in the County of Donnegal & Barony of Innishowen, which Barony takes in from Birte inclusively all the Peninsula to the North, & this is in the Diocese of Derry; The rest of the County of Donnegal if I mistake not, is in the Diocese of Rapho. I crossed the river which rises near Muff & came to Fantham commonly called Fawn; very pleasantly situated on Lough Swilley opposite to Inch Island. This Lough is formed by the river Swilley, & the tyde which overflows the flat. That river rises near the western Coast, & running by Letterkenny, a litle below it Spreads to near two miles in breadth, it then forms a bay to the south, which with the lake below makes a peninsula of what they call Birte Island, & a litle further on the opposite shoar a bay is formed by the river which comes from about Tully; below this is Inch (Island) a high ground which covers all this bay to the point on which Rath mullen stands, where there is a ferry from Fawn about a league over, in passing of which last month a boat was oversett, & almost all the people thirteen or fourteen drowned: It then takes a pretty direct course to the sea, being all the way about two miles broad; & it is a very pleasant lake: I walked out on the banks of it towards the sea, & in the way came to the Church, where there is a very old Cross,[61] an oblong-Square Stone with a Cross work'd on it in Bas relief & many ornaments round it, there was also a Cross before the churchyard. I then came to a well called St. Mary's well; they have a religious regard for it, & it is arch'd over. A litle beyond this is a slaty rock, which opens on the shoar & is very curiously shaped in most of the members of Architecture; I brought a way a piece, which forms on each side a different compleat Cornish; this I take to be owing to the rock on which this slate is formed, as it is supposed to be under that head of natural productions, which is formed by incrustation; & it is not at all improbable that the several members of Architecture were taken from some such natural formations in the earth, There is an account in History, that St, Patrick was at this place & crossed over to Rathmullen.

    On the 14th I set out to go round Ennishowen & came in two miles to the Strand, where I saw people at work with wooden Shovels, in turning up the Sand, as the sea left the strand, & enquiring what they were about, they told me they were catching Sand Eeles. I observ'd that the moment the wave leaves the Sand, they run in the Shovel, & turn up the Sand & the fish are taken; they are about 4 or 5 inches long, very small for their length; are made like a Whiteing & they say are very good. We came to Burn Cranmer a village of one Street on a litle height over the sea, between two rivlets, one of which gives name to the place,—Burn signifying a rivlet.[62] Here Mr. Vaughan endeavoured to establish a linnen Manufacture & erected buildings for that purpose, but the people breaking, his design came to nothing. A litle beyond the Village Mr. Vaughan has a house pleasantly situated, with fine fields & plantations about it: I went on towards Desert Egnè—& passed by the Old Church, there being a Chapel below for divine service. From this place we ascended still higher & found all bog & heath, & passing two or three hills, we crossed a river, which I suppose is that in Petty called Owen Kirk, & even here the herdsman who keep the cattle have two or three acres under corn, gained out of the heath & morass. On a height near Desert Egni I observed some Stones set up an end as in a circle round a Single Stone, like those in Cornwall. We had high rocky mountains to the north, the barriers against the northern ocean, & going over a high hill, came to the Country called from the parish Clanmany, a very rough Spot of ground, but surprisingly improved, where ever a plough & spade can work: Coming to a rivlet which runs into the bay, I saw a road which leads to Bigny a hamlet to the north west of the point made by these hills, we went on & came to the Strand Strabeghy (the deceitful Strand) by reason that it is full of holes & difficult to pass. I was too late & was obliged to go all round it, having been directed this way in hopes of getting the Strand; for otherwise the short way is directly across the mountain by Carne, which road they told me was not very good. The way was on the south & east Side of the Strand & crossing a rivlet at the east end of it on a bridge, I came into that peninsula which is called Malin: The Morass to the east is called Monei reilta (the Starry bog), for there being Several holes in it full of water it appears in a moonshiny night like Stars, which may serve as an instance of the significancy of Irish names, which commonly are descriptive of the Place. We went westward near the Strand & turning to the north passed by an Old Church called Malin Church, where they say there was a Convent, & going over two hills I come to what they call Malin well, which is the most northern point of Ireland in the degree of 55.19, they told me they had not above two hours night in which they could not read in the longest days, & that the Sun was excessively hot in Summer. This is farther North than ever I was before. Coming near the sea cliff I look'd for the house I was going to, & could see none, but came to a passage down the Cliff where I found the house on the beach under the rocks, & enquiring for the well, they showed me a hollow under a rock at the south end of a high small rocky Island, which at low water is a peninsula: Here people bathe with great success, the water being very Salt, as not mixed with the fresh. & the Roman Catholicks plunge in with superstitious notions that the water receives some virtue from the Saint (Terence Marialla) who lived in a cave in the rock of the cliff, where poor people lodge who come for cure. The house for accommodation is exceeding bad. There is a high beach of pebbles which are esteemed the best in Ireland, except those of a port in the north of Green Castle. They are mostly Jaspar, some jaspar Agates, Cornelian & Agates; & I met with one which seems to be Chalcedony. I had a letter to Mr. Harvey within a mile of the wells, which I sent to him, & soon followed, & met with a most hospitable reception: they presented me with Several curious pebbles & a very curious Crab dryed,—the legs of which are mark'd with winding lines that are white, & from the variegated colour 'tis supposed that it has obtained the name of the Highlander; they are exceeding scarce, & it may be they do not meet with one in seven years. I observ'd a fine Square head of land to the west called Malin Arde, which is under corn & appears very beautifull, being a peninsula: To the east are very high rocks, where there are eagles which frequently carry off lambs; & a man being let down by ropes to the nest of one of them, in which he found eggs, he met also with a salmon & a Breme; the former swimming in Shallow water might easily be taken, but the Breme, keeping deep in the sea must have been supposed to have been thrown up. The fishermen observe an extraordinary thing here, that if they find a Stone in the Cod fish that it is a certain sign of an approaching Storm, & it is supposed they Swallow it in order to sink themselves to the bottom of the Sea, that they may not be dashed against the rocks, as they frequently are, & are taken up dead sometimes in great numbers; it is supposed also that they have a power of disgorging the stone;

on the 15th Mr. Harvey sent his man with me to Coledaff, passing the bridge which I came over to this Country: I observed a fine habitation over the SW to the North east, Mr. Donorty's called Catridge. In five miles we came to Coledaff, where there is a church, & Mrs. Young has a good house with a plantation of trees about it. We soon passed by Redfort the house of Mr. Elwood Minister of the place, which probably had its name from a red vein of soil about this place; I observed an Island at the north east point & saw Clonkan Church to the South west, which is the Parish Church of Mallin: We had an unpleasant road across the mountains to the south west; & came to the rivlet, which runs along a valley that meets another which ends in the bay of Clanmeny, that I had pass'd & going eastward three miles, came to the Lough of Derry near Moville Parish where Mr. O Neal has a house pleasantly situated, & I went two miles to the north along the Shoar to Green Castle where I dined. I went to see the fine Old Castle[63] built on a rock, the entrance is defended by two towers, where the Chief apartments were; the north end is also defended by towers & it is a strong & delightful situation. It was the Strenght of the O Donorty's, the last of which family going to London to Queen Eliza. was Knighted, but afterwards being in rebellion: his estate which was all Ennishowen was forfeited, most part of which now belongs to the Earl of Donnegal; This Castle may have its name from the green fire Stone it is built of. A quarter of a mile from it is a Chapel which seemed to have been built with pinnacles & with large windows, & is very uncommon in this Country. This is the passage of two miles from the opposite point of Magilligan; near which I had passed before from Colerain. I set out Southward & came in five miles to Red Castle, where Mr. Carew has a very handsom house near the sea: I went two miles further to White Castle & two to Turn, near which the direct road from Mallin comes in, which it is said is through a most pleasant vale, in which I suppose the river runs, that is placed in the large map of Ireland near White Castle. I came five Miles to Muff, where the poor Inns were all full, being the market day of Derry, from which it is five miles distant. So I sent to Mr. Hart half a mile from the town, a pleasant Situation near the Lough of Derry, brother of Alderman Hart, who has been Ld. Mayor of Dublin, who sent me a welcome, & his son received me, as the father was gone to repose.

On the 16th Mr. Hart treated me with great civility, invited me to spend the day, & sent his son Captn. Hart to show me the neat Chapel of Muff, & a pleasant view from a hill, from which among other things I saw Culmore Church: He accompanied me with great civility as far as the Strand which crosses to Birt. I crossed that Strand the southern side of which is bad, enter'd on it, two miles from Fatham or Fawn Dr. Ledwiches. On the other side of the Strand is a large Meeting house to which there was a great concourse of people from all parts being the Fast day before the Sacrament, & they had a sermon, to which they come fasting & afterwards take their repast. I went on three miles & passed by Mr. Forwoods, having had a view of the fine hill of Birte a peninsula called an Island, on the top of which are the remains of an old round Tower; This is part of Mr. Forwoods estate: a litle mile further brought us to Newtown Cunningham, the estate of Mr. Hamilton, where his brother the Curate now lives, they are Sons of Archdeacon Hamilton, who formerly lived here, he is a very fine Old Gentlemen between 80 & 90, I dined here & came to the top of a high hill, by an easy ascent, from which there was a most glorious view of all Lough Swilly seen behind three or four heads of land which lock in & divide it in a most beautiful manner; To the South west we had a view up the river Swilly beyond Letterkenny, a very fine Vale to the South, the Country of Mannor Cunningham & some adjacent villages, as an Amphitheater, encompassed with hills well improved, rising gently over one another to a considerable height, on the other side of which is Rapho. I came to Mannor Cunningham three miles from Newtown. It is a large village; I went a litle beyond it to the Charter School of Ray founded by Dr. Foster late Bp. of Rapho on 22 acres of land given by John Leslie Esqr. at a small rent, & 2 in perpetuity without rent, for 20 boys & 20 girls. I went on five miles westward to Letter Kenny. Nothing can be imagined more beautifull than the winding of the Swilly & several streams running into it, all at that time full with the tyde; The view of LetterKenny of Mr. Spaws house beyond it & opposite to it Captn. Chambers[64] & above it Major Staffords page to King James the 2^d, who has been some time dead, add greatly to the beauty of the prospect. This high ground on each side the river being most like the fine Views on the Aire in Yorkshire. At Newtown Cunningham I came into the Barony of Enishowen being in the Diocese of Derry, I was informed that the place of residence of the Bishop of Derry was first at Newtown-Stewart & then at Marra, they had no Episcopal house at Derry, till Bishop King purchased the present house of the Normans by the lease of Fawn which they now enjoy. Nor could I be certainly informed that there was ever any Cathedral Church at Derry, & the present seems not to be properly a Cathedral, but only made use of by the Bishop & Chapter, the parish belonging to the Deanery, as most of the parishes do near Derry—Letter kenny seems to have its name, as some other places from being the grant or letter to one of the name of Kenny,[65] so in Boyhlagh Letter—McWard was probably granted by patent or Letter it may be from the head of a Clan to a family of the name of McWard—Letterkenny is more beautifull in prospect than when one enters it, consisting of one Street meanly built, with gardens behind the houses & there are remains of an Old Square Castle. The chief trade of the town consists of shops to furnish the Country to the north, & a market for oats & Barley, wheat, some yarn & flax. We here enter'd the Barony of Kilmacrenan, & I was detained all the morning of the 17th by rain. In the afternoon I cross'd for five miles over two hills excessive bad roads to Kilmacrenan, on the road I saw a new kind of round fort, common here, made of loose Stones well put together the walls are ten feet thick & about eight high encompassed with a fossee & about seventeen yards in Diameter within, Kilmacrenan is a very poor village on a river called Gannon, which runs through rocks beautifully adorned with trees, & all over the Country there is an agreeable variety of Hills, Rocks, Wood & Corn fields, The church is thought to be part of an Old Convent of Minorets founded by O Donnel,[66] over the door is a relief of a mitred head. We here come to the fine new road which is making from Letterkenny to the north west point of this Barony chiefly carried on under the direction of Mr. Wray of Ardes: It leads over a very high hill, on which there is a fine lake call'd Lough farne which is about a mile long & a quarter of a mile broad, the new road being carried on three sides of it, & the hills rise above it all round being very high to the South, & on this side is the extraordinary old road, which seems to have been very difficult as well as frightfull to the traveller, being over a precipice with the deep lake directly under it: To the right of the passage down to Doe is a small lake on the side of the hill into which this empties it self & from that the water runs down into the sea, To the East coming up to this lake, I saw another about a mile in circumference it is called Lough Castle Culane: Going up the low hills to the north of the lake, I was extremely surprised at the view of the Country, consisting below of a great number of small Loughs, in a heathy[67] Country & some spots of Corn to the north & east, two bays winding in & forming several Strands for some miles, many of them appearing when the tyde is in like Serpentine rivers, not without many Spots of corn & wood. The countries here are distinguished by general names, probably the old names of the Clans, by which they are now called & also by the names of the parishes which have generally the same bounds: As the country to the East comprehending the parish of Clandevadoge is called Fanet, a parish finely bounded by the sea, by Lough Swilley by the bays & Strands, which are formed by the sea, which comes in at an opening between this & a division to the westward, call'd Rosquil named by the Lord Boyne whose estate it was Rosapenna & now belongs to Mr. Clements. This opening is mark'd in the map of Ireland by the name of the river Mullroy, & by a river in Petty's Map, but neither of them show the large bays & Strands which are formed by this inlett: Dr. Bedford lives in that parish, which tho' hilly is all under corn, & is a most delightfull retirement. This Clergyman is greatly regarded by the people, to whom he is a father, & there being plenty of Corn, he has put them in a way of exporting it, by freighting a Ship & advises them in every thing for their interest. Rosaquill is another head of land, the parish if I mistake not, is called Carrigart the church of which is just opposite to Rosapenna house. The next division is Doe, divided from this by another bay, which is called Ship haven, this is the parish of Clauda hurky; taking in Ards Mr. Wrays & Horn head Captn. Stowarts. The fourth part is Clo ha heny, which takes in all the country to the west, as far as that which is called the Rosses & has in it the Parishes of Ray & Tullaghobegly, of all which I shall be more particular, when I passe thro' them as I determine on this most romantick prospect of these Countries. I returned to Letterkenny.

on The 18th I set out for that Country by a diferent way, going towards Tully in a road about half a mile distant from Lough Swilly & passed by a fort of the same kind as the other called Lis Ballyart, the walls of which are twelve feet thick, the Diameter within twenty two paces, the fossee fourteen & the rampart is eight broad; I observed that the houses are built with sods, supported within by a wooden frame, which the poor people sometimes leave with their effects, when the collector of the hearth money approaches: The roof indeed of all their cabins built with Stone & Clay are fixt on wooden posts within the wall, which is not strong enough to support the roof. I came to Tully consisting only of a few poor scatter'd houses & an Iron work, there being Iron mines at Lismonokan about a mile west of Letterkenny & at Pluck two miles from it. We had seen Rath mellan a mile to the East a small town at the south west corner of the bay, on which Rathmellan stands opposite to Fawn where Dr. Ledwich lives. I was informed that there are remains of an Old Convent here called Kiloghdonogh which is probably the Convent of Franciscans called by Ware Kilodonel, We went on & crossed the river Gannon which runs through Kilmacrenan, & between the same beautifull rocks & trees; which are seen all over the the country [*sic*] especially about Mr. Grove's at Balymoyle to the south, with an agreeable variety of corn fields. Over this seat is a fort of the same kind as the others called Lis Brunhal, & in the Country below are four small Loughs. A litle beyond Tully to the west is Lough Ferne above a mile long, & winding round the north end of it there are at that end two or three small Islands in it. In two or three miles from Tully we come to a village call'd Berenenalagah: From this place for three miles to Cranford, the seat of Mrs. Cunningham the road was most pleasant, being in the sight of a wood & by the edge of it. We descended towards it & came to Brinian bay, a Strand, which winds round from the great Strand to the west of Clandevadoge, & is formed by the inlet of the sea between Rosquil & Fanet: we crossed the river which falls into it at the west end, & went along this Strand at the edge of a wood which covers the hill, & from this place between woods & rocks & other Strands two computed miles to Cranford Mrs. Cunninghams, a most exceeding pleasant ride: Afterwards we rid by the great Strand, the bay appearing like a large Lake & saw Rosurkils & near it the Church of Clande vadoge, the country to the west being rough; We passed by several litle Strands, saw some ruined Salt pans & works for boyling the Salt: & came near the Church of Carrigart, which is the parish in the division of Rosa penna or Rosquil; & passing the end of the Strand on which Rosa penna house stands, I dined on the west Side of it: Here I observed a long sort of sea weed, much like a rush peeled for lights & pretty long, they call it Raff, I found it five or six yards long & growing to a Stone: They say, it is sometimes twenty yards long, & that it twines round people in the water to such a degree, that it often occasions drowning: We went on mostly through Sandy banks, which are rabbit warrens & came near the Strand, which from the opening to the west of Rosquil forms a bay, that extends first to the South & then to the west beyond the Castle of Doe. We came opposite to Ards Mr. Wrays seat[68] & fine plantation & afterwards to the Castle of Doe, to which we might have crossed, if the tyde had been out, but were obliged to go above a mile farther, & came into the new road from Letterkenny & Salt hill & turned to the north. I here observed a Stone, which appear'd like a Slaty grey marble, but they told me yt it is not a lime Stone; it is formed like the slate at Fawn in the form of several members of Architecture. We passed a river on a bridge which rises from Lough Vah, a Lake in a very Romantick Vale, called Glysivah which is to the south of the mountain called Muckish judged to be one of the highest in Ireland: Coming near the west end of the Strand, on which the Castle of Doe is built, I saw a beautifull fall of water which descends from Lough meur; & going northward I passed by a Chapel of ease to Clonharhurky Church, & a litle beyond it a remarkable Fort on a high rocky hill, of the same Kind as the other walled forts, which is called Lismore (the great fort) & passing over a bridge observed a rivlet falling in beautifull Maeanders into the sea. Half a mile farther we come to the New Church which is now building for this parish, with rustick Quoin stones of grey Marble, which they have near Dunfanahy, & the upper Members of a basement round the church, the design is a Venetian window at the end & four windows on the South side, the frames of which are to be of the Same Marble: it is a very fine Situation, & the ornamental part is very much to the honour of the Gentleman who is to be at the expence of it, Dr. Obins, late fellow of Trinity College, the Minister of this place. We descended down to Jeshiah Lough, about two miles in circumference with a small island in the middle, but it is one of the finest Lakes I ever beheld; the beauty of it chiefly consists in the hills, that are to the south side of it which rise gently from the middle of one side of the Lake & are covered with wood, on each side of which the ground is bolder & afords a most agreeable variety of rock & wood. We then soon came on the strand & turning westward, arrived in less than a mile at a very poor small town called Dunfanahy on a small creek in this great Bay, which is made by an inlet of the sea to the East of Horn head; I found I could get no sort of accommodation here, & so sent a note to Mr. Stewart at the west end of the bay, who returned a Welcome in answer; I went & took up my quarters at his house. As soon as I was set down to Supper a messenger come to me from Mr. Wray six miles with a letter in which he informed me, that hearing I had passed & knowing there was no accommodation at the place, he desired me to come the next day to his house & that on Monday he would ride with me & show me the Curiosities of the Country.

On the 19th I rid with the family to Church & preached, met Mr. Wray & family there, who came & dined at Mr. Stewarts. This Gentlemans house is situated on the Side of the hill over the bay, which extends to the north east & makes Horn head; The house is fortifyed in some manner, & stood a siege against a privateers crew in the wars at the beginning of this century; There is a bay on the main sea to the north west, called Trahimore (The great Strand), between that & the other Strand is a great bank & hillocks of Sand, which gain on the ground to the east, this & some ground bordering on it, make a very large warren belonging to Mr. Stewart, of which he makes about £500 a year, Killing commonly 14 or 1500 dozen a year, the Skins of which he sells for about nine Shillings a dozen, & the flesh for six pence a dozen. In the evening we rid across it to the bay; on each side of which the rocks are very fine, the beach consists of large pebbles, & finding ridges of them farther from the sea under the Sand, they conclude that the sea looses here. We went to the north west side of the bay to the sea Cliffs to see that great Curiosity MacSuines Gun.[69] The Cliffs about 100 feet high form a litle triangular creek at the bottom of which is a hole in the rock like a large arch, it may be fifty feet wide, this may go in about thirty feet, & over it is an opening which is irregular, but at the top forms a triangle it may be fifteen feet on one Side & thirty on the two others; on the arch mentioned on the outside we saw the waves roll in & filling the hole, they tumbled back with a great noise, 'tho it was a very fine calm evening; but in Stormy weather when the waves are drove in with great violence & one succeeding another very quick, the water is forced up to the top with the very Stones, & Sometimes with such force that it forms a jetteau in a large body rising very high, some said, a height hardly to be believed, but probably an hundred feet, the wind blowing the water with great force over the land, so as that there is no Standing against it, not only on account of the water, but likewise of the Stones which it throws up. From this I went over the Stony ground, in which the Stones are laid along in rows in many places as for bounds, but in some places so near to one another, that I concluded many of them, were pickt up by the herdsmen to clear the ground. The rocks at Horn head are very high, & it is a curious Sight to see the birds when they are brooding, being much like that of the Isle of Wight; They are of three sorts, the Puffin about as big as a partridge, called also Coulter neb, they have a parrots bill: the Razor bill or Auk, as big as a Pheasant, with a parrot bill likewise; the [Funin?] with a sharpe picked bill, on the Strands they have a seapye with a red bill & legs, which lays in the rocks on the Shoar & does not go into the sea, & I was informd that Curlieus lay in the rocks of inland mountains. Passing through the water over a Strand, I was made to observe that the birds follow'd the horses, & dived dawn where'ere they had trod, which is to take up the Sand eeles, & other small fish that are pressed out of the Sand by the feet of the horses. I went to see the Marble quarry near Dunfanahy, it is a white marble with some Blewish veins, the bed may be about six or seven feet thick, in which there is one layer near three feet thick, of much better Marble then the rest: It lyes in a large patch from the mountain to the sea, where a Stream Spreads it self from the Mountain; By the look of it & by the manner in which the bed lyes, I concluded it to be an Alabaster made by the running of the water, which brings the fine particles of the Stone that unite & form the Alabaster as in the Stalactites. Asking the quarriers whether it was an Alabaster, they said it was not, but a lime stone, which I imputed to their ignorance, if so be that Alabaster will burn to lime, as if I mistake not, it does. Going from church in the morning I observed a Circumstance, which added to the Romantic view of the mountains to the South: In the Side of one of them a Sort of Amphitheatre is formed in the rock; here I saw several hundred people spread all over that plain spot, the priest celebrating Mass under the rock, on an altar made of loose Stones, & tho' it was half a mile distant, I observed his Pontifical Vestment with a black Cross on it; for in all this Country for Sixty miles west & south as far as Connaught, they celebrate in the open air, in the fields or on the mountain; the Papists being so few & poor, that they will not be at the expence of a public building.

On the 20th I went with this family by invitation five or six miles to the South-east to Mr. Wrays & saw in the way Doe Castle, it is a fine Square turret of five Stories & near Sixty feet high, it is encompassed with an inner Well & Turrets & with a second almost all round. This was the Strength of the Mac-Suines, who were masters of this Country; & after the wars the head of them being offered part of his lands, as they say, refused them, unless he had all, & the books being Shut, he lost all. Near this Castle are some small remains of a Convent of Minorites, which must be that Monastery called by the Historians Baley MacSuine near Doe: They also mention another called Beleaghan, which I could not hear of, no more than of Muchish Abbey put down in the Maps. To the north of this, is what they call the Marble-rock, it is a bad white, with large Spots of a sort of Ash-colour, what they have raised does not polish well, but if they dig deeper, they might probably find a better vein; it is a very uncommon marble. I went on to Mr. Wrays called Ardes, on a rising ground on the North side of the bay, which is formed by an inlet of the sea, half a mile to the east of it, the gardens are on the descent to the bay, that forms a beautifull basin before the house, which is well shelter'd not only by the hills to the north, but by the fine plantations about it, & from those hills there is a beautifull prospect of the sea, & of the Country & the bays that are near, here I saw Melons ripe, & fruit in great perfection. This gentleman is married to a daughter of Archdeacon Hamilton mentioned before who in the troubles went to Magdalen College in Oxford, & is above eighty years old with all his senses & understanding in great perfection: To the publick Spirit & activity of Mr. Wray those fine roads are owing, which are made over Lough Salt mountain & in other parts, laid out so as to be finished in about seven years, by allotting such a measure of road yearly to each house, according to the value of the land they hold: they are twenty one feet broad, with a margin on each side of green turf about two feet wide; they are first raised with the earth that is thrown up to make a fossee on each side, then they lay a coat of broken quarry stone, on that some earth & then gravel at top. These roads considering the Cheapness of Carriage on litle truckles drawn by one horse, almost answer the end of water carriage, for they will draw a hogs head of wine, or anything not exceeding 600lb. weight & one man will attend three or four of them: they commonly feed their horses on the grass they find in the road, so that they will carry a hundred & fifty miles for about three Shillings a hundred.

on the 21st I took leave & with Mr. Stewarts family went three miles beyond his house to the west to Ray to the house of Mr. Hartley the minister who had invited us to dine with him. Mr. Babington who met us on the road, went with me in the way to see the Marble quarry. At the Church at Ray is a very Curious old Cross broken in pieces. I here met young Mr. Orphilts a very accomplished young Gentleman, married to another daughter of Archdeacon Hamilton he carried me half a mile to his fathers house, where I lay, walking out to the sea side; they here thatch with a Course grass called bent, with which also they make cords.

on the 22d, Mr. Orphilts went with me a mile to Mr. MacSuines, where I set out with two hired men & horses to Carry my provisions, as well as to Show me the way; there are no more gentlemen to the west nor to the south for near thirty miles, till one comes to Eniskeel: Mr. Orphilt accompanied me some way farther, but whilst I was waiting in the last place, a large Eagle flew directly over the yard & the fowl came all running towards us, & making a noise, from which I judged that they were alarmed by the noise of the eagles wings when he flies. They have in these parts two doors to their Cabbins, keeping one only open on the side that is not expos'd to the wind, as they have no light commonly, but by the door. In all these parts the drinking of Whisky very much prevails, they call it in Irish Usquebaugh, which is I suppose the general name for Spirits, as Arraki is in the east, so the eastern Spirit is called Arrack, as the spirit for which Ireland is famous is called Usquebaugh. Whiskey is made of Barley, they also distill it from water press'd from potatoes after they are boyled to a mash, which they ferment with barme; they have a notion here that it is the wholsomest of Spirits, tho' I have reason to think it is the worst of that kind; & has tended very much to debauch & corrupt the Common people. We passed by a hamlet called Ballinascagh, where there is a very large Stone of Granite so equally poised, that a man putting his shoulder to it, moves it very easily, after the manner of the

rocking Stones in Cornwal. I here saw the Machine for twisting Straw ropes, which has been thought to have been one of the Egyptian Hieroglyphics, in honour of the person who invented it, it is in this shape the straw is fixed to the top, it is held at the bottom & turn'd round being a swivel at P. this instrument they call in Irish Corhougan.

Going on farther I saw stones set up an end, seeming to be of that kind of Monument which is seen in Cornwall & Wales call'd ye Cromlech, of a large Stone laid on three or four Stones & are called [*text illegible*]. For three miles we went through a very rough road over the hill called Crocheniniary, having Morass to the South full of litle loughs & a rivlet to the west, which falls into the sea at Clanashour bay where there is a village. I observed at the top of the hill we passed some of the Grey Granite extending from east to west mostly in two lines, which probably is the top of some bed of Granite, there being no other pieces about the hill, which rises much higher to the north: A mile further we saw a bay called Olignio, where there were some Cottages bordering on the bog, which we passed with some difficulty; being now come to the western shoar; & having turn'd our faces to the south, we had another hill to the north called Culsolich, which is the hill that makes the north west point, we came to Bolileneu, where I sat down by a river & dined, having passed these bogs; some poor came about me & I bless God Almighty that I had to feed them! The Irish

Grace was said, Raghnakoude nrahan, agles da jesk ring Dieu erna Koub Mille; diring Dieu rockown re dering ren en ring er argoud, agus er argoron. In English thus, God blessed the five loaves & the two fishes & divided them among the five thousand; may the blessing of the Great King who made this distribution descend on us & our provision.[70]

We went on half a mile to Glashan, here I observed a sort of ash coloured Granite, of which all the rocks are to the sea; & then travelled between sandy banks a quarter of a mile to Carig & about two miles to Lognian & a mile further to Makery Clogher, in half a mile came to a river & in a mile to Nickart Wullery,

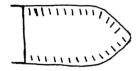 where I proposed to cross over the river Slady on the strand in a Curragh & to swim my horses. A Curragh is a very extraordinary boat, about seven feet long & three feet & a half wide, & about two feet & a half deep in this shape, it is made of strong wicker, covered over with the raw hide of a horse or bullock. It is set up an end on the frame which is continued on each side as at a a in order to dry it when they take it out of the water, as they always do; I saw a woman carrying one to a Lough & two children following her, she paddled it along at the head, sometimes on one side, sometimes on the other, & when a puff of wind came she held up her gown for a sail. We cried out to her Brahaskin (well done) & she answered Maugiliore (well enough). The horse that swims at the end of these is held with a bridle by one in the boat. The tyde was come in too far, so I took up my lodging in a Cabbin at the village, where the farmer told me I was the first that ever eat of his own provision in his house.

On the 23d. I set forward & in less than a mile pased over the river Slady on a bridge; which runs beautifully down the rocks & here they have a salmon fishery; we now entered into the Country called the Rosses, or as I suppose the heads,— probably an old word derived from the Arabick Ross—a head or Cape of Land, & it is the parish of Temple Croan; here the rocks are of the same red Granite as that of Egypt, of which the Obelisks are made. We then went a mile & half & came to a Strand called Trakern bay, & in a mile more to Molah Durack & in two miles to strand Bernientileh, having all the way a most agreeable variety of Strand; rocks & litle Loughs & views of Strands or Bays, with rocky Islands in them: We had also islands in the seas all along on this Coast—A litle farther south is Colain, then Ennisboy, farther south Enisurnak & then Enniskoul left dry by the tyde, here I was to have crossed over: The mountains from Doe westward are Muckish, Iacca, Altam, behind which is Glyn Vah, then Mulock, then Argile, a most beautifull pointed mountain the highest of all, as some think, & the top when seen above some hills appeared like the great Pyramid: Then Slea Snaiteh (Snow mountain): & the low Chain of Hills running west of these & to the South are called Carantricanah. Having passed the Strand we came to Kedu, & had in our view to the left a long beautifull Lough called Wellan, appearing like a serpentine river. We passed by Temple Crowan Church, which is a mean low, thatched building; this Living of £80 a year is in dispute & is lapsed to the Crown, & is ye most desolate & I may say uninhabited part in the world. We came on to a boggy part of the Country, & having past some difficult places, the guide desired me to walk a short way to Glasbegginmill & went in search of a good pass but could not find any & was obliged to come back & go in the comon way near a rivlet which turns that Mill, which I passed with great difficulty on foot; I saw they were obliged to come to it; the Miller came to meet us, & I asked him if there was a door or a board to lay for the horses to pass; he said there was not; but the guide went to the mill & brought a board & an Oxes skin. So laying sods & heath the skin & the board on that, & sods on each side of it to keep the horses from slipping in, we cross'd on them safely, & passing on still over bog, when we came to any narrow passes, the horses leap'd them, & taking another guide we came to Letter McWard, a hamlet of three or four houses: I observed they chose to go on the edges of hanging grounds over rivlets or low places which are driest. We had this Morning the Isle of Arran to the west, which is about two miles long & a mile broad, & some other Isles South of it, & passed the rivlet called Cloghnehich (The grey Stone) on which there is held a yearly Fair for Cattle: Before we came to Letter McWard, we went two miles on a Strand called Trianah into which falls the river Goninesh & when we had pass'd over the hill of Letter McWard we came to a Strand & the river Gubarrow, which is crossed in a Curragh, & the horses are led in & swim across. This river rises to the North east; & directly west is a high hill, on the side of which is Lough Fin, out of this Lake the river Fin rises: Then there is the chain of hills between that & the Swilly: The mountain to the North of Gubarrow is called Dirliaconnel, then going North, follow Croiveh, Craheh, Carvan Trianch & Bloody Farrel. This Country being entirely unknown I have been the more particular in relation to it, for my own satisfaction. From the Ferry I west westward along the Strand, & passed under an old Church called Kilkenny, a Chapel of Ease to Enniskeel, a mile farther I came to a village called Balyaristan: & having a letter to Mr. Stewart the Minister of Inniskeel I came in two miles to his house, the first half on the Strand & the remainder within the Sand banks; opposite to it is a Small Island called Keel or Inniskell (Island Red) in which are two churches, about one the Protestants bury, & at the other the Papists; At low water they ride over to it. This Parish extends for near thirty miles from the western point as far as Lough Fin; near that Lough there is a road from it to Strabane, & all that Country on the Fin & the Swilly, is called the Laggan. There is a voluntary division of the parish for this turn, there being a chapel to the west served by a Clergymen who has half the profits:

On the 24th I set out in the afternoon & going along the Strand for a mile, ascended the hill to the west & came to Lough Kildairar, & observed an Island in it, with a building on it; We then came to Locrasmore bay, & to a bridge over the river O Neck, where there is a Stone set up an end & nine feet high, four broad & three thick, they call it Fin McCoues Shoulder Stone, with which he used to divert himself by throwing it like a Quoit. We then went over the Ardragh on a bridge & soon had Locrasbeg bay to the west. There are three Chains of mountains which run the length of the head of land, one on the Northern Shoar, another on the Southern, & the third running along the Middle of the Country are called the mountains of Boylagh, from the half barony of that name; the other half barony of Banagh being to the South, we came to Mugurny on the entrance between the mountain in the middle, & passing several Streams came to Mulmussack mountains which are part in Boylagh & part in Banagh & at length to the long bog called Stragate mountain, over which there is a very good road made to a village call'd Carrignabouhil on a rivlet called Bougoshton that falls into the bay of Killibegs, at which place we arrived; a very poor town or rather village, Situated on the west Side of the bay, about a mile from the sea, & from the north end of the bay; it is esteemed one of the finest harbours in Ireland: there is a narrow entrance to it, on the inside of which is an Old Castle & over it the foundations of another, call'd CatiCastle. At the lower Castle the East india Ships when they came in during Queens Anns war, planted a battery & another on the opposite side, & there is a height over the town, where they say, there was a Castle: There are a very few fishing boats here; but ships belonging to Baley-Shannon Merchants come here & unload, having Ware houses for that purpose; BaleyShannon being a bad harbour, by reason of a barr which hinders any Ship of Burthen from coming into a safe place. To the west there is an open bay call'd Ti[   ] or Tilcers, where there is a curious Cave, & beyond it at Mount Sleavebag there is a bed of Marble.

On the 25th, I set out for Donnegal: in three miles we came to Dinhonely & a mile farther to Brocla's bay, on which there is a Castle; two Streams fall into the bay of Killibegs & three into this. We had St. Johns point to the South, where there is a hole like that called MacSuines Gun: there is also a large Cave with a table in it, cut in the rock, which they call Temple Sugan. Three miles farther we came to Inver another large bay, where I observed a kind of granite lying loose in the bay of a light liver Colour with large grains in it, of a kind of Sparr. The Country to the north is mostly beautifull & well improved & more particularly three miles farther about Mount Charles on the Bay into which the river of Donnegal falls: Here the Country Consists of Small hills all covered with herbage or Corn, & some wood to add to the beauty of it. The land running sometimes into the bay in such litle hills, makes the view from Mount Charles which is almost all covered with Wood one of the most delightful I ever saw. Three miles more brought us to Donnegal which stands on the East side of the river Eask that rises out of a Lough of that name, three or four miles to the north west of the town. It is but a poor small town built almost all round a sort of triangular Green: There is an old Castle which had been improved into a good

W.H. Bartlett, Ballyshannon, County Sligo, 1842

house with the help of some addition to it, particularly there is in it, a very well designed Chimney piece in the Style of Inigo Jones but not executed in the best manner: It was the Castle of the O Donnels formerly Lords of this Country, & now belongs to Sr. Arthur Gore, whose Grandfather lived in it. A quarter of a mile out of the town are the remains of an Old Convent of minorites said to be founded by Odo sirnamed Rufus O'Donnel in 1473 & that there was a good Library in it. The Cloyster Consists of small arches, supported by couplets of pillars on a basement, in one part are two narrow passages one over another, about four feet wide, ten long & seven high, which seem to be places for depositeing valuable effects in time of danger; the upper one is covered with Stones laid along on the beams of Stone that Cross it, & the lower one with Stones laid across on the walls, both exactly after the Egyptian manner; & in a building over it are plain marks of a regular Roman pediment tho' there had been some other building raised against it, which made me conclude that this was the remains of some very ancient building either converted into a Convent, or it may be now founded by O Donnel. Donnegal is a Corporation consisting chiefly if not altogether of out Burgesses.[71] There is a way when the tyde is out to Balintra five miles off, but I went the inland way & struck out of the high road to the South east to go to the Caves called the Pulleins near Colonel Hamiltons house a mile from Balintra, by which place I ought to have come instead of going

Chiefly along by a rivlet a very bad road for three miles: These Caves are large & a river runs at the bottom of them, goes under ground & afterwards comes out, but they were so overflowed that I could not go in. Colonel Hamiltons is a fine plantation & a well improved estate.[72] I came through Balintra a very poor town, & in five miles more came by a very fine road to Ballishannon, where Mr. Conelly being to make some short Stay there was such a concourse of people, that the Inns were full; So I sent to Mr. O Neal the Minister to accommodate me with a bed, which he did with great politeness. Ballyshannon is most delightfully situated near the mouth of the Erne, on the north side of it on a bold rising ground, this river rises in the County of [   ] & forms that beautiful lake which is known by the name of Lough Erne, & perhaps exceeds any in the world for the beauty of Land round it, & of the Islands in it covered with wood. The mouth of this river is blocked up not only by sand, but by a ridge of rocks that cross it, above which there is a fine basin, above this is a Shelf of rocks crossing the river which forms most beautifull cascades of water, that fall about fifteen feet which has a fine effect from the height under the church, as well as from the other side; & here is a famous salmon leap.

On the 26th I walk'd to see it & met Mr. Conolly, who was pleased to take knowledge of me, & to desire me to joyn—& to go & dine with him at Colonel Foliots: We went to Church, where a dependent of Mr. Conolly's preached before him, after church Colonel Foliot invited me to dine with him, & introduced me to Lord Adam Gordon brother to the Duke of Gordon, an officer of his Regiment, who is with him at his Country house,[73] & his Lordship took me with him in the Colonels Chaise, & we dined a large Company at Colonel Foliots, who brought me back near two miles in his Chaise.

On the 27th Mr. O Neal rid with me to Badeke three miles where there is fine hanging ground; wood, Islands & several Cascades, altogether making a most beautifull appearance; we rid four miles further opposite to Sr. James Calwells house,[74] this gentleman has spent most of his time abroad, was Aid de camp in the Austrian service to General Odonnel, whose father dined with us yesterday, & they say is the head of that family descended from the Earl of Tyrconel & tho' he has only leases, yet he is the head of the Roman Catholicks in this Country, & has a great interest, is a sensible man, & well versed in the Irish History, both written & traditional: & it is said that Sr. James being agreeable to the Empress was made a Count of the Empire, which title he does not take upon him. Lough Erne & the Islands appear very beautiful from this Hill, there being many considerable Seats on it as at Bel Turbot Ld. Lansborough's, Castle Hume,[75] the seat of Loftus Hume, where there is a black marble with a brown cast & so not an agreeable black, but polishes pretty well, & many others. The Lough is divided into two parts the communication being by a narrow Channel, on which stands the town of Enniskilling: The road we were in is the way to Lough Derg, where is the famous place of pilgrimage, called St. Patricks Purgatory.[76] There is a good road also as far as to Pettigoe where Mr. Skelton lives,[77] who has lately wrote very well against Deism. Lough derg is three miles beyond it through a very rough road, I return'd & dined with Colonel Murray (who had come to see me in the morning) I dined in Company with Mr. Conolly & many others, this Gentleman is brother to Lord Elebanck & to Mr. Murray who made so much noise in the Parliament of the year 1750 & is Lieutenant Colonel of foot.[78] I had also in the morning been to visit Mr. & Mrs. Moore & Mr. Taylor her brother, son to Sr. Thomas Taylor, who with two four wheel'd Chaises were come from Lough Erne & were going to Giants Cause way &c.: I walked in the even to see a Cascade three quarters of a mile above the town: The river falls in a narrow Channel between the rocks, & there is a descent for a great way, which makes the river very rapid. I observed in the rocks of Marble the Trochi, Entrochi & Asteriae. I walked also down towards the mouth of the river on the east side to a house of Lord Foliot to whom this estate did belong, but descending to the Heirs General, it was sold to Mr Connelly: The house is particular as it is brick on the outside & stone within. The Ancestor of that Lord came over from England in office; And the Colonel & Captn, Foliot are descended from Collateral branches. The Lime Stone is seen here in many places on the Surface of the ground, & the Softer parts being worn away, it appears in many odd figures above ground. On the opposite side Colonel Foliots estate is well improved. Beyond it is Clary Castle, the Strong hold of that family who have since taken the name of Clark, & beyond that is a curious Grotto, the top of which appears like a fine Arch.

On the 28th Mr. O Neal went out with me three miles to the South to see Lough Melieri, which to the South is bounded by the mountains in the County of Leitrim & extends from the north east to the South west about eight miles & may be between two & three miles long; there are about half a dozen Islands in it covered with wood, a river runs into it from Lough Cane which has a communication with Lough Nilly, & the water of it falls into the sea at Bundroose, & all these waters are this way the bounds between Ulster & Connaught & between the Counties of Donnegal & Sligoe. I went to take leave of Mr. Connolly & Col. Murray, the former was not at home: & I set out for Sligoe, stopped on the other side of the river at Bundrose, where there is a Castle on the river which comes out of the Lake Melvin. Here I sat down in the County of Sligoe in Connaught & dined, the river being beautifully divided into four Streams, by beds of pebbles on each of which are boxes to take salmon. In the road from Ballihaven in two miles I passed by Finnah Church & then travelled two miles to the river Drook, at the mouth of which is a Castle called Bundrouch, in half a mile we came to Castle Duncarberey, & in a mile more to the Mannor of Ward-house belonging to Mr. Gore who has a jayl for Debtors for a certain

sum. Half a mile further we came to a rivlet there being an opening to the South
in the mountains called Glanedy, through which there is a road to Bally-Hamil-
ton. I observed beyond this a fine mountain called Gartne, which seemed to be
detached from the rest, but when I came to the west of it, I saw it joyned on to
them: beyond this is the most beautiful mountain I ever behold called Ben Wall
ben. The upper part is perpendicular, but being worn in a sort of rough pillars
by the rain, it appears like a Gothic work, the rest of the mountain is a Steep
descent & a fine verdure; I saw on it many flocks of Sheep which added to the
beauty of it: the top of this mountain is flat & here the hills turn to the South. I
came to Bundutt in about a quarter of a mile, & had Millino head to the South
west, a mile further to Castle Buiskin, in two miles to Der Innis & as many more
to Rahamly, in a mile to the river Grause, where we turned to the south, in three
to Feranangam river & in a mile to the river Drumdive, where in a Churchyard
is a curious Old Cross, on one side of which is a relief of Adam & Eve at the
tree of knowledge, & some other defaced reliefs on the other side: Turning to
the west I came in three miles more to Mr Knoxes fine farm to Sligoe, having
been informed of something curious this way, on the shoar seven miles from
Sligoe, but omitted to make a particular enquiry concerning the nature of it.
Sligoe is situated on the south side of the river Gilly: There is also a sort of suburb
to the north in which there is a barrack, & there is another barrack a little way
out of the town, called the Strand barrack, both which are for horse; There is a
foot barrack on the other side, within an old regular fortification built in Olivers
time, without any fossee, that now appears the bastion being built high. It is a
town of some small trade, tho' a Ship of 100 tun can come up only at Spring
tides, & the Ships of any burthen commonly lye down at Poole about a mile or
two below the town. There are remains of an old Convent here, in which the high
altar is seen entire adorned with Gothick reliefs, & there are two or three old
Monuments in the Church; In the Cloyster are remains of a Stone Pulpit, The

Church of Sligoe the design of Mr. Castels[79] is in this
shape with windows at W, & galleries at every end except
the east; the roof is a curious piece of work & every way
it is one of the best designs I have seen. Mr. Ormsby has
a large house in the town; but the thriving country round
next after the barracks & Colonel Wynnes improvements,
is chiefly owing to the industry & Spirit of Mr. Knox; &
it may be reckoned the Capital of this north west part of
the kingdom.

On the 29th I went two small miles to see Col. Wynnes house on Lough
gilley,[80] & in the way viewed the Charter school, which is building out of Erasmus
Smiths Charity:[81] there are three good rooms on a floor, a kitchin & two Schools,
being built for sixty Children, the Governor of Erasmus Smiths Schools gave
first £500 & then £200, & Colonel Wynne gave 4 acres of ground for ever; They

W.H. Bartlett, Hazlewood House, County Sligo, 1842

have raised it to the first floor, it is built of the Slaty lime stone near it. Col Wynnes house is situated on an eminence which has the Lough to the South & east, wch is most beautiful in Islands & in the fine rocky hills that are on the South & east Sides of it, both the one & the other in great part cover'd with wood. The house is built of a marble in which I saw Shells, as in the Kilkenny marble, it appeared as if it would polish of a black Colour. It is Mr. Castels design, six rooms of a floor & very well finished insomuch that it may be looked on, as one of the best houses in the Kingdom. I had met Captn Wynne the second son on whom I waited, he introduced me to his older brother, who in the fathers absence, with great politeness showed me the house & pressed me to stay dinner, & invited me to stay two or three days. I took leave returned to Sligoe & waited on Mr. Knox Mrs. Stewart of Hornhead her brother, & afterwards Mr. Mitchelburn Knox, the person to whom this Town & County are so much indebted. After dinner I set out on my journey, going first southward three miles to Belerejoneh bay & soon to Beleseclair bay, where if the tyde had been out we should have crossed the Strand, but being obliged to go round, we passed a road that goes to Clonine & came to Beltrace, where there is a Church; we had almost all the way gone round a fine[82] hill called Knockrach which makes the head to the west of Sligoe, on the top of it is a remarkable Kerne or Mount, which if I mistake not is called Muscarrow. I saw in all this road the Stones full of that petrifications [*sic*] of Coral. I have reason to think from observations I have since made, that they extend all the way along that Country to Newport Pratt on the western

Ocean. We turned to the west & in a mile came to Balinley rivlet, & saw near it the ruins of an Old Convent called Balinley Abbey, for here they call all Convents Abbies & in Irish Monastere. Just beyond this we passed by Bureen Castle & in three miles came to Arnaglas, where there is a large Old Castle & two mounts near the village; a mile farther we passed by a height where there were some foundations of Castle Arragh & had to the right Garagandouch, a hunting Lodge of Mr. Wynnes. We then came to a bay & turned up Donecoi about two miles from Castle Arragh, where there is a large Old Castle on a rivlet that runs on a rocky bed, in which I observed the Stones lay very much as in square rocky pillars & in their Strata. I saw Grange Castle about a mile to the east & passed by a Danish Mount & in two miles came to a poor Village called Doneel where there is a Castle & rivlet; here I lay in a very indifferent Inn.

On the 30th I set forward & in a mile came to Bellonrow rivlet, in two miles to Eskan bridge, here is the Shell of a good Church & of the Priests house adjoining to it: Towards this place I had seen the Mycetites or petrified Corralline growth of the fungus kind, & saw towards the sea a place called Leaught, I here also observed a sort of large Square pillar on each side of which there are niches as for Statues, which probably was a Cross. We came in a mile to a rivlet called Finich & being come to the bay of Killala turned Southward; & here the Country is no more Stony except a sort of a rubble Stone under the good Soil; I observed that it is a very fine pasturage, which is converted to Sheep walks. In a mile we came to Ricleheny rivlet, & as much farther near to Castle Ducani, which is on the sea & two rivlets run by it, having an old Church on the East called Kiliaglass, we passed thro an old Rath, opposite to which to the South is another a rivlet running between them in half a mile we came to Carrihubbuck village & rivlet, in as much more to Inniscrual, & at the same distance to rivlet Belavaddy & in a mile to Seummore village Castle & river, & here there is a boat to the opposite side & horses swim over: To the north of this is Delakish, & about this part there is a lime Stone, which is full of the Conchae Anomiae, as well as Cockles & continue for some way: In a quarter of a mile we came to Doneen, & soon after to Kileh village & rivlet, & in a mile to Castle Connaught where there is a rivlet. This Castle is situated on a height almost opposite to the Abbey of Rosserick, we afterwards passed these rivlets not above a quarter of a mile from each other Rallenon, Farengrohen, Tramiliese, Cayeck, Conquiseen, & Baurive which latter is large & falls in beautiful cascades down its rocky bed; & so we soon came to Ballina[83] on the Moye which rises to the South falls into Lough Conn & passing out of it again runs by Foxford & so it falls into the sea below Killalla: We here enter'd into the large County of Mayo, bounded by the northern & western Ocean, being the North west part of the Kingdom. Ballina is pleasantly situated on the west side of the Moye & is a market town by which, & a foot barrack it is chiefly subsisted. It is but a poor place & belongs to [   ]. On the east Side are the remains of a Monastery, where there is a very good Gothick door case, which consists of about twelve members. From Ballina I took a ride to Lough Conn, which extends in length about eight Miles from Newtown Gore, Sr. Arthur Gores seat near as Foxford & is about a mile broad; the high mountain of Nevin is to the South of it, & it is a fine Lake. I returned to Ballina & rid to Killalla, the bishop was expected home on Saturday, so I took up my abode at his house.

On the 31st Mr. Carter the Curate of the place came to see me, & I set out on a journey into Erris along the Northern Coast. In a mile I came to Palmerstown, a village on a rivlet that falls into the sea a litle below it, Mr. Palmer lives at this place, & there are some litle remains of an old Castle. Here they have a lime Stone, & a litle further a yellow free stone, which I observed also in the Cliffs near Killalla. in about half a mile we passed near the ruins of the Abbey of Rafrane, which must be the Monastery of Rethbran: further on I observed some Stones as in a Circle & some set up an end, after the manner of the ancient burial places in Cornwall. I saw Castle Cariganas to the left, & in about three miles came to a village & river called Gartetui where Mr. Bark lives. We went on about two miles to another hill & began to ascend towards Donfiny where there is an Old Parish Church, & from this height the high rocks are seen off the eastern point, which makes the harbour of Broad haven: These rocks from being very high & sharp, are called the Stags of Broad haven: but the weather being very bad I put into a Cabin, & din'd & returned in the evening to Killalla, the rains making this journey impracticable. On the first of August, I rid with Mr. Carter along the Strand two miles Southward to Abbey Moye, which is remarkable for having a Square tower built, on one side (that is not on the point) of the two Gable ends that form the quire & the body of the Church; Hexagon arches being turned on Consoles from east to west, fixed in the Gable ends, which is a bold execution: there is much good Stone work & Masonry about the Church Convent & Cloyster, the latter is built on plain pillars in Couplets as at Sligoe, this is called in Ware a Friery. We went on about two miles to Rossurk or Rosserick Convent,[84] where the tower is built in the Same manner, but exactly on the middlepoint of the Gable ends: It is remarkable in both these Convents, that there is a Closet built of hewn Stone for two Confessors to sit in & hear Confessions, with a hole on each side, for the persons who confess to Speak through. We went to the side of a rivulet & din'd, & I distributed what I had prepared for my western journey among the poor. In a wall I Saw many of the sunci Lapidei & petrified Corals called by some Conchae-anomiae. Mr Linat a neighbouring Gentleman farmer came & invited me to take a glass of wine, I staid with him half an hour, & found the Bishop come home at Killalla. This is a poor town but very pleasantly situated on the east side of the bay near the mouth of the river Moye, which runs on the east Side of some Islands that are between the river & Killalla; this river is easily crossed in fair weather: The Islands in the bay afford a very delightful prospect.

Francis Grose, Rosserick Abbey, 1791

On the 2nd I preached at the Cathedral, & on the third I went through Balina, where by Captn. Owen in whose company I had dined there, I received a very kind & pressing invitation from Mr. Vaughan near Lough Conn, but being engaged to go on, I excused my self & went forward: There is a road on both sides of the river to Foxford, but the new road is on the west Side, & after riding about 4 miles, we crossed a hill from which we had a view of Lough Conn, & particularly of the South-east end of it, from which as I was inform'd, there is an outlet into the river Moye, on which Foxford stands. We had a view also of all that Morassy ground to the west of Foxford, to which place we came, it is situated on the edge of the bog & under rough rocky hills to the east in a very bad air, & all the water about it exceeding bad, except a spring a mile distant; it is a very poor town, but they are building a New Church: They have a barrack for foot, & formerly had iron works here, which before the revolution were in judge Wards family, who was born in this Country, but on the wars that family retired to their own estate in the County of Down. They brought the iron ore from the mountain called Nevin to the west for all these mountains as far as the sea are full of Iron Ore; They work it up with the ore of Lancashire, which hardens it; otherwise it would be too Soft. They have now iron works at Mullamore, nine miles to the west; And they Collect together the washings[85] of the Ore here & carry it to those works. I dined here & visited Mr. Evelyn the Minister, & went on: They are searching for Coal at Sleave Horn a mountain near. In a mile I passed by Baky Lough Castle & went over a river of that name on a bridge & I saw Toramore Castle to the left. In about a mile more we passed by an Old Church called Temple a Strada & soon after I took a view of a Convent called Strada[86] where the high altar is beautified with Gothick ornaments & in the middle is a dead Christ in the Virgins lap, & a person in relief in a Compartment on each side. There is also a tomb adorned with curious reliefs, of four Kings in different Compartments, in another one Kneels before a mitred person & there is a relief of St. Peter & St. Paul: In a mile we passed by Ballicurry & saw Currane Castle to the right & Turlans-Church on a height, where I thought I saw one of the round towers; A mile further brought us to Minola, a poor small town Situated on a rising ground to the West of a rivlet: It is chiefly a Colony of Protestants, settled here as Freeholders by Mr. Brown of the Neal, who founded a Charter School here for 12 boys & 12 girls, by giving 10 acres for ever & twenty at five Shillings an acre [   ] which I went to see & travelled on towards Castle bar three miles farther, I saw to the west Elm Hall, a Seat & good plantation of Mr. Cuffs of Ballinroab, passed by [   ] the house & Estate of Mr. Domick Brown, & about a mile from Castle bar saw [   ] Mr. Millars. Castle bar is very pleasantly situated on a rising ground to the east of the river which falls out of the Lough of Castle bar that has communication with several beautifull Loughs round about. It is a pretty good Small town, having a good market & a Horse Barrack, & they have lately built a handsome Church of Mr. Castles design, it is the Greek Cross with three galleries: The windows & Cornish are of hewen lime Stone which is the finest black marble, & it without mixture

Francis Grose, Strade Abbey, 1791

polishes well.[87] The Church is covered with a very good light Stone Slate of which there is a quarry in a mountain near called Sleanbawn; & about two miles from the town they have a quarry of good flags of the same kind of lime Stone as the ornamental parts of the Church: There is also the black Medicinal slate in some mountain near. This is the estate of Sr. Charles Bingham now abroad on his travels, who has a small house near the town, built on the scite of an Old Castle after the revolution: The two large round towers of the Castle remain in which his Grandfather lived with his Father-in-law Dr. Vesey Archbishop of Tuam in King James's wars & defended themselves against the enemy.

On the 4th Mr. Ellison the Clergyman of the town & Mr. Johnson a neighbouring Clergiman came to see me: I set out at noon & observed the road from[88] Killalla which comes to the West of Lough Conn & to the east of Nefin; & going near a mile Saw another road which leads into Erris, we soon came near to Lough Honey to the [   ] which falls into the lake of Castle bar & passed by Lough barry from which there is a Communication by a river into the other. I observ'd here that the rocks are chiefly a cement of pebbles a litle like that of Hertfordshire, & many fine Stones might be found among them that would polish very beautifully with a variety of good colours: In two miles we came to a rivlet & a litle farther to the river Broheh which rises out of Lough Belta, call'd in the Maps Blata about two miles to the north east & in about two miles falls into the bay of Newport.

We came to Newport called anciently Bally vicken or Baley vaughan, it is most beautifully situated on a height to the north of a Small river which about a mile [   ] lower falls into that famous bay which is full of beautifull Islands: Westport a much older town being at the South east angle of it. This estate was a lease of 999 years from the Ormond family to Commissioner Medlicot & 'tho consisting of 70,000 acres, yields at this time but £1700 a year, it was then valued only at £600 a year, of which £200 a year was fined off. Mr. Pratt who was Clerk of the Treasury had a lease of it from Medlicot, built this litle town, which from him was called Newport Pratt. On his failing he suffered himself to be ejected: & now Mr, Medlicot has bought the reversion of the £400 a year of Ld. Arran after that Lords death. It consists of the Mannor of Burrisool, which has great priviledges as a Court for Civil Causes not exceeding £40. The old Mansion house & Castle, are on a litle Peninsula on the bay of Burrysool, which winds up from the harbour towards Lough Furren, it was Converted into a barrack where Theophilus Bolton late Archbishop of Cashel was born, when his Father was a Captain quartered here. Opposite to it is the Convent of Burrisoole which is a poor Church & building, tho' it makes some figure at a distance; in it I Copyed this inscription on a tomb, Orate pro anima Davidis Oge Kelly qui me fieri fecit sibi et heredibus suis Anno Domini 1623 et ejus uxori Anabla Barret.[89] It is said that this Convent was founded in the time of Henry VII by the Butlers, & they have a great Pattern or festival here on August the 4th St. Dominicks day: near it is the ancient Parish Church of Burrisool, removed by an act of Vestry & council to a Glebe about a furlong above Newport on the Opposite Side. At this place there was formerly a little town, & at present there are a few scatter'd houses. This being the port & a place of some small trade untill Newport was built: The Market of Newport consists Chiefly of frieze, yarn Stockins & different sorts of Corn; the provisions are very cheap in this place from June to Christmas. Beéf a peny, Mutton five farthings a pound, chicken pence a piece, a fat Goose for six pence, a Turkey for the same & fat Ducks two pence a piece, fish also is very Cheap, & they have a Merchant who imports very good French wine at £16 a Hogshead.

On the 5th I set out with a guide on hired horses for the Barony of Erris & particularly the Mullet. We came in a mile to a rivlet they call the Ford, which falls into the bay by the Abbey, half a mile further we were to the east of Lough Furren a beautifull Lake into which the tyde comes, tho' we could not see the communication: it is about a mile long & half a mile broad, Lough Rafarn falls into it from the north & is much higher, this is almost as wide & long: on the east side of it, the hills are cover'd with wood, & on the west are high mountains; I observed here a reddish free Stone: We went over a hill from which there is a fine view of these lakes & the bay, which appear all like one Lough full of Islands extending for twelve miles to Crow Patrick. We came[90] to a river which we crossed several times, & another falls into it, which we also crossed often & went frequently along the bed of it, & in my return I observed in it towards the Lough near which I went in another road, several bodies of trees lying in it, which they say grew on the spot, & were washed down by the torrent. We past Letikeyn a few houses to the east of the rivlet, called four miles from Newport: We here turned to the west, going up the hill for some way along the bed of the rivlet; here I found myself as in an Amphitheater encompassed with high Mountains which made a very Romantick appearance, To the east Bockwoth & Billing Carragh to the north Carnen, & west of that Mamarakty & of that litle Nefin. To the west Crooknegrah (sheep mountain) to the South Furcleogh: We gain'd the top & descending had a Small Lough to the right, passed through some very difficult bogs, & ascended on the Side of Mamarakty having those high mountains to the south which stretch towards the Island of Achil to the west & make the northern point of the bay of Newport: These mountains about five one beyond another have a very Curious aspect, the tops of most of them appearing with escallop hollows in perpendicular broken rocks; They are full of Red Deer, which are very indifferent food, being never fat, however the hunting of them affords good diversion to those who traverse the mountains on foot, but they frequently escape the dogs. This mountain that I had ascended was of a sort of silver mica, which is not a lime Stone, for they have none beyond the first hills we crossed to the river, but there is from that to the bay a vein of blew lime Stone gravel which is good manure, they have also in many places about Newport a marle with Shells in it, but the land being Stiff, it is not a proper manure for it. We here sprung a cock Grous the only one I had ever seen flying & appeared very beautifull. Having gained the height on the Side of the hill, we turned northward, & dined at a Stream which gushes out of the side of it, from which place I had a glorious view of the mountains of the Isle of Achil, of the sea & some fine mountains to the North east; descending for a mile, we crossed four rivlets & ascended along the foot of a mountain called Kormestity, which appears very beautifully like two grand bastions, We travelled on & had to the east another high Steep & rocky mountain, & we went by a road which is over a rivlet & coming to a large vale, in which there is a house & farm, we crossed a mountain torrent & ascending went round the side of the hill for three miles, to what they call the river, in the Map it is called the salmon fishery, & the mouth of it is part of the black sod harbour; I here observ'd a Stone, a sort of silver Mica, which lyes very much in the form of the members of Architecture, & one I saw much like a large Cornish: As soon as we had the mountain to the east of us, we had to the west a morass extending to the sea now full of litle [fords?]: The most dismal looking country I ever saw, & they say, the greater part irreclaimable; Here are however not far from the foot of the hills, three or four litle farms which chiefly belong to herds. The river we crossed was a rough bottom & very dangerous in time of floods: there is a road by this river to the east into Tirawley which rises out of the mountains near Lough Conn, but it is very boggy & almost impassible, except after that there has been dry weather for some time: We here got into a Cabbin where they had clean Straw & clean blankets—but the man observing the smoak was very troublesome to me, he made me a low seat near the fire, & I found it was not so inconvenient, the smoak rising up & condensing above. The guide called for an egg, broke off the top & emptied it into a Scollop Shell, as I thought to dress it, for the poor here use Scollop Shells for all uses they can, as they do on the Red sea, but I was surprised when I saw him give a dram about in the egg shell; the woman also melted tallow in a Scollop & dipt the rushes in it, & another time they twisted several rushes together, to make a larger light, & stuck it on a Slit Stick, the base of which was a large turf into which they run one end of it. The common people of the Country live too much on these poor wretches when they travel, Seldom bringing any thing with them; & they were Surprized when I distributed my bread & meat & what I had among them, & that I gave them a piece of money when I went away. All their vessels are of wood, most of them cut out of solid timber, their stools are long & narrow like a stilion,[91] & their table is a long sort of stool about twenty inches high & broad & two yards long; their food chiefly oat cakes baked on the gridle & potatoes with their butter milk: they had killed a goat & were boyling part of it; but I suppose it was not very good, as they industriously concealed it from me; but they offered to prepare me what they had to eat, which for strangers, is new milk, Eggs, butter & oat cake: They have here a french potatoe with a purple blossom, it is something like an apple, but is watery & not so good as the other kinds. However this potatoe does best in sandy & I believe boggy grounds, &

the cold & moisture of the potatoe is a good Corrective of the heat of the oaten diet. It is the Custom for the poor especially the Children to come in & sit by the fire of those who are in better circumstances as well as travellers of all Kinds, & they give to all, of what is going in their own way.

On the 6th We set forward the Gratefull Host accompanying us above a mile to show us the way through a bog to a large Lough to the north west called Curraghmore Leterahery out of which the river Munry rises, which we crossed: The lake does not appear very large in this Situation, but seeing it from an higher [*sic*], I observed two large bays extending to the east & west, there is a small Island near the side we pass'd the ground to the South being on a declivity, I observed that the bog hung over at this part of the Lake, & in some places hung down for two or three yards, kept together by the heath, tho' the hard ground did not appear to have been lately worn away, but was greenish & some plants grew out of it, & I was informed that especially in wet Seasons water runs between the bog & the hard ground which made me inclined to think that where bogs are on a declivity & the lower part of them as here is broken away, that they do actually move by their gravity; as the ice in the Glacieres of Savoy certainly does & falls down into the valley, & they affirm, that the ice when it moves is attended with a great noise. We had a boggy way for a mile, & passing by two houses soon came to a vale, in which there runs a rivlet, & there are two or three natural mounts in it, one of which has been fortifyed; here I stop'd & took some refreshment, & crossing over the foot of a hill, came to a Strand which is made by the Blacksod harbour to the South & stretches along the South east side of the Country within the Mullet; A very beautiful Peninsula stretches out into the bay, joined to the eastern land by a long narrow Isthmus. They have a bed of small oysters here, which at Spring tides is left by the sea, & the people go & pick 'em up, pickle 'em & send them to Dublin: They sell them here for a peñy a hundred, & on the bank they will load a horse for four pence. We continued riding round the Strand to avoid the bog above, on which the sea has gained in some places, insomuch that there is in some parts bog on the Strand, & one cannot ride on the sea weed, there are also several Stumps of trees on the Strand. From this Strand in my return I went up to the height to see the bay which is formed by Broadhaven to the north, & with this bay forms that neck of land which is called the Mullet, & joyns that long strip of land to the mainland which is called Erris within the Mullet: on the south side of this neck of land Sr. Arthur Shanes, whose estate it was began to build a litle Town, & actually cut a Communication across the Isthmus large enough for a small boat to pass, which is now choaked up: They laid out also much money on roads into this Country, made along the sides of the hills, by cutting away the bog, but this was found to be a bad way, for it makes a course for the water, & the rain washing away the earth, leaves it a very stony rough road, & where[92] this is done in a flat Country, it has not only this effect, but the bog fills up the trench again: for the true way of mending their roads is by raising a Causeway of gravel, & where it is very soft, by laying a litle heath under it. All the half barony of Erris consists of two parishes, Kilcommon taking in all without the Mullet; & Kilmore all that is within the Mullet; & they have some time ago obtained an Act of parliament to build a Church on the Mullet for the united parishes. We came within Mullet to that fine peninsula which is about twelve miles long from north to south & about a mile broad one place with another; the north end is chiefly high heathy ground, from which I saw the Stags, as they call 'em, off Broadhaven, which are high pointed rocks of the eastern head that makes the bay of Broadhaven: the rest of the land is partly in small hills, & partly consists of long rising ground, of good land & some Sandy banks & loughs; being altogether a most delightful Spot in Summer. In these Sand banks they find a great variety of Shells, & lately they found some very curious Vertebrae of fish, of which I procured[93] a Specimen: They have also discovered some tombs, which they call the tombs of Lugnad-umme they say they are of an extraordinary size, but now they were all covered over again by the sand. I went to the house of Mr. Anthony Odonnel to whom I was recommended by Mr. Odonnel of Newport; I met his Nephew on the road, who very politely showed me the way, & among other questions had asked me if I had any acquaintance there, which was on purpose to have invited me to his house, tho' he had the good sense not to say it; I dined at Mr. O'donnels, took a walk & saw the old walls of the Church of Tarman Carra buried in sand, which they say was the Church of a Nunnery. I took a ride in the evening along the sea shore to the north east, which consists of litle bays made by the low rocky Cliffs, & the waves rolling in on these rocks in calm weather, has one of the most beautifull effects I ever saw. I observed a small detach'd rock, which had had some fortification on it, & going further saw a litle head, which was defended by a modern fortification, made across the Neck of it in Queen Elizabeths time, as they say, in order to deposite goods that were ship wreck'd that they might not be plundered by the Country. They had also built two barracks, one at Carne on the Mullet, the other at Learne on the east side of this Land within, in order to prevent the landing of privateers, but Queen Annes peace prevented the turning them to that use. I went on further & returned seeing a litle to the westward a passage under ground from the sea, where the tyde goes in about fifty yards & is seen from a large hole over it.

On the 7th I set out with Mr. Odonnels Son & Nephew to ride to the south of this land. To the South of this part is a Strip of land called Annah joynd only by a small neck; & the Strand east of it, as well as that to the north is called the Strand of Annah; this in the Map is made an Island, & called Emlokrash, the reason of which is this, it was in one form with the land to the east of Tarmon Carrah, which goes by this name. We then came to an open Strand called Baludurish; in which there are several rocks under the water which render'd it terrible to the sight, even in a Calm when the tyde was coming in; but when we return'd & the tyde was going out, it was very beautifull: on the point to the South of it, are the remains of a Convent called the Convent of the Cross & near it is a Church of the same name, which the Protestants had begun to repair, for Sr. Arthur Shane planted about twenty Protestant families here, on leases for ever of small farms, mostly under a hundred acres: This Gentlemen left two daughters, one married to Mr. Bingham of Newbrook,[94] the other first to Mr. Wynne, & now to Mr. Carter second son of the Master of the Rolls, these ladies hold the estate in Copartnership. Opposite to this is the Isle of Ennis Clory, which is a great burial place, of this Island they say no rat or mouse will live in it, & go so far as to affirm, that if they bring the earth & shake it in a rick of corn, none of these Vermin will touch it. To the South of this is Enniskerah & South of that Enniskeah, where if I mistake not, is a mineral water; & to this land people frequently go to pass some time for their diversion. The people in this Country are very hospitable, if you cannot stay to have a Sheep killed they offer Ale a dram, Eggs & butter, & the woman of the house sits at the table & serves you: They have an odd way in some parts in the north, I did not see it here, when they would preserve meat; they put it into meal to preserve it from the flies, as I suppose, but it becomes very musty & very disagreeable. We came to Lough cross, a beautiful lake about two miles in circumference, here are wild Ducks, which as we rode within a few yards of them did not move into the Water, & when I rode towards'em, only walked gently in like tame ducks, & there is a litle Island in it, in which I suppose they breed. An extraordinary thing happened in relation to this lake a few years ago: there was a rivlet run from it, to the sea, with a mill on it, in a great flood, it carried away the mill, & the passage was stop'd up; on which the lake retired near a hundred yards from its western bank, so that probably there is some Communication under ground from the sea. We came soon after to the Lough of Leame near which is the building designed for a barrack; Riding on we came to Castle Tarah, the ruin of a large old building: Towards the South point of the land we ascended Mount Tarman, a round hill not long ago covered with herbage, but the rabbits, burrowing in the sand, ye wind[95] blew it away, & has left a more curious top all cover'd with beautifull large flat Stones of grey granite: From this hill is a fine view of the Island of Achill, which is very mountainous & about 2 leagues distant: There are in it 25,000 acres of land, & it lets for £300 a year; the inhabitants have a kind of Sheep here, with a coarse wool fit for yarn stockins, which they spin & knit & sell the stockins for about ten pence a pair; & with this produce they pay their rent; They have oats & potatoes sufficient for their own use; this is part of Mr. Medlicotes estate. There is a great Knowledge gained by experience, as to feeding their Cattle on all these mountains, they find that for six months or some certain time they thrive on the same Spot & then fall off, so that they move 'em to other parts, some parts are fit for cattle of different ages, & some at different Seasons of the year. We came down from this hill to Mr. Gambles house, & took some refreshment there; which was very Civilly offer'd us: & returning we went to the east side & near Mr. Markhams the pleasantest Situation in the place which command a view of the Lough, of the sea & Islands & of Blacksod harbour, of Mullet & Erris to the east, as well as the Isle of Achil; that Island is represented as divided in the Middle by a Chanel; there is water goes almost through, but not so as to divide it into the greater & lesser as represented in the Map;[96] but little Achil as I was informed, is only that very small Island at the South point, which is placed in the Map without name. They have a Custom of raising heaps of Stones called here laktch, in other parts Kerns, to the memory of the dead, mostly in the Shape of Sugar loaves, which are kept up as long as their friends remain, & are raised commonly not far from the Church, in the way to it from the house; some are built with Mortar & have inscriptions on them. We came to the Mullet & when we were out of it, we took some refreshment, I parted with my friends & the Cattle they had mounted me on, & set forward the same way I had come with Mr. O'Donnel the gentleman I had met at my entrance into it, who was going to the Fair of Balyheen. The way I was coming into this Country by Broadhaven is round by that bay very difficult & boggy & is two days journey from Killalla. Going along the bog I saw an Eagle & crows about a Carcase, for these birds never take notice of their brethren the Carniverous race. It was of the large kind, & he seemed to attempt to raise himself, but remained very near us, & when we went towards him, he flew low to a turf Stack at a litle distance, for in a Calm they sometimes find it difficult to raise themselves from the ground. About half an hour after we saw him fly over us to the North east to the sea. We took up our lodging about a mile to the north of the river at Mr. Hashes farm house where we had a fine view of the lake; here is an old Square Castle in ruins called Clonatekilly; a litle below it are two Caverns, about six feet wide & high & ten long, covered with Stones laid across, within one of them was a narrow hole about three feet Square like a drein; these seem to be places to hide in upon any danger. They have a way in this Country of burying Children in some litle plat near the house, when they are at a distance from the Church, & such a burial place I saw.

On the 8th We set out & crossed the river on each side of the banks of which towards the sea are litle spots of arable land & several houses; & one part of it goes by the name of Kilkeny, where they have a considerable salmon fishery. Several people joyned us going to the fair & we made up a litle Caravan of about Seventeen horses: & when we stop'd twice & I divided my brew & liquor among them, & to the two or three protestants my meat also,[97] I was had in great esteem among them, & so early in the evening I finished this curious uncommon journey & arrived at Newport; where my friends of Newport spent the evening with me.

On the 9th Mr. Herne the Minister came to see me, & I preached at his Church. He, Mr. Odonnel & Mr. Moore the Collector invited me to dine with them; the last very politely by a card the night before, being a litle indisposed with the

Francis Grose, Burrisool Abbey, 1791

Gout, the other that even:—But I was first engaged to Captn. Cantillon the commanding officer of the foot here. I drank tea with the Collector, rid with Mr. Herne to see the Monastery of Burrisool,[98] & spent the evening with the Collector, & lodged at Mr. Hernes.

On the 10th At noon we set out, all the officers, Mr Herne & the Collector on an expedition in the Revenue Sloop to the Islands, & had a most delightfull voyage through them to the South west. The sea gains on them & some are almost divided into two; there are fine Stones on the Shoar round them, some of the petrified Coral rubbed into pebbles & some of the Mycetites; They are Islands covered with pasturage & some with Corn; forty of them belong to Mr. Medlicot, some to the Arch bishop of Tuam, some to Mr. Brown of Westport & other proprietors on the bay; they say that there are[99] 300 of them, & it is look'd on as the Archipelago in miniature & is a most singular beautiful bay,—At the mouth of it is Clare Island, belonging to the old proprietors the Omellies,[100] I was told it was worth £200 a year; To the South west of it is Buffin, belonging as I was informed to Lord Clanrickard & worth £150 a year; They have in these two Islands a pretty breed of Small horses: they do not Submit to pay any tax but the hearth money, & have good water in them, & so have many of the small Islands. About ten leagues off is a bank, where there are plenty of Cod, & it is supposed that it is part of that bank which extends to Newfoundland, being supposed to be hills in the Sea where the fish lye: on this they have between 40 & 50 fathom water; the fish have very much failed on all the coast since they have burnt the sea weed for Kelp, which they not only take away as the sea leaves it, but they cut it off in the sea that it may be thrown up, the fish Spawning on this weed. We returned to Newport & they spent the evening with me. In the river of Newport they have the large fresh water pearl Muscle.

On the 11th I set out to the south & all the officers went with me & dined with Mr. Brown of West port, who had sent compliments to me that he should be glad to see me. The road is very pleasant near those litle bays which are westward from the harbour & in sight of the delightfull Islands. I went to the top of some hills to have a view of them; At about two miles & a half distance we came to a rivlet called Moinah, which goes under a hill about a quarter of a mile into the sea, & the tyde comes in by the same passage. A litle farther we came to a well wall'd round which they call Omeles Well: concerning which there is a tradition in the Country, that a female child of this family, being dipt in it became a Male, which was probably some trick in order to secure the estate of the family in that Child. We desended to West port a small village situated on a rivlet which falls into that bay, & makes the South-east corner of the great bay, in which there are some small Islands. The foot of Crow Patrick mountain comes into it which is called (the Eagle mountain) by reason that it appears like an Eagle stretching out its wings; tho' from the North east from Castle bar it does not appear in that manner: It is not determined whether this mountain or Nefin is the higher. The Coast extends about ten miles farther to the west beyond the river called Killaurs, where there is a great salmon fishery & so far the road is good. Then the Barony of Morish in the County of Mayo extends about ten miles farther to the County of Galway, where the Country on the western Ocean is called Connemarrah ([   ]) probably the name of some ancient Clan;[101]—this it is likely is about the extent of the Barony of Ballynehinch; to the north east of this is the Joyces Country on Lough Mash & Lough Chorrib, probably the Barony of Ross. To the South east is the Country of Eyre Connaught, taking in I suppose the Barony of Moyeulau. I had designed to have rode along the sea coast, but the weather was so unpromising, that I laid aside that design. Mr. Brown's house[102] is very pleasantly situated on the South side of the rivlet over which he has built two handsome bridges, & has form'd Cascades in the river which are seen from the front of the house; which is built of Hewen Stone, a Coarse Marble they have here; It is much like Bedford house In Bloomsbury Square, except that it has a pavilion in the middle over the Attick Story in which there is a large Convenient Bed chamber for the young people, of the size of the hall, the design is with nine windows on a floor & for five rooms; one of which a back wing is not built: It is an exceeding good house & well finished, the design & execution of Mr. Castels: Mr. Brown designs to remove the Village & make it a Park Improvement all round; there are fine low hills every way which are planted & improved, & the trees grow exceedingly well: the tyde comes just up to the house; & the Cascades are fine salmon leaps. In the house are handsom Chimney pieces of the Castle bar marble, which are a good black without any white in them like the Touchstone, which the Italians call Paragonè & value very much.

On the 12th I rid out with Mr. Brown to a hill to see the prospect & to the Park, where he has several red as well as fallow Deer, & in the afternoon I walked out to the quarry & to the side of the bay. I had forgot to mention a small Island called Ennis Turk to the south west of Clare Island, there is a good Slate quarry in it. They have here a Marle with which they manure sandy lands, but I could not be informed that it had any Shells in it. Mr. Brown makes use of oxen to draw dung, stones, &c.: on Sledges which they easily load.

On the 13th Mr. George Brown a younger son, who is at the College, & Mr. Blake a young gentlemen of Estate, going my way accompanied me, & showed me three miles off, a litle beyond a village call'd Baleyburk, a Cave to the right, into which the river Anne falls, & goes for some way under ground, & coming out again falls, as they told me into Lough Carray, & is a river which in the maps is represented as lost in a very small Lough to the west of Lough Carrah. It is a very fine face of rock, consisting of about fifteen Strata which lay very regular. I believe most of them are of plain black marble, as I was informed it is of that colour, but some of them when broke are of a brown colour. The river runs principally into one hole, which is as a beautifull arch, the Strata rising one over another & each beyond the other, until it extends to the face of the rock, the passage may be forty feet wide & long, about 20 high, this leads to the grotto in which the river runs about sixty feet wide from the passage, seventy long, & 50 high, through this the river runs, but being then a flood, it was all over flow'd; To the west of this are two or three other passages into which the river runs when it overflows. Returning to the road we saw Kil Turk a litle beyond it to the left, a fine old ruined Mansion house of Mr. Browns in which his father lived, & to the North of that we saw Holy hill, Mr. Chambers's. About three miles farther we came to Balin Tubber Convent; Near Kilturk we passed through Balikeen, where the famous Fair had been held just 3 measured miles from Castle bar. This is an handsom Convent, called also De Fonte, from the Irish name which signifies the Town of the Well or Spring; there are handsome pillars & arches in it, & at the east end are two windows of the Saxon Architecture. The Lords of Mayo have their burial place here in a Chapel in which there is a handsome altar piece & an altar of hewn Stone, round the latter are the figures of our Saviour & the eleven Apostles in relief. Here I took leave of those gentlemen who went on in this road, which leads first to Castle Burk, the seat of Lord Mayo, where I heard there were some petrifyed Stumps of trees & some underground passages to the Castle; beyond it is Rusk Garrah, Sr. Henry Lynches on Lough Carrah, it then goes to Holy Mount,[103] the Estate & Seat of Vesey Archbishop of Tuam, which was esteemed a fine place in those times, & so it goes to Tuam. But I crossed to the Ballin robe road I had left a litle before; we soon came near Lough Corra at Ballikeneh & I went to a rivlet & took some refreshment. I saw to the North about two miles Newbrook[104] Mr. Binghams, & going on came to the bridge of Fere, under which Lough Carrah passes into Lough Maske, tho' it is spoken of as a great work, yet it is only a long Causeway, with one arch in the middle which is not large. We passed over a greater work, a road made across a morass, having had a view of Lough Mask to the South for some time, I came to Balinrobe, a very small town pleasantly situated on the river Robe, which about a mile below it falls into the Lough Mask. The large map of Ireland makes a small lake here which is wrong. They have a handsom sessions house built of hewn Stone, the assizes being held at this place & at Castle bar alternately: They have here fine quarries of a dark grey Marble which rises so well that they make ashler very litle inferior to hewn Stone. This town belongs to Mr. Cuff who lives close to it, & is endeavouring to improve the town. There is a Charter School here for thirty children which I went to see; where Mr. Miller, Minister of the place & Mr. Lanorgan a Clergy man of a Neighbouring parish came to me & they Spent the evening with me. There are remains of a Church of a Monastery of Augustinian hermits near the town.

On the 14th I breakfasted with Mr. Miller, having received an invitation from Mrs. Cuff in her husband's absence to breakfast with her, but her hour being too late, I was obliged to send an excuse. Mr. Miller set out with me towards Lough Mask. About a mile from the town I saw a large Kern of loose Stones, it may be twenty feet high & forty feet diameter, another about a mile to the South with a fossee round it, & a smaller between them, the tradition is, that two armies engaging there, Kerns were erected over the Slain of the principal of them: We came to a fine Old Castle called Castle Mask, from the top of which I had a beautiful prospect of Lough Mask, with many Islands in it cover'd with wood & one in particular with a pleasure house belonging to Mr. Cuffe: We had also a view of the mountains of Joyces Country. This Castle belonged to one of the Burks of Ld. Clanrickard's family. On the top of Benlevegh in Joyces Country I was informed that there was a large Lough Near this Country of the Joyces in Lough Cherrib is an Island called Castle Kirk which is the name of Mr. Middletons house in Denbighshire in Wales. I was told that at Long Abbey there is a stone head said to be design'd for Roderick O'Connor King of Connaught.

Beyond Lough Mask to the North west towards the sea is a mountain called Ferramore on which there is such a debt to the Crown that no one will occupy it; on it they say are traces of a town, sd. to be begun to be built by some Stranger who came to settle in these parts, & as it is supposed by those people who afterwards built Galway. In Lough Mask is an Island Call'd Inch en Keill, consisting of about sixty acres, in which there are two Churches. There is also another Island called Innish Enearton (The Earls Island) to which they say Strong bow fled & was killed there, & if I mistake not they show some place for his tomb.[105] We got into the road from Balin robe to Hetford, which passes thro' the Nail, from which we had gone from Cong to Tuam three years ago: We came to Garn Church a mile from the nail, where I saw a quarry of fine marble, which pollishes a brownish black, they work it with the hammer for about sixpence a foot. We saw on Lough Chorrib a point of land called Baley Cumea, a very fine Situation of Mr, Lynches, & to the east we saw Skrool famous in History for a very horrid Massacre;[106] In this road I observed what they call the Terloughs, that is Meadows that are cover'd with water in the winter, which goes off as it comes in, by underground passages; some of them are good meadows & some only marshes. We crossed Ross river into the County of Galway, & saw the large Abbey of Ross. About a mile lower on the Same water: We came to Hetford a small town where there is a barrack & a Mansion House of late Lord St. Georges, now of General St. George, but leased by the late Lord to his daughters heir, married to Mr. Usher now Usher St George, who lives there; I was met two miles from this town by the Revd. Mr. Fletcher brother to my Agent in Dublin, to whom I had sent that I would come & dine with him, he conducted me half a mile beyond Hetford to his house, where after dinner taking leave of Mr. Miller, Mr. Fletcher went with me six miles in my road. I passed over Achlin bridge & saw an old Castle Ballinacort lately fitted up, it is in a fine Situation & the Seat of Mr. Kirwall. In three miles I came to Baliclareh, & near it on a rivlet saw Clare

Galway Abbey, where the high tower in the middle of the Church built on arches is a curious piece of architecture; I saw the Chapel of the Church converted into a Mass house. Three miles more brought me to Galway; where I went to the house of my Old friend Mr. Simcocks Warden of Galway.

Galway is pleasantly Situated on a fine bay, which is a very good harbor, & on the river which comes out of Lough Chorrib, which spreading here to the east, they call it the Lough, the river runs on a rocky bed, & dividing into three parts it forms two Islands to the west of the Town, on one of which there is a Nunnery. This town was inhabited by the Hollerns Fishermen till one Lynch in 1280 got a grant of the lands of it, from Edward II, & as tradition saies built two Castles, both called Reinville, one against the Hollerns the other against the Flakerts of Cunnehmarrah. This was anciently in the Diocese of Anadown, which place I saw on the right on the Lough coming to Galway, it is now absorpt in Tuam. The people of the town got an exemption of this & Several other parishes from the Pope, on account as they pretended of the ill behaviour of the Clergy the Bishop sent to them: Some say this was when Anadown was united to Tuam. This exemption they got Confirmed to them by Charter from Edward the 6th, who gave them a power to elect, a guardian & three Vicars of the Church exempt from all jurisdiction whatsoever; the Guardian & senior Vicar preach alternately in the morning, the other two in the afternoon, & the three Vicars take their turns weekly to read prayers & visit the sick. The Corporation also have a power of punishing or even removing them within the year. This town was formerly of great trade, to which they apply'd themselves when the other parts of Ireland were very unquiet: they had a great trade in Spanish wines, which were formerly drank; but above all to America, till the act pass'd which obliged all ships from America to touch in England, from which time the trade of this town began to decay.[107] When the town was in this flourishing Condition, there were many large houses built in it of hewn Stone, after the Spanish manner, most of which remain & one sees a great number of fine carved windows, Doorcases, Chimney pieces, & bow windows in these houses. The trade is now mostly carried on to France & Spain by the Roman Catholicks, who have correspondents there, & are jealous of others coming into any Share with them. When the town was in this flourishing Condition, the merchants here purchased almost all the Lands in this Country which doe not belong to the Church & the Earl of Clanrickard: The descendents of which merchants are now possessed to the value of £100,000 a year, & others have forfeited or sold to a much greater value. They were of the name of Blake, Darcy, French, Linche, Kirwan, Joyce, Martin, Brown, Bodkin, Terrets, Athy, Funt, Penrice, the three last are extinct or near it. If they had Submitted to Oliver Cromwell, it would probably have been much better for the town. The remains of the forts he built to attack the town & defend the passes between the Loughs & the Sea, are still to be seen. Lord Mountjoy built the Citadell at the South east part of the town. They have a large Church adjoining it, the Lynches have a Chapel in which they bury: In the Vestry on three large Stones are cut as big as human life, Our Saviour, the Virgin Mary to the right, & to the right of that God the Father & over his head the Dove, they were dug up some where about the Church: To the north of the town are the remains of a Franciscan Convent, & the face of an altar or tomb with some reliefs of Saints on it. Both ye Franciscans & Dominicans have Convents here, & there is a Nunnery which serves also for a Boarding School: Just without the gate is a mineral water of a Strong taste, which they use for purging, & when drank plentifully, it is said, they answer the end of Scarborough waters. About two miles to the north east in the way I came is a rivlet, which comes out of the river that falls from Lough Chorrib, it is call'd Pool Hurley, it goes under ground there & comes out into the bay of the sea which extends to the east. From a hill about a Mile above the town by the Canal, is a very fine prospect of the sea, of the Country on the other side of the bay, of the isles of Arran, Of Eyre Connaught, the Joyces Country & Lough Chorrib. They have in Galway three barracks, which hold two Regiments & a half of the present Compliment: for it is a garrison town with a Governor who has a salary of £300 a year, but he does not Commonly reside, & then the Commanding Officer acts as Governor.

On the 22d at Galway I walk'd out morning & evening, & Mr. Heathcote in a regiment here, who was one of Lord Chesterfields pages, came to see me, & spent the day with me: In the evening I look'd into the Assembly to see the Company, for the Clergy go here in their Coats.

On Sunday the 23rd I went to wait on the judges & attended them & the Corporation to Church & preached before them, Warden Simcocks not being well, I dined with the judges at the Mayors, the Gentlemen of the Grand Jury being there I came home & Dr. Lynch spent the evening with us.

On the 24th I took a litle ride, but the weather did not favour. Mr. Darcy came to see me & brought an invitation from the Grand jury to dine with them, but I was engaged to the Wardens; that Gentleman spent the even with us. A very remarkable thing happened here in relation to one of the Lynches, so long agoe as that he was the fourth or fifth Mayor of the town: His Son was coming in a Ship from Spain, murder'd the Spanish Captain, brought the ship into Galway & Sold the goods. When this fact come to his fathers Knowledge, the son was tryed by the father & condemned, who sat on the bench, & intercession being made for him; he bid the persons come to him in the afternoon, & when they return'd they saw the son hanging out of the Chamber window. This house remains as a Specimen of an inferior sort of building, & over the door is a Deaths head & bones of a Skeleton. I examined some of the records of the Town;—found that in 1511 butter was a peny a pound & a hundred of Eeles here sold for two pence & a Cod for a half-peny in 1526 a Carpenter & mans pay was two pence a day with diet. When six & eight pence only was allowed for the Mayors dinner the twelve Aldermen & such others as he should ask, & there was such plenty of fish in 1701 that a thousand Herrings were sold for eight pence. In 1646 they condemned a book as against the King, entitled Disputatio Apologetica et Manifestativa de Jure Regni Hiberniae pro Catholicis Hibernis adversus Haereticos.[108] There is an order that no corn be burned or scortched in the town. In 1632 the oath of Supremacy & Conformity in Religion being required the Mayor & officers resigned, & others were chosen who took the oath. In 1649 they had the plague. In 1654 the Irish were dismissed from all offices, & English Protestants Chosen in their room. In 1691 the Town surrendered to Genkle on the 26th of July. Having mentioned the Bishoprick of Anadown or Enaghdun, it is to be observed that the Bishoprick of Mayo was united to it in 1210. The Bishoprick of Enaghdun was long disputed by persons who pretended a right to it from about 1250 to 1318. In the Episcopal Register at Exeter I find Bps of Annadown suffragans to ye Bp of Exeter in the following years viz.

> Henry . . . . in 1395 & 1398
> John 1438
> Thos 1458

On the 25th I was at the doors of Mr. Brown & Mr. Darcy, took leave of Captain Heathcote & after dinner set out, young Mr. Simcocks accompanying me three miles to Oranmore, where a rivlet falls into the bay; two miles farther we came to Daren bridge, & half a mile farther to Shilcollogan bridge. I observed several large entrenchments on the mountains of Burien to the west, in the County of Clare, one of them they say was the Residence of O'Laughlin King of Burien, & on the Bay about four miles distant is the Abbey of Corlumro, which they say is a fine ruin, & that on the graves are laid tombs of wood, many of them being of yew, with some remains of inscriptions on them: It was anciently called St. Marie's Abbey: within a mile of Gort we passed through a village called Kiltorton. The Sheep in all this Stony country produce very fine wool much valued & is sent to Dublin & Cork. I was at Gort in 1749 in our Tour through Munster & Connaught, it was the estate of the Oshognusses & was forfeited; & now there is a Barrack in an old Mansion house of that family built within the walls of the (in the) Castle, it is a very poor market town like a village: In my way to this place about six miles from Galway, I had a view of the house of Mr. Walter Taylor, whom I had seen in Galway, he is above four score years old, & told me had seen about 460 descended from his Father, & several great grand children; he rid lately from Dublin to Tullaghmore in one day, which cannot be less than sixty english measured miles, it is 45 computed irish miles if I do not mistake. As his passion has been to encourage a good breed of horses, so at this time he is a constant attender of all diversions in this country, relating to the improvement of that noble animal.

On the 26th I went two miles south west, passing by an uncommon oval Castle at Newtown; the mountains of Burren appear to be Stony, but the summits of most of them are round & appear as in beautifull Terraces. I came to Kilmacduagh Situated on rising ground over some litle Loughs which are to the west. It is the See of an ancient Bishoprick now united to Clonfert & consists only of Old buildings & of two or three Cabins; It was called the Church of Duah: About the middle of the 6th Century, it had the name of Kil-mac-duah, that is the Church of the Son of Duah, commonly called it seems Kil-macough. The first building that offers is the Cathedral in the form of a Latin Cross; on the South side of which is an ancient Altar in good taste; under a relief of a Bishop is this inscription Sanctus Coloman Patronus Totius Diecesis Duacensis: In the middle is a crucifix & a person on each side with Ave Maria & some devotion round it: In the Oshugnussy Chapel, the Old Proprietors, is their tomb of the Corinthian Order, & I observed their arms the Castle of Gort supported by two Lyons. In that Chapel there is a tomb with this inscription. Orate pro anima Edmondi ocahel Praepositi et Coninici Duacensis 1742.[109] To the South is a Chapel called Shatrany. To the west in the Church yard is a small Cell where they say the Patron Saint was buryed, & that the body was afterwards carryed to Agheraim. Between this & the church is Macduaghs Chapel, in which there is a standing large dead Tree, of which they take pieces by way of Relicks; & to the South of this is a raised work of Stone, which they call the Saints Bed. In this Church yard is one of the round towers, if I mistake not; fifteen feet in Diameter: it is finely built of Stones well chosen, but do not seem to have been hamerd & they are not all laid in regular Courses, the lower Tier sets out 9 inches, the entrance is about twenty feet above the ground: there are five small windows round at top with pointed arches, & there about six others without any order in different parts: By measuring the Shadow I concluded it to be about 82 feet high, a litle of the point at top is broken off;[110] This I think is the best I have seen after that of the Church of Ardmore. To the east of the Church is our Ladies Chapel & to the north of it St. John Baptists. To the north west is the Monastery of Kilmacduagh, said to be of Regular Canons; it is on a neck of Land between two Loughs, of which authors mention, that they empty in Summer by whirlpools, but I found that the water goes off only in a very dry Summer & that rarely; when they do empty they catch Eeles & other fish. The Church tho' small is a very neat building the pillars & arches of the entrance to the Altar part & of the east window are in a beautifull Style, & the Angles at the east end, are work'd as in pillars, as at Lismore Cathedral: To the South of the Church is a Sacristy, & adjoyning to that a room, in which they probably deposited the valuable effects of the church, which because it is arch'd they call the jayl. There is a Chapel on the South of these, & a room which I conjectured might be a Refectory, & from the buildings, I imagined the Canons might live in separate houses not built in the best manner. To the north of the Church is an old wall about two feet from the other, it is out of its level, & they have a Story of its being a place of penance, & that penitents were used to get in between the wall & let themselves down by way of punishment. The Bishops house to the north of St. Johns Chapel, or as some call it the Seminary is a building of two rooms on a floor; what is Singular is a building on the outside like a Chimney, but from what I could gather, it was the Stairs to which there is a passage, by a sort of a bow window which rests on one Stone in the wall, from which they say the Benediction used to be given.

27th. In the way to all these buildings is a Holy Well with a circular enclosure. From this place I came again into the high road at Crusha two miles from Gort, where there is a tolerable Inn. At Tuberein we crossed a Stream from the County of Galway in Connaught, to the County of Clare in Munster, we came to Loughed bridge which I conjecture to be the river which in part forms those Loughs that are to the west of Crusheen: Half a mile further we crossed another stream & in half an hour more came to Crusheen on an eminence where there is a very good Inn, at which I dined: Till we come to the County of Clare the face of the country is all rocky being a greyish Marble as I conjecture; about Galway it is full of Cockles & the Conchae anomiae, & in almost all parts the petrified coral more or less. But here the face of the country is entirely different, all in litle well improved hills, not without wood & something like Northampton Shire. We went on & immediately Crossed a Stream & had a fine view of Lough Rinchacrounah, we passed three Streams in a mile & come to Brin-Castle, & crossed three more below, I come to a village called Span[   ] Hill, where the road strikes out to Ennis which I had formerly gone in. This place is three miles from Crusheen, we soon came to Molieth Mr. Macnamarrahs, well improved & a fine Situation, & at the end of three more came to Quin, having had a view of Col Hickmans house & of the plantations of Mr. Burton & Sr. Edward Obrien we had passed in our former journey through this Country. Here I saw fine lime-Stone with much of the coral in it in it [*sic*] entirely Consolidated with the Marble. We had also in this ride a view of that pleasant bay beyond those Gentlemens' Seats, which extends to the north from the Shannon & is full of Islands. At Quin is one of the finest & most entire Monasteries I have seen in Ireland, it belong'd to Franciscan Minorites, & is called in Ware Quinchy;[111] it is Situated on a fine Stream, there is an ascent of Several Steps to the church, & at the entrance one is Surprized with the view of the high altar entire, & of an altar on each side of the arch to the Chancel; To the South is a Chapel with three or four altars in it, & a very Gothick figure in relief of some Saint probably of St. Patrick: on the north side of the Chancel is a fine Monument of the Macnamarahs' of Ranace: On a Stone by the high alter I saw the name of Kennedge in large letters; In the middle between the body & the Chancel, is a fine tower built on ye two Gable ends. The Cloyster is in the usual form with Couplets of pillars, but particular in that it has buttresses round by way of ornament; there are apartments on three sides of it; what I supposed to be the Refectory, the Dormitory & another grand room to the north of the Chancel with vaulted rooms under them all; to the north of this large room is a closet over an arch, which leads to an opening, that seemed to be anciently a private way to go down in time of danger, in order to retire to a very Strong round tower, the walls of which are near ten feet thick, tho' not above seven or eight from the ground; it has been made use of without doubt since the dissolution, as a pidgeon house, & the holes remain in it. In the front of the Convent is a building which seems to have been a Forastieria or apartments for Strangers, & to the South west are two other buildings: On the other side of the river is the parish Church, with a tower built to the Corner of it. Half a mile to the north east is a beautifull turret of a Castle. We went on three miles further to a small neat town on a fine Rivlet.

On the 28th I went three miles to six mile bridge, where there is a handsom new church, & near it Mr. Ivers has a pleasant new built house. The ride from this place to Limerick is very delightful, being well wooded & in sight of the fine river Shanon, & of the beautifull Country on the other side of it. The appearance of the Country on this side Galway is very different from what it was farther north for I observed the corn ready for the Sickle, & when I passed Gort, I found the harvest in several places far advanced: It is all a hot lime Stone which makes the harvest very forward; & I was told that the Cattle turn themselves frequently in the night on account of the heat of the ground. In about 2 miles I saw a large old house, near the river called Bunratty,[112] which was the Mansion house of the Obrians, the ancient Earls of Thomond. I came to Limerick very strongly situated by nature on the Shanon: To the east of it is Irish town, which is pretty strongly fortifyed, the whole being about two miles in circumference; excepting the principal Streeet; All the rest of the town Consists of Narrow lanes, & it is a very dirty disagreeable place; Tho' so large there is not one good Inn where Strangers can be well accomodated; they have a tavern indeed which has lodgings in it, commonly filled by Officers: Both the air & water are looked on as unwholesome, & the army Commonly loose many of their men here: They are Chiefly quarter'd in a barrack within the Citadel on the west side of the town, & this large city, which has Such convenience of Water, has not so much as a fire Engine to make use of, in case of any accident of fire. The Cathedral is a very mean heavy building, but the Quire is fitted up in a neat manner; & in it is a magnificent tomb of black marble, erected to the Memory of the Grandfather the Earl of Thomond who lived in the time of King Charles the second, in the place of an Old one defaced, of which two Couchant Statues remain; This Cathedral was built by Donald O'Brian King of Limerick, & there is a Church in Limerick call'd St Munchin, now a Parish Church, which is said to have been the Cathedral, & that it was founded by St Munchin first Bishop of Limerick. It is remarkable that the present Cathedral stands near North & South; & they have a tradition that it was a palace of the O'Briens: the Bishoprick of Ardfort probably taking in the County of Kerry is united to this see, & in that is the absorpt Bishoprick of Hoghadoe the church of which I formerly saw over the lake of Killarne. There is an old Convent turned into a Tan-yard, which they call the Abby it is on the north side of the town. They have a good Mole for shipping to lye in: There is a great manufacture of Serges here, & a very great number of working people in the town, greater perhaps then in any place of the Size; & I cannot think they can be less than 40 thousand Souls in the town & Suburbs. They import wine, timber & all Sorts of Goods for the Supply of this Country, & great part of the County of Tipperary, as well as the Counties of Clare & Kings County: But Cork lies much more Convenient for the Export. I walk'd round the town either on the walls or within them & went to the Cathedral service.

On the 29th I rid to the west & in a mile crossed over Brater bridge in another mile to Money or Monterel, commonly called Mongrel, where there are remains of a poor Old Convent with a tower, at one corner of the Church. I was informed that monks never had towers to their Convents, by which I suppose they mean Mendicants Fryars. In two miles we came to Cloynreen village & rivlet & in two more to the ferry over the river Magel, on one side of which is Clogtotacheh Castle, & on the other, Column Castle; Mrs. Hartings house near being called Court, as in the Map.[113] In a mile we came to Kildaimon; in another to Lacerane Castle & Lough, & in another mile to a very Small church on a litle height called Killallatring,[114] the walls of it are very thick, with only such a window in the east end, as is seen in the round towers in this Shape ∧ so as that it is probably one of the most ancient churches in this Kingdom. ⊓ I came in a mile to a large Old Castle called Palace with a village near it of the same name, to the South west of which Mr. Bury has begun a new town called Newmarket, & is endeavouring to establish a market there. I soon came to Shanon Grove[115] where Mr. Bury has made fine plantations & enclosures. The first thing that offers is a fine orchard with a Syder house built in elegant taste, the plantations & fields between this & the house are very beautifull; the situation of the house is pleasant; commanding a view of the Shañon & of the fine Country on the other side between the great bay to the north & Limerick. I then went to see the Charter School which was founded by Mr. Bury, who keeps it in very good order. This Gentlemans Mother was daughter of Archbishop Pallasor, & his Lady being sister of Lord Tulloghmore, his son is next heir to that Nobleman, who has no children. I returned two miles in the same way, having the Castle of Carigaginiel on a fine high rock near the Shannon in view all the way, as I had also from Limerick. We returned to Kildaimon & Struck out of the road we came in, to the South east, & in three miles came to Adair on the Magee. This place now a poor village, was they say anciently a walled town, & there are great marks of its having been a place, of some Consequence; In it are remains of a large Old Castle,[116] which belonged to the Earls of Desmond, & of three monasteries; one at the west end of the village, & is called if I mistake not the Abbey of West gate; & in the middle a small Church; there is a tower about 30 feet square, which gives it the air of a Castle. Another monastery is near the bridge, & is called the Steeple Abbey; the openings of the Cloyster of this & of the third are like Gothick windows. There are several niches in the walls, besides the Seats for the administering persons; which were probably so many tombs of ancient families: on the north side of the river a quarter of a mile higher, is what they call the Poors Monastery, tho' it is not inferior to the others in building.

On the 30th in the morn I saw the Convents & went to Church, Mr. Quin a Gentleman of considerable estate here, having met me in Dublin, invited me to dine with him, I went to his house & lay there, it is Situated on the river, the tyde coming up just to his house.

On the [   ][117] I set out & travelled near the river two miles to Croom, passing by the park & house of Lord Carbery where he lives; his Lordship has another very fine park between Bruff & Limerick. On each side the river at Croom, there is an old Castle: We went on three miles farther to Alakee or Athlacha crossing a Stream which falls into the river; & leaving that stream we went eastward three miles to Killmallock, where I had been in 1749, as at all the other places I Shall mention as seen this day. This is another ancient wall'd town, in which there are if I mistake not, two old Monasteries & as this town Athenree & Adair had a Monastery or Monasteries in them, & do not seem to have been situated for trade, it is not improbable that the Monasteries built walls round these towns, for the security of themselves & their tenants, who probably built some of the oldest houses in them, with windows of the Gothick arch; & as the Papists in King James's time were ordered to build houses in walled towns, this might be the occasion of building the greater part of the houses the windows of most of them being in the style of that time. I went to see the Charter School near the town, & from that three miles to Kilfinane; where I visited another Charter School; & meeting Mr. Graves minister of the place, I dined with him & rode six miles to Charleville.

On the 1st of September I went to visit Dean Bruce who was out of town, view'd the Charter School; this town is finely situated on an eminence which commands a fine view of the Country to the South; it is the estate of the Earl of Orrery & the town is chiefly supported by the Dragoons, for whom there is a barrack, & by the thorow fare which is very considerable since the road from Limerick to Cork is carryed through this town which before was farther to the east; near Ard Patrick I crossed over the hills to the valley in which the river Snider runs, & first came to Buttavant, which gives the title of Baron to the Earl of Barrimore & the eldest son by Courtesy takes that title: Here are large remains of an Old Convent as well as Castle. We crossed over the Snider & saw Donerail to the left & came to Malloe famous for its waters, which are on a lime stone & have something of the virtue of the Bristol waters. There is commonly much company here every Summer, & they have a Long Room for Assemblies: It is situated on a small river that here falls into the Blackwater, which we crossed, & going over the hill we passed by Sr. Robert Deanes house, & came to four mile water where I dined, having met in the way Lady Dean & Mrs. Oliver in their Chariot & six, with both of whom I was acquainted & paid my Compliments to them. I came 8 miles to Cork finely situated on the river Lee which divides above the town & running on each side of it, makes it an Island, as it does also below & forms the litle & great Island, below which it spreads again & makes the harbour of Cork. There is a town on the north side of the harbour of Cork called the Cove, near which there is lately built a strong fort to defend the entrance of the harbour: The part of Cork which is built to the river is pleasant; but most of the Streets are narrow & dirty, which makes Chairs of great use here, & there are several of them ply in different parts of the town. This See & Church was founded by St. Finbarr in the 7th Century, to whom the Cathedral is dedicated & is commonly called St. Barrys; the See of Ross, is united to Cork, supposed to be founded in the 6th Century by St. Facknan who built there a Priory of Canons of St. Austin. This place is situated to the west on [   ].

There are six parish churches in the town, Here was one Abbey, four Monasteries, & a Nunnery. The History of a Settlement of a tower of a church here like that of Pisa, & of their Management of it is a great Curiosity: there are several Hospitals in the town; but the foundling Hospital is most remarkable, they have in it about 40 kept [*text unreadable*] nearby, & between 2 & 300 abroad, they are well clothed & kept neatly. An act passed lately for their changing Children with the Poor house of Dublin, in order to prevent any persons putting in children, with design to get them afterwards to their own disposal. The Exchange & Custom house here are handsom buildings. The County jayl at the South gate, is a noble building of three Stories, all Rustick, & of the Tuscan order, & appears more like a palace than a jayl. There are in the town 7366 houses, & the Souls are computed to be above 73000. There is a great export from this Port of Beef, butter, Wool, & yarn, besides a very Considerable import of all Sorts of Goods.

On the [*text scored through*] I rid to Kingale crossing the Oun Boy on the road: it is called eight miles, but is a very unpleasant road all up & down hill, & it is four good hours ride. Kingsale is about a mile long situated over the harbour at the mouth of Bandon river, consisting of one long Narrow Street, & one or two over it on the side of the hill. There is a Charter School here for twenty boys, built by the encouragement of Mr. Southwell. It is a very fine harbour & there is a great resort of Ships in time of war, & this is the only place in Ireland for refitting the King's Ships. The harbour is defended by a Strong Fort called Charles's Fort. The resort to this place is so great in time of war, that their leases pay double rent during any war. As soon as I came to Kingsale I walk'd towards the School, & meeting Mr. Woodward who has a Living near, I din'd with him:

I set out in the Evening for Innishanon six miles up the river Bandon; this village is pleasantly Situated on the East side of the river, having high ground over it, & on the other side is fine hanging ground cover'd with wood: here Mr. Atherly has established a linnen Manufactory in all Kinds, where I saw several Children apprenticed from the Charter Schools & the workhouse in Dublin; on the heigth is a Charter School finely built for forty children which is just opened, & was founded by Mr. Atherly's encouragement.

On the [*text scored through*] I saw these things & went three miles up the river to Bandon Situated on each side of the river Bandon; it is entirely a Protestant town, & they will not suffer a Papist to live in it: They have a great Woollen Manufactory here, if I mistake not, chiefly of Camblets, & now begin to come into the linnen trade. I went to visit Dr. Brown Brother to the Bishop of Cork, who was out of town: so I went about three miles in the road to Cork, & leaving it on the right went almost directly north through a very uneven Country about six miles to Inniscara, a pleasant Situation on the Lee, between two hills which are not improved. I went to the parsonage house of Dr. Philips which is a beautifull plantation & fine retirement, but not finding him at home, I crossed the Lee again over a large bridge, & came five miles to Cork, seeing the Castle of Ballincolly to the right, of which there are great remains. I went to Mr. Falkener my Banker & then to Mr. Penrose where I was invited to lodge.

On the 4th I went three miles on the South side of the river to Riverstown,[118] a fine improved estate of the patrimony of the Bishop of Cork: I dined & lay there.

On the 5th I set out & came to the river, & going eastward passed in four miles through Carigrohil, where is the burial place of the Cotters; in two miles more to Middletown, a small market town & burrough, near a seat of Lord Middletons, with a fine park belonging to it; this is within two miles of Cloyne. I went three miles to Castlemartyr & saw the Charter School for 40 children; founded by the encouragement given by His Excellency Henry Boyle one of the Lords Justices & speaker of the House of Commons, who has a seat near. He has made an artificial water, it may be beyond any thing in Europe; for it encompasses the litle town to the east of this seat, & one may be rowed four miles on the Canal & Serpentine rivers. From this place after I had taken some refreshment, I crossed the mountains to Tallogh in the County of Waterford, having had a fine view of the sea, & of the mouth of the Blackwater. Talogh is Situated about a quarter of a mile south of the river Bride which two miles lower falls into the Blackwater; It is a market town & a Burrough, & they have a Barrack here: It is the estate of the Earl of Burlington. At Curryglas[119] not far distant in the County of Cork is a pleasant seat & plantation, lately Mr. Maynards but now belongs to the Crown; The author of the County of Cork saies that there is a fine white clay here with which the park walls are plaster'd & look very beautifull. I came in the evening to Lismore, which is a village most pleasantly situated: The Castle & Cathedral are on a hanging ground, some of which is covered with wood over the Blackwater: From the Castle & the Warren behind the Cathedral is a fine view of the river both ways, of the meadows on each side, of the wood on the hanging ground & of the Cascade from the Salmon Weer; one sees the beautifull rock of Killree making out like ahead to the north; & below that Cappoquin & its Castle: To the south a mountain torrent called Oen shad falls into the Blackwater directly opposite to the Castle through a Glyn or narrow vale, between the mountain, the lower parts of which are adorned with wood, from this there is an opening into the County of Tipperary, & a way into that Country by what they call the Devil's Causeway; on one side of it there is a fine Lough, in which there is the black Trout; & on each side of this Glyn are high mountains & particularly to the East the highest of them Knockmeildown: the Quire part of the Cathedral is very old, built with sort of Pilasters at the Corners, & long narrow windows on each side & at the end. It was founded by St. Carthage als. Mocoddy who was driven by King Blathmac out of the Abbey of Ratheny in the County of Westmeath. He first founded an Abbey of Canons Regular of St. Augustine, where the Castle now is: He also founded a School or University here, which was afterwards governed by St. Cataldus, who in process of time became Bishop of Tarentum.[120] This Cathedral was repaired by Munchus King of Munster in 1130. The body of the church is a modern building, probably of the time of King Charles 2d. The Chapter house is a good room, there are remains of the Staircase in it, & Signs of a room above in which they might keep the Archives of the Church. In the Church are remains of the tomb of a Magrath in 1557 probably a relation of Bishop McGrath. The Chapter Consists of a Dean, four other Dignitaries & nine Prebends, & it is founded on the rule of the Cathedral of Sarum. There are five vicars Choral, who ought to be presented by the Dignitaries to the Dean as they were formerly, & admitted by him. But the Dean puts them all in. The Author of the County of Waterford saies there was an Anchorite here, to whom Baleyhausay or Anchorets Town & [*text illegible*] did belong. & that there was a Lazaret or Hospital here, the Master of which was called the Prior of Lismore. Tis said the Castle was built by King John, but soon destroyed by the Irish; & when rebuilt was the place of the Residence of the Bishops till Miler McGrath about 1588 granted it & other lands for a chiefry to Sr. Walter Rawleigh, from whom it was purchased by the first Earl of Cork. There is a Free School here founded by that Earl. Sir Robert Boyle was born in this castle,[121] & if I mistake not Congreve the poet.[122]

I lay at Dean Jervais's & on the [   ] I rid through the old Park of Lismore, now disparked two miles to the Blackwater opposite to Drummannah Lord

Grandisons, leaving the old mount or Fort to the left in the way to Cappoquin, from which Lismore (The Great Fort) has its name & also Kilbree an estate of the Bishops, where on a hanging ground over the river is an Old House, said to be on the site of an Old Castle built by King John. A litle further to the west is the rock of Kilbree already mentioned, it is to the left over the river, & is a glorious Situation for a house; & also Cappoquin over which one passes by a long wooden bridge; it is a very small town of one Street with a Barrack at the end of it, for one troop of horse: The Castle over the town is a beautifull Situation & Commands a fine view of the Country every way, & particularly of the rich vale to the east, as far as Dungarvan. Between this & Lismore at Salt bridge north of the river were Iron works & Iron mines near; & a vein of Iron runs through the Park. There are at present Iron works at Araglas to the west of Lismore. I crossed the Blackwater to Drumanna to the Earl of Grandisons, situated on a rock over the Blackwater, where there was formerly a Castle; the hanging ground & wood on it to the South of the house is beautifully laid out in Terraces, Slopes & walks down to the river which is navigable to Cappoquin for large vessels, & the tyde goes up near to Lismore. There is a handsom avenue to Drumanna house from the east: To the north of which is first a wood & several pieces of Water, & then a Park & fine enclosures down to the Phinisk, which is the bounds between this Estate & Affane; to the South is a new planted wood of many Sorts of trees, with firrs on each side of the ridings, & near the house is a Green, on one Side of which my Lord has built seven houses; that in the middle is a handsom edifice for an Inn, the other are for necessary tradesmen.

On the [*text scored through*] I went with Ld. Grandison in his Chaise half a mile to see a New town he has built called Villers Town; the design is two Streets crossing each other with a square in the middle for a market & Chapel. There are 24 houses built with a garden to each of them & his Lordshp is bringing in about eighty acres of Land at great expence for pasturage for the town for as they are all linnen weavers they are not to be diverted by farming: Here are above twenty of the Charter boys apprenticed to the Weavers; & My Lord settles a Curate here & intends to build a Chapel; This Chapel is since built.[123] One of the Streets is to be carryed down to the river, at a place where a Small rivlet runs into it, on which, above the town, is a very good bleach yard. His Lordship is about to build a wall to enclose the land for a park between what is designed for this town & the other lands which he has cultivated. I walked in the afternoon about the garden improvements, & went to see the houses on the Green.

On the 1st of September. I took leave of the Earl & Countess for so that Lady is distinguished, the Daughter being made Viscountess Grandison by Patent to discend to her Heirs Male & is married to Mr. Mason. I crossed the Phinisk on a bridge & came near Affane famous for a particular Sort of Cherry, something like a White heart, which Sr. Walter Rawleigh brought from the Canary Islands.[124] At new Affane is a quarry of black & white marble; & a litle below it at Torrein Mr. Nettles is a Marble of many Colours mostly Brown, white, yellow, & blew. This place is also famous for Cyder; the plantation of apples having been made in these parts, by the tenants of the Earl of Cork. I crossed to the other road leading from Cappoquin to Dungarvan, leaving the Parish of Whitchurch to the right, in which at Baley lemon they have good marle, & in digging for it, they found the horns & most of the bones of a Mouse Deer or Elk, which I saw at the Earl of Grandisons, a rib also was found a mile from Whitechurch, thought, to be of an Elephant, but possibly might be the rib of a Whale. At Bally lemon also there is a quarry of fine dove-coloured & white marble, & at Kilcrump in the parish of Whitechurch is a black marble, which lies deep & is therefore neglected. I left this road & got into the Clonmell road which crosses the Parish of Modeligo, in which I saw some litle remains of Mountain Castle & another entire Castle called Slady, both belonging anciently to the Magrathes. I came into the road from Cappoquin to Clonmell & passed by an old Redout for Soldiers against Raparees now an Alehouse called Ballinemult in the parish of Seskinan: Ascending the hill beyond this place, I had a glorious view of the fine Country of Tiperary & of the river Sure, which runs towards Clonmell: We crossed here a small part of that County & descended to Four mile water or the Nier, at a bridge over it, where there is a small village at which we dined; & crossing the river come again into the County of Waterford. This river rises out of the Same Mountains as the Tey which runs by Killrossanty, & the Malon which runs by Kilmac Thomas, & runs into the sea at Knockanmahon, & the Clough which runs by Curraghmore Ld. Tyrones seat & so by Portlaw in the road from Waterford to Clonmell & falls into the Sure. Ascending the foot of an hill, we had a view of Kilbruantine a very pleasant seat of Mr. Rode Greens over the Sure; just opposite to it is Knocklofty[125] an exceeding fine situation of Mr. Hutchinsons in the County of Tiperary. near Clonmell is a Spaw water, not much frequented at this time. About two miles further brought us to Clonmell on the other side of the Sure in the County of Tipperary, a very pleasant Situation & a thriving town well laid out. Here they have a Manufactory of Serges & other woollen goods, the Assizes are held at this place for the County of Tiperary, & at that time great Contracts are made for wool: It was the Capital of the Duke or Ormonds Palatinate of the County of Tiperary, which was dissolved on the forfeiture of that Noblemans Estate. There is one parish Church in this town, & the Church of the Convent of Minorets, is converted into a Meeting house. Near this town is a very neat well regulated Charter School, for 20 boys & 20 girls, founded on a legacy left by Mr. Dawson. There is a horse barrack in this town: on the County of Waterford side is a spaw water formerly frequented. I visited Mr Ware who was not at home, met him on the way going to the Charter School, I return'd & spent the even with him.

On the [10th *crossed out*] 12th Mr & Mrs Crawley were with me, & I Set Out[126] for Cashel, call'd 8 miles but cannot be less than 12 measured miles. I passed by Donoghmore & in Sight of the large Castle of Mocklerstown. Cashel is situated in a very fine Country two miles from the Sure, & at the foot of the hill on which the Old Cathedral stands called the rock of Cashel; It is a poor town, but as the new road from Dublin to Cork is to pass through it, it is probably that will improve the town. There is no certain account of any thing relating to the See of Cashel before Cormac King & Bishop of Cashel in 901, who is said to have built that Curious Old Chapel adjoyning to the Cathedral, called King Cormac's Chapel; which is arched over & adorned with many litle pillars like the buildings about the time of William the Conqueror: In 1134 Donald O'Brian King of Limerick build a new Church, probably the Old Quire, & made a Chapel or Chapter house of the Old Church: there is a fine arch now decaying over the middle of the Cross Isle: To the West of the Church & adjoyning to it, is a building called King Cormacs palace which was the habitation doubtless of the Succeeding Bishops. There are remains in the Church yard of a very ancient Cross. This Church is built on a very fine high rock, the top of which is cover'd with Verdure & Archbishop Bolton made an easy ascent up to it; it commands a fine view of all the Country round about. In 1569 the See of Emly was united to this Arch bishoprick. In Archbishop Price's time, a few years ago the Cathedral service was removed from this place to the parish Church. There are remains of a Convent here, for there were two, one of Mendicants & the other of Minorites. Near this town is Hore Abby of St. Mary which belonged to Cistertians. A very fine house was begun here by Archbishop Goodwin & finished by Bolton, with offices for Registry & Library & he left the best part of his Books to it: The late Archbishop Price was a Benefactor towards building a Sumptuous Charter School for sixty children. I went to see it,[127] 1 set out to the west & passed by New Park,[128] Mr. Pennyfeather's Seat two miles from Cashel, & in three computed miles more came to Killenaul, a small poor town near the Collieries of Coal, which go by that name, a swifter coal than the Kilkenny coal, & not so full of Sulphur;

here I lay, & the next day the 14th (by the Change of the Style from the old to New[129]) I went forward & travelling five miles to the north came to Kilcooly where there is an old Castle & near it the seat of Sr. William Barker just on the edge of the bog of Menela. There is another road from Killenaule to Kilkenny by Callaghan but much worse. I then turned to the east, & entering the County of Kilkenny in two miles came to Killaghy & saw near it Kilrush, the seat of General St. George, which his Brother the Dean who is in remainder has taken from him; this is a very fine County. We soon come to St. Albans, a handsome park & plantation of Councellor Cuffs, who has a good house here. Ascending a hill we had a glorious view of the fine Country Northward along the Nore beyond Durrow & Southward to Callaghan & all the country below Kilkenny on the Nore: & after riding about four miles came to Kilkenny most pleasantly situated on the Nore. Kilkenny Consists of two parts, the city to the south, & the Burrough of St. Kennys to the north belonging to the Bishop. The See of Ossory was first fixed by St. Kiaran at Saiger now Seir-Keran in Ely O carol in the time of St. Patrick, which about 1052 was removed to the Abby of Aghabo, of which in 599 St. Kenny was first Abbot & was there buryed: in the time of Henry 2d. the See was removed to Kilkenny: Bishop Hacket is said to have built the Belfery of polish'd Marble. There is a fine round tower here, probably built to the honour of St. Kenny. The Bishop had houses at Aghore & Freinston, repaired by Bishop Canewell: This Cathedral is looked on as one of the best in Ireland. Near it is the Bishops house most pleasantly Situated on a height over the river. There was a Priory on the east side of the town for Canons of St. Augustine founded by William Marescall the elder, Earl of Pembroke, which I take to have been where there are the remains of a Convent on the east side of the Nore; The sides of the Church are all window, & it looks very light. There was a Convent of Minorites on the bank of the Nore, which I take to be the church lately rebuilt near the bridge. There was also one of Mendicants founded by William Marescall junior Earl of Pembroke in 1225, There is a free school here with an endowment, if I mistake not of £120 a year, a house & pleasant meadows on the river; & is the only one in Ireland that has some face of a publick School; but the prices are risen so high, that it is to be feared it will fall in its Credit. This school was I suppose founded by the Ormond family, who resided in the Castle here, which is a noble house situated on a height over the river with a hanging ground under it, covered with wood. There is a grand Corinthian gate at the entrance of this house, & at each angle in front a noble round tower: it was very finely furnished, & the furniture was bought by one Hacket a Creature of the family, who when he came to take down the hangings & tapestry, found a second sett under them, which no one knew of, the others being as tis suppos'd put up in haste. They are building here a handsome Session house & Jayl of Kilkenny Marble, with which marble the houses are built, & the Streets are paved: of this place it is said that, There is fire without Smoke, Water without Mud, & Air without Fog; The former is not a benefit as the Coal is so full of Sulphur, that people who are not used to it, cannot bear it in a room; but when burnt first in the Kitchen, the Cinders make a good tolerable fire, but it never flames, must not be stir'd & looks like red hot iron, it makes an excellent Kitchen fire: This coal is found in the hills about five or six miles to the north east of the town; & the Collieries belong to Lord Castlecomer. The Kilkenny marble quarry is half a mile to the South of the town, & is a very fine one; they can raise Stones of any length; I have seen them fourteen feet long in entire pillars & jaumes of doors of one Stone; They have Machinery turned by water for sawing & polishing, & formerly they had them even for turning, & made punch bowls, tea dishes, Saucers & frames of pictures. The marble is of two or three kinds, the white being mostly made by petrified Shells, but there is a sort called the feather marble from some resemblance of feathers. Some of the Marble of the County of Kerry, is still more beautifull than

John P. Neale, Thomastown Castle, 1818–23

this, in a variety of petrified Shells: This Marble makes very fine Cisterns, which have been carryed into Italy & much valued. The park of Kilkenny is on the Nore & much esteemed for the pleasantness of it; & beyond it are some remarkable Caverns. The Charter School for forty boys is a mile out of the town & is very well regulated. I dined at Kilkenny, walk'd to the School, & rode three Miles in the evening to Bennets bridge, on the Nore; Here frequent Camps have been pitched in order to discipline & review the army, particularly one in 1745.

On the 15th I crossed this bridge & went on the east side of the river, & soon saw on the other side a very pleasant seat on the hanging ground over it, belonging to Mr. Griffith; I soon after passed by [   ] the seat of the Lord Ikeran now Earl of Carrick, with fine plantations about it, & I saw to the east Dungarvan, where there is near the Church, one of the round towers. I come to Thomas Town, a small market town & Burrough on the Nore, to which place it is navigable for small boats: Between this & Ross is another burrough town called Innisteag. At Thomas town are remains of a fine large Church: A mile beyond the town in the way to Waterford are great remains of the Abby of St. Mary of Jerpont, it was for Cistertian Monks, founded by Donald King of Ossory in 1180, whose monument is here, as well as that of Felix O'Dallan, who translated the See of Ossory to Kilkenny; the Abbot had a seat in parliament. A litle lower the river [   ] falls from the west into the Nore which rises at Kilcooly, by which I passed out of the bog of Monela, then runs by Callan a small town which I have been at, near Lord Diserts seat: & afterwards by Kells, through which I have passed in the way from Kilkenny to Carrick, at which place there is a round tower; here was a Priory of Augustinian Canons. Going on over the heathy mountain I saw to the west Knocktopher, where I have often been, & where there was a Carmelite Convent founded by James the Second Earl of Ormond in 1356. In seven miles from Thomas town we passed by Lukes Well, a place of great Devotion, & in seven more came to Waterford, a City which stands very pleasantly on the river Sure, having the finest Key in Europe, except that of Messina in Sicily & is half a mile long & of a good breadth. This City was built some hundred years before Henry 2nd by the Ostmen or Danes. The old town was in a triangular form with a tower at each Corner, first Reginalds or Ring tower at the South east Corner, then it went along by High Street westward to Turgesius's Tower in Baron Strand Street, from which it extended to St. Martin's Castle by Lady lane & so to Ring tower: It afterwards took in all to Johns Gate, Stephens Gate, Patrick gate & to the Key, & it is probable the river come anciently to the town walls & that the pill or mill race from it washed the southern walls: The City was then enlarged by the English, & I observed the old walls to the Key were built of large Stones, which are a cement of pebbles & must have been brought from the other side, all the Country being of that kind of Stone. Near Patricks Gate was a Square Fort by way of Citadel, where the Barracks are now built. The Cathedral called Christ Church dedicated to the Trinity is said to have been built by the Danes; & Malchus was the first Bishop in 1096. It is a plain building consisting of the body, the Quire, two Isles & the parish Church of Trinity behind the Quire. To the North was Rices Chapel & the Chapter house, both now pulled down: In the former was a Curious Monument of Rices now in the parish Church: On the South side is St. Saviours Chapel, now the Bishops Court, & St. Nicholas now the Vestry & Chapter house; There is also a chapel opposite to the Bishops Court. The Quire has lately been much ornamented if intermixture of Grecian with Gothick Architecture can be call'd an Ornament by a Corinthian Altar piece, which is the gift of Mrs. Susannah Mason & cost £200;—by a very handsom Canopy over the seat of the Mayor & Aldermen, & by the same over the galleries, & the seats of the families of the Bishops & Dignitaries, by making a Gallery to the north for the Soldiers, to the west over the Organ for the Charity boys,—by adorning the Galleries with handsome Ballustrades, & New seating the Church & paving it with black & white marble, to which besides the white marble The Revd. Dr. Jeremiah Milles, Chantor of the Cathedral of Exeter as he was likewise formerly of this Church & Treasurer of Lismore, gave the sum of fifty pounds:[130] St. Olaves & St. Patricks Church are both paved with black & white marble, adorned with handsom Altar pieces Pulpits & thrones, & all the seats are so disposed, that the people Stand with their faces to the east, the men on one side & the women on the other: These Churches were order'd in this maner & adorned under the care of Dr. Thomas Milles Bishop of Waterford & Lismore;[131] who published a learned edition of St. Cyril of Jerusalem, & writ a Treatise against Dr. Dodwell of the Immortality of the Soul.[132] There was a Dominican Convent in this City, called the White Fryars, the Church of which is now the County Court house: The Benedictine Convent of St. John, founded by King John, & the Franciscan Convent of the Holy Ghost, the Church of which now belongs to the French; another part of it is an Hospital for twenty four Popish widows, founded by the Walshe's. Lastly, St. Catharines Priory for Canons of St. Victor. The Lepers Hospital was founded by the Powers Lords of Tyrone, & the lands are now applied to an Infirmary, & £100 a year to ten decayed House keepers; & adjoyning to it is another Infirmary founded by the late Countess of Tyrone, which are attended by the same officers: Opposite to the Cathedral is built a very handsom House called the Apartment; for ten Clergymens widows, & there are two houses more; they have £10 a year; all the Benefaction of Bishop Gore; it is built on the place where King Johns house was situated. The Bishops House is a fine building of hewn Stone begun by Bishop Este, but is not finished. The City Court house & Exchange, the City jayle & the fish market, are also handsom buildings of hewn Stone, & the Custom house of Brick, with hewn Stone windows. The Charity School founded by Bishop Foy, for 75 boys, is also of Hewn Stone, a low Decent building, they are cloth'd & taught, the Master has £60 a year & the Catechist £15; & there is a fund for binding them out apprentices. Mrs. Mary Mason also erected a good building of Brick, with Stone window Cases for thirty girls, who are clothed, fed, lodged, taught to read & work. Behind the Bishops House where the Mill dam was, is a fine walk, planted with double rows of trees, & is called the Mall; just beyond which at the end of the Key, is a fine Bowling green on the River. Mr. Barkers hanging gardens are very beautiful. Mr. Wyses Mills are well worth seeing, in which the preparing of wheat to make flower is performed by Water Wheels; he has also a Smelting house there, a manufacture of pins & several other works— There is also a Dock in the Marsh for repairing of Ships with water pipes laid to it. They have a considerable trade here to Cadiz, sending Butter, Herrings, &c: [   ] & bring back, fruit, spanish wines, &c.: [   ] They send butter to Holland; the Newfound land Ships come here & take in Pork, Coarse Linnen & other provisions. They send work'd Woollen yarn, Raw hides & Tallow to England. The Linnen Manufacture is carried on here of late years with great success. Near Waterford Kilbarry is a parish where there was a Preceptory belonging to the Knights of Jerusalem, & the lands of the whole parish belong to it.

On the 18th I went from Waterford to Tramore bay, passing by Balinemona the Seat of Mr. Carew. Tramore bay is about two miles broad, & has an exceeding fine Strand, a rivlet falls into it at the east end where the tyde coming in, makes the north Strand, divided from the other by a Strip of land & some Sandy hills, & it contains if I mistake not near 2000 acres, & when the tyde is in, it appears like a fine lake. There is a great Concourse of people of late to this place, in the Summer to bathe, & to drink the Salt water: & My Worthy friend Dr. Thomas Archdeacon of Lismore & Vicar General of the Diocese, has built a turret here, in a beautifull situation, with one large room up one pair of Stairs, & great conveniences under it. At this bay are a great variety of curious granites, marbles & jaspars, that have been rolled from the sea; some of which I have had polish'd & are very beautifull; & to the west is a litle bay called, if I mistake not, Carols Bay, in which I have been informed are many curious pebbles. There is a bed of excellent oysters in the river which falls into the bay, but they are very scarce. On the other side of this rivlet, on the north side of which is a harbour for small craft, Mr. Wyse has a small Country house, to which one fords the river; on the Sands near it, I have seen Asparagus grow wild, as Eringo does also in great plenty.[133] Going along the sea Coast towards Waterford harbour are several Caves from the sea, with openings from them to the Surface above: one of the finest of them is called the Bishops hole; a litle within the mouth of the harbour is a very Small bay, called White house bay: on one side are the remains of an old Castle & opposite to it, is a pleasant box call'd Nymph Hall belonging to Dr. John Alcocks Dean of Ferns & left him by Mr. Henry Mason: Beyond it is Dunmore Castle, & a litle further Woodstown the seat of Mrs. Motloe, from which there is a Strand to Passage; but before one comes to it in land is Crook Castle & a Church that belonged to the Templars. Passage is the place where ships lye that wait either to go up to the town or sail out of the harbour. The litle town is Situated on a narrow slip under a Steep high hill. Further on is Faith leg Mr. Boltons house & estate,[134] on it is Cheek-point hill, from the top of which is a glorious prospect:

The Nore & Barrow having joyned above Ross fall into the Sure. Opposite to this place, having made [   ] what is called the Great Island, tho' it is only a peninsula; Going on towards Waterford is Ballymakill the seat of Mr. Dobbyn, a very ancient family, opposite to which is the litle Island, a fine spot of ground of about an hundred acres. There is a Castle on it but no Spring. Inland Killure a Preceptory of the Knights Templars, & Bishops Court a ruined Country house of the Bishop of Waterford. Passing Waterford & continuing up the river first is Grace Dieu where there is an house on a height, a most pleasant Situation & beyond it a good house by the water side which belongs to Mr. Anderson. About two miles further is Skilloteran, a very neat Church on a rivlet, & opposite to it is the Charter School for forty Children, founded on the encouragement given by the City of Waterford & neighbouring Gentlemen. Near this is a very fine Slate Quarry, & about half a mile farther in a bottom on a Small rivlet is Whitfield, a seat of Mr. Christmas's, a small house with a handsom Apartment added to it; the gardens are pretty & a proper advantage is taken of the great command of water; Mrs. Christmas made a beautifull Shell-room of a Summer house, in which there are a great number of fine Shells, Corals & pieces of Statuary & Grotesque China. Near Lisnekil Church in an ancient Danish fort were found two urns of Coarse earth, in one there was a black earth or Ashes, in the other a bracelet of pure gold, weighing about five ounces. At the Mouth of this riylet on the Sure is a pleasant box, late Mr. Ivies, now the habitation of Mr. Southwell. To the South east of Lisnekil is an old Castle called Butlers Castle. It is to be observed that all along on this Side of the Sure there is no lime Stone, but plenty of it on the other side, except that about Kilmeaden they find it in a marle they have there, some of which is in large lumps: but this marle is of such a nature, that tho' it has been tryed every way, they cannot find it does any good to the land. At Kilmeaden just over the water is a small house of Lord Donerails, now inhabited by Mr. Usher; there is also a Spaw water at Kilmeaden: & Mr. Wyse has lately made a rivlet navigable from the Sure about half a furlong [   ] to Mills he has built for rowling Copper, smiteing Iron & Several other works. Going further up the river, close to it is May field, the seat of Mr. May built adjoyning to Rochets Castle; near this the river Clodugh falls into the Sure, on which about two miles higher is Curragh more, the seat of the Earl of Tyrone, situated in a bottom. The house is grand & comands a view of the mountains to the South west. To the west of it, is a fine artificial Serpentine river & walks are cut through a beautiful wood of well grown oaks. Lady Tyrone is making a fine Grotto near it, in which there is a great profusion of Curious Shells & Corals. They have a piece of Chrystal in this family of which the country people have a notion, that if is put into ye water which the Cattle drink, it will cure the Murrain, it is sent for even from distant places for this purpose. In a bog near this place, two of those brass heads of an ancient offensive weapon Call'd Celts were found, of which so many have been dug up in several parts of England.[135] Lord Tyrone has rebuilt in a very elegant manner the parish Church of Clonegam. Following the course of the Sure above Mayfield is a ruinous house in a pleasant Situation

over an height caled Montpelier, & belongs to the Bolton family. We then came
to Carrick-beg opposite to Carrick in the County of Tiperary; here was a Minoret
Convent, the tower of which is remarkable, it is built on the side wall of the
Church from one point as in the middle of the wall below. At this place is the
Church of Kilmolleran, a parish absorpt in that of Desert, form which it is called
the Prebendary & Vicaridge of Desert & Killmolleran, but the bounds of the two
ancient parishes are not known, tho' probably it was the stream at Coolne-
muckey: At Carrickbeg is a large Stone bridge over the Sure. In a quarry of Soft
Stone above this place are many Dendrites, formed by the Shooting of some
minerals, but they easily wash out.[136] To the South at a distance from the Sure,
is the large parish of Mothil; near the parish Church are remains of an old
Convent of Cistertian or Augustinian Monks. Coolnemucky on the Sure is an
old Castle of Mr. Walls, to the East of it I saw formerly an Oak standing called
the Blahoge, the trunk of which was about ten feet diameter, & the boughs spread
as it is said, over near an acre of ground: On the side of the hill to the south of
Cool ne Muchy, is a fine plantation of 20,000 firrs, which thrive much: A litle
further is Church town the seat of Mr. Disney on the river where there is a ford,
& there is another about three miles higher, & on a rivlet a litle beyond the Church
of Desert is Glyn a house belonging to Mr. Congreve, formerly a Castle of the
Everards: At Bolenhendeport upon the Mountain, saies the Author of the County
of Waterford, was an Abby, rather a Convent of St. Madock for Canons regular
of St. Augustine. On the first mountain are the houses of several gentlemen
farmers, who have small estates here, mostly the Powers. This flat on the top of
the hills is a pretty good Country, & extends two or three miles to the high
mountains of Cummora, which stretch near as far as Dungarvan: on the top of
them I have been informed, is a large Lake.[137] This Country & the eastern part of
the Barony of Decies, Is called the Powers Country because it was mostly
inhabited by people of that name. Within two miles of Clonmell is an old Castle,
if I mistake not, called Tuchencore, belonging to Sr. William Osborn: about two
miles above Clonmell on the Sure, they find excellent Marle, & from it the estate
of Mr. Moore is called Marlefield. As I have before given an account of this
Country, as I travelled through it as far as Drumanna & Villerstown, I shall go
on with it to the South from those places. & first on the west side of the
Blackwater. To the west of Tallon is the Castle of Lisfinny formerly belonging
to the Earls of Desmond. Towards Youghall on a rock over the river is the Castle
of Strancauley, from which there is a passage cut through the rock to the river;
There are traditions of the Earl of Desmonds confining people here, leaving them
to perish, & seizing on their Estates, on which part of the Castle & rock were
blown up. Lower are the Castles of Temple Michael & Rhincrow alias Kilcrow,
of which there is a tradition that it was the place of the Knights Templars. Near
this is Balyntray, the house of Mr. Smith, opposite to which is an Island called
Der Inis & sometimes the Isle of S. Molanfioe or Molanna, from a convent there
of Regular Canons founded by that Saint in the 6th Century. Here they say
Raymond le Gross was buried, who in the time of Henry IId. had a great Share

in the Conquest of Ireland. Near this is the bounds of the County of Cork round by a rivlet to the South: Going on the other side of the river we met with a large Castle, said to be built by King John, & is called in Irish Clough, I should before have mentioned that on the Phinisk north of Drumanna is Bewley, where there are ruins, said to be an house of the Tomplars, but there is no account of it, At Balline Multina there is a quarry of Good Slates. About Clashmore the river Lichey falls from the east into the Blackwater, on which is the Castle of Balyheny; At Clashmore there was a Convent of Canons regular founded in the 7th Century by St. Cronan Mockoa.[138] Kinsale beg is opposite to Youghal, where the church was roofed & covered by Bishop Milles, but all the Protestant inhabitants leaving the Parish it was not finished. Near it is prospect Hall, the seat of Mr. Bernard, from which there is a fine view of Youghall on the river which is built up the Side of a hill, a litle like the situation of Constantinople, to the South west was a fine Strand four miles long, but by some accident was spoiled for riding: Pilestown is the estate of the Walshes where judge Walsh lived, who is supposed to be the author of the forged Commission in favour of the Irish Rebels, in the time of King Charles the first, according to the Author of the County of Waterford. We now leave the river & turn east ward along the Shore & soon came to Ardmore, the great (head or height) from a head of land at this place, It was anciently the See of a Bishoprick founded by St. Declan of this county who was the first Bishop, about the time of St. Patrick: They say he founded a Monastery here, which might be at the old Church over the Sea-Cliff, where are remains of a very ancient building; the Cathedral probably was where the present parish Church is, at the west end of which are some curious old reliefs of Saints, of Adam & Eve, &c.: the Chancel only is covered for the Parish Church. Near it is a small square building where St. Declan is buryed: there is the finest & best built round tower here in the Kingdom, fifteen feet in diameter & above a hundred high, it is divided into five parts by four water Tables, There are at top two or three beams of timber for hanging a Bell, for which use it certainly served, there being very plain Channels in the Stones at the bottom of the door worn by the ropes. There are also remains of an old Castle here; on the head of land were formerly lead mines, & searching of late for ore they found they were worn out. This parish extends a great way into the mountains to the north & four long miles to the eastward. There is a great Pattern held here on St. Declans day & penances are performed by creeping under a Stone, concerning which they have Some Strange tradition:[139] old mines also are seen over the mountains, which if I mistake not, are said to have been Iron mines. They have a fine Strand here & a pretty good fishery: Between this & Dungarvan is Rineogonah parish, from which one may pass over the Strand to Dungarvan: but the more Common way is over very dismal Mountains, which are near on a level with the ground towards the sea, but there is a great descent from them to the vale in which Dungarvan is Situated on a Bay into which the small river of Colligen & Briskey fall, the latter is a great torrent after rains. It is situated on the South side of the river & is a good fishing town, & famous for an export of potatoes to many parts of Ireland, & I have been told they export the yolks of eggs boyl'd hard & Salted for Spain to be eaten as sauce with their Salt fish; There is a bank about ten leagues from Dungarvan, where they catch great quantities of Hake & Haddock, Cod, Ling, & many other kinds of Fish. They have also a bed here of very large oysters. There is a Barrack built in the Old Castle, of which there was formerly a Constable: on one side of Dungarvan is Shandon, the seat of the Hores, & on the east side Clonkasteran, Mr. Nugents;[140] opposite to the town on the North side of the river is an old Convent of Augustinian Eremites, founded by the MacGraths in the thirteenth Century. Going along the Coast eastward, Clonea is a flat Country, & under the Strand is a bog, the turf of which is disagreeable to the Smell when it is burnt Within[141] land, in Killrossanty parish are the Castles of Barnakill & Beleykeroye. In Stradballey at Ballivony is a large building & two remarkable wells, which communicate with each other & they are fed by water, brought by a Subterraneous passage: there is a descent by steps to one of them: it is thought to have belonged to the Knights of Jerusalem. At Kilmacthomas is a strong Castle of the Powers, & a litle farther about two miles from the sea is Newtown, laid out in Streets, & paved & a few houses built, but now ruined all by Mr. Greatrakes.— Going along the Coast is Kiloarimeden, where on Lord Ranelaghs estate some lead mines have been discovered, which did not answer, but on Knockanmaham the Bishops estate they have worked some Copper mines with good success, tho' now they say the vein is grown very small & hardly worth pursuing. I saw some Ore which looked like glass & like broken bugles[142] & some pure native Copper: Between this & Tramore is nothing remarkable but Island Ikane, so called from very small Islands opposite to it, about two miles from Tranmore bay.

On Monday Octr. 2d 1752 I set out from Waterford to Ross & crossed over to the County of Kilkenny, in about two miles I passed by a small Kern with a Cross on it, & had soon to the left a rocky hill of that Cement of pebbles, chiefly of the Alabaster kind, which abound all over the Country & of which the walls of Waterford are built; after riding about two miles farther, we passed by an Old Church call'd Kilmacoivow: We had a fine view of the river Sure & then of the Nore & Sure & going up to a height, I had a delightful prospect of the Mouth of the harbour, of the winding of the Nore & of what they call the great Island, which is only a Peninsula. We came to the Nore & crossed it into the County of Wexford to Ross; all the Country we passed over is a union of Vicaridges in the gift of the City of Waterford. Ross is very pleasantly Situated on the river & on the side of the hills over it, a rivlet runs down the middle of it through the street in a litle hollow between the two hills; it is encompassed with a wall defended by turrets: on the top of the hills the large Church of the Convent of the Minorits, the east end of which serves for a Parish Church; there is a handsom tower to it, which commands a view of the Country, of the Barrow falling into the Nore about a mile higher, a fine flat on the river below, a litle like the Campo of Scio,

Francis Grose, Tower of Hook, County Wexford, 1791

except that instead of wall'd gardens, it is laid out in beautiful Meadows. In the Church they show the tomb of Rosa Marra, who they say built the Town walls & the Church, & near it is what they call the tomb of her son, who being drowned as they say, she built Hook Tower at the mouth of the Harbour of Waterford. Under the South cross Isle are two or three vaults which are open. The body of the church is cover'd with lead. There is a good Town house here, built of a very fine white mountain Stone or Granite. The Key is a most pleasant walk. Half a mile from the town in the road to Inniscorthy is a Charter School for twenty boys & twenty girls.

On the 3d I set out & went about a mile to the South west in view of the river, & leaving the road to Ducannon Fort struck into the road to Nash Belligarvan & Clamines. I went near Slea quiltah which is over the river, in about a mile we came to Castle Terri [   ] & soon come to Aglamau & in half a mile further to Dunmain Mr. Reyleys having lost the way to Nash further to the north, but came into it at Balligarvan: The house of Dunmeen was the habitation of Lord Altham, where it is said he parted from his Lady, & when afterwards a dead Child was born of one of the name of Esther, they afterwards came together, & then it was, as I understood that it is said she was delivered in the house of Mr. Annesley, who now again sets up for the estate & title. We soon passed near Abbey Kilbrayney belonging to Mr. Cliff: & further to the east saw on a height Brianstown Mr. Tenches; we came in half a mile to Castle Boley, & in half a Mile more to Dungulow Castle & soon after to Clamines, which they say was formerly a town of trade, tho' there is now only one house in it, but there are three old towers or Castles remaining in it, one of which is near the Parish Church of St. Nicholas, & in it was an arch'd Chapel with an apartment over it. The other two are in a line, & they say there was a row of houses between them & another row built so as to make a Street, & part of the Cross of the Market place is remembered as standing: Just over the river are remains of a Convent, which I was informed was of Augustinian Monks; near it is St. Maria's chapel: Just above, the Blackwater from the west, & Folkes's mill river from the north unite, & make the river of Clamines, which lower is called the river of Bannoe; The Tyde comes up here making a sort of a bay & at low water they cross over on a kind of a Causeway they have made, but the water comes three or four feet over it: This is a Burrough, Mr. Annesley's estate, but the Burrough is in Lord Loftus. I here dined on the provisions I had brought, & a dish of fish the Farmer provided for me, of the white Trout & Plaice, the latter very litle inferior to Turbat. He had a Son who is dumb, but very sharp in Country business & has a very strong sense of Religion. I here left my horses to cross over to go to Bannoe & took horses to ride four miles south to Fethard; Having travelled about half way I came to the old Convent of Tintern, turned into a mansion house of the Colcloughs; The church is large with a great tower in the middle, the Chancel part was converted into a house with three floors & Chimneys, of which I never saw an instance before;[143] I was informed that this family come over in Queen Elizabeths time, that an Ancestor marrying a Papist went over to the popish religion, but in the present is a Convert who has fixed a Spinning School here & a linnen Manufactory & built a litle market house in the village. I came to Fethard pleasantly Situated on the north side of a small river, about a mile from the Bay of Bannoeo. It is a Burrough belonging to Lord Loftus who has built a litle town here; It was a Mannor of the Bishop of Fernes, but exchang'd for another Estate. The Castle was the Bishops house one of the name of Ram was the last that liv'd in it: It was afterwards the Mansion house of the Loftus family.[144] There are remains of an old Chapel & of a building which they say, was the Bishops Study & that there was a Terrace to it from the Castle: There is a turret near the town built like a Castle, which is on the Glebe, & is supposed to have been the Parsonage house. In this bay there is a small oyster bed for Lord Loftus's use; I had been formerly at this place & the places I shall describe—Bag & Bun a mile to the South east where Strongbow landed in the time of Henry 2d. in a litle bay made by that head & the head to the north of it at the mouth of Fethard river: It is said he come with two Ships, one named Bag, the other Bun; there is a double entrenchment round it: A narrow Strip of Land extends to the south on the east side of the harbour of Waterford, on which stands a Light house called Hook Tower & there being a place call'd Crook opposite to it, 'tis said that on landing the General declared he would take Ireland by Hook or by Crook. Here is Loftus Hall[145] the Seat of Lord Loftus a descendent of Primate Loftus; no tree will grow above the Shelter of the walls; The mulberry tree thrives best of any with that Shelter: this strip of land is exceeding rich, as it is constantly manur'd by the spray of the sea. About two miles farther to the west is Duncannon-fort, which was built to command the passage up the river, the lower works are cut out of the rock, & the Channel being close to it, no ship can go up but must be within Canon shot; some soldiers are always here in Garrison;[146] near this fort is a very good chalybeat spring. King James had a ship ready here in case of any disaster, & after the battle of the Boyn he lay in Dublin; & came here the next day & embark'd for France. About two miles farther is Ballyhack opposite to passage & under the hill in the same manner; here are some great Fairs held for tame fowls of all Sorts which sell very cheap, as also white Coarse frieze at low prices.

On the 4th I left Fetheard & walk'd a mile on the South Side of the river to the Mole, in which a vessel of an hundred tun can lye safe, but in a Storm a Ship cannot be secure abroad, except it may be from a westerly wind. I crossed over in about half a league to Bannoe & landed on the Strand at that Creek of land which joyns what they call the Island of Bannoe to the land: here they say was the old & safe entrance when Clamines was a town of trade; but now the entrance is to the west of it, & is choaked up by several barrs of sand that would make it very difficult, for a ship to pass with Safety when the tydes are high: This Peninsula is is [sic] fine low round hill, covered mostly with Corn & appears very beautifull. There are only three or four houses at Banoe & ruins of a good Old Church, in which there is an old Font, a tomb with a Latin inscription on it, in the Old Character & a Stone Coffin with a hole cut in it to receive the head. This is in the Barony of Bargie, which as well as that of Forth is a great corn Country, insomuch that they say these two have sent some years from Wexford, as one told me 140,000 barrels of Barley, that is half that number of quarters. These Countries are entirely different from any other part of Ireland exceedingly well inhabited, especially in & towards the Barony of Forth; a gentlemans house is seen almost every mile, & besides Villages & Hamlets one sees a house at every quarter of a mile distance, the farms being from five to Sixty acres & mostly above twenty, the people neat well dress'd & very honest. The barony of Forth are a Colony from England about the time of Henry 2d., & they are so wedded to their own Country, that they have not gone much out of it till of late years, they are become so very populous that they now go to Newfoundland, to England, & also to harvest to many parts & take farms in Bargie & about Eniscorthy where they have manure of Marle, for having been used to those improvements which are the gift of nature, they do not care to go where they have not either lime or marle, & this has raised the price of land very much in those parts: In Bargie which is not altogether so populous, there is a greater appearance of wealth; notwithstanding in Forth they live as neat as can be on such small farms & keep all clean about 'em, their food is Potatoes, barley bread, Bacon, Cheese & milk; at the great festivals they have the old English way of making a feast; inviting their friends & their Neighbours, the Landlord & the priest, & they have beef, Mutton & pudding in great plenty: as they sow horse beans very much & grey pease, so they eat both the one & the other with bacon dry as well as green. Near the sea they manure with sea weed, sowing every year & Manuring every year, & Change the grain, Barley, oats, beans, pease, but no wheat; what they want is bought at Wexford. If they lime it holds nine years, & marle I believe the same. As to their particular Customs, it has been said they go to bed in the middle of the day, which they might do formerly; & now, as the Irish, they lye down for an hour in hot weather: All Contracts are transacted by exchanging money, & so the contract of marriage is made here; the young man goes with his friends, gives the woman a piece of money; & it having happened sometimes that among people not of good Character consummation has ensued, this has been the ground for saying that it was Commonly so, & that they married in form afterwards. We went on Close to the sea side; in two miles came to Cullingtown & soon after to Bali Teague Island, as it is called, tho only a Peninsula it is a warren & is a long Strip extending westward, & at the West end of it the sea enters & makes those bays to the north of it, which are called the Broad water; in half a mile we came to Coolhill Castle, & in a mile more to a litle town called Duncormuck, where there is a Church & a bridge over a rivlet, I saw Kai Mr. Wilsons to the north, & to the east of Ballykenny Mr. Vigors; I then passed by Kilcooly Castle & rivlet, & observed a singular building on it, like a small house, this castle seems to have been destroyed on purpose to get the limestone out of it, for from this rivlet, if I do not mistake to Bridge town they get a reddish lime Stone, for which they dig in pits, finding it in pieces mixed with the Soil, & this has made this Country very populous, probably by Colonies from Forth. In a mile we come to Baldwinstown where there is a Castle & rivlet, & all about it is great plenty of lime stone, which they carry to the distance of four or five miles, they make Kilns of sods in the field they would manure & build up the lime stone in a Cone, & burn it with furze & the old kiln remains till they want to make use of it again; but when once a field is arable they keep it for a long time under corn by manuring it again; for in all the road to Ladies Island I saw only one piece of fallow. Opposite to this part are the Saltee Islands, which abound in rabbits & sea birds, there are good Springs in them but they are not inhabited. In a mile I came to Bridge town, where there is a large bridge over the river; near it is the Church of Mulranchy in which parish it is: in the Church yard is this inscription on a tomb—

Here lyes a jolly merry blade
Who's gone;—but now he's but a Shade
To teach the Ghosts a Masquerade:
But Pluto likes not such a Guest,
Bids him depart & go to Rest
William Hoskins, Dancing Master, 1748.

The estate on this side of the river belongs to the Ivery family, who set leases of lives renewable for ever to Protestants; & then sold the estate: so that there are as they say more protestants in this Union, than in all the two Baronies of Bargie & Forth; that is I suppose Gentlemens families excepted; However that may be, there are, as they say, about fifty families, & they have all sorts of trades & seem to be very happy & wealthy; & truely the face of these two baronies appeared to me like an enchanted Country, so different from anything I had seen indeed any where. I took some refreshment here, & in about two miles came to the Bridge of Bargey, where there is a Castle; here I came into the Barony of Forth, the miles before were so long that three make about five, but in Forth they seem to have introduced the English mile, for here I found the miles very Short: They call it six miles to Ladies Island; & here I saw the marle pits, for manuring the land: I saw Hia Castle about a mile from Ladies Island, & at the Same distance passed through a village called Broad way, & passing over a bridge near an old Church, I observed just opposite to the Island the white Sand which is famous here, it is a Stratum a foot below the surface, & is carried to all parts for the use of Sand boxes,—but they have the same sort on the sea side to the east. Ladies Island is about a mile round, it is now become a Peninsula one sees where there was a fossee for the water to pass, & at that place there is a Tower called Maidentower which has settled on one side, the foundation appears to be laid on the green sod; here they say was a Draw bridge, there seems to have been a wall built on each side to this tower, & there is a Causeway of large Stones to it, to pass over when the Lough was full; within this about fifty yards is a Gate way & another wall built at about the same distance within; that is the Old Church, where there is a Font of red Granite of which there is Great plenty In these parts, there is also in a nich an alabaster Statue of the Virgin & our Saviour & before it an old brass Cross, with one of the four Evangelists in each of the ends of it. This is a place of great devotion among the Roman Catholicks, probably set on foot by the English Colony, that they might have every thing within themselves; & they come to do penance here by walking once round the Island barefooted, & three times round the Church & sometimes they perform this three times over, & some on their Knees: The tracks of their feet is seen all round the Island; There is an enclosure by the Church for the acoomodation of pilgrims, who come mostly between the Festival of ye Assumption in August, & that of ye Nativity of ye V. Mary in September: & all the roads are exceeding fine in those parts. But the Lake here is a natural Curiosity, it rises so high in about seven years, that it would overflow the inland Country round it; & then three or four hundred people come in & mark out in the Sand banks to the south west a fossee about an hundred feet wide & begin to open it in the middle, narrowing it as they go down, they then open it to the sea, & at last work upon it towards the Lake; if they find the water coming they must instantly leave it, for it gushes out as a great torrent & falls down in a Cascade into the sea, the bottom of the lake being about ten feet above the Surface of the Ocean; Sometimes it breaks away the bank at night, but if it happens by day they take great quantities of fish, mostly Plaice; but if it goes out by night as it did the last time they loose the fish: the first high wind fills up the opening, the lake fills slowly, as it leaks out for some time at the place they open, but when that is closed up with the Slime & earth from within, it fills faster, & in about Seven years begins to overflow the lands; the water with the Spray of the sea is brackish; great quantities of wild fowl lye on it. I saw the black Gull & green plover, for this Country is famous for Wild fowl; the widgeons are excellent, but the best sort we call'd the Wynniards, so also is the Barnicle, the first go inland to the bogs & breed, the Barnacles go to the parts from which they came, to the North, & are seen by the Ships at sea northward with the Tyde; when they are attack'd by Eagles or Hawks by a wonderful instinct, they gather all together & keep beating with their wings & raise the water, so that the bird of prey cannot see to attack 'em, but if any one is disabled & cannot close with them, they are surely taken; they have bounds of furze bushes round this Island to lye unobserved & Shoot at them.

I Set out on the 5th & went two miles to Carne village & Head, where one Mr. Pallasur lives the Landlord of the place. Carnehead is the south east point of Ireland & makes out to the south in Rocks of Granite, chiefly of the red kind, such as at the Cataracts of the Nile of which the Obelisks were made, some of it is greyish in large veins like some in Cornwall. I went on to the point which is covered with muscles, that fix to it with their beards, there are also welks &

limpets on these rocks, & a boy seeing me walk on them, came & grop'd for Crabs, & I observed he knew every hold tho' it was under Water; the seals also came very close to the rock & I whistled to them, to which they seemed to give attention, but when they saw me they div'd. I then went along by the sea side northward passed by Carne Church & afterwards St. Margarets Major Nuns being a great Landlord in these parts, then by Baley Trant Mr. Hughes's, & by an old Church; I went along the Strand for some way, & saw the Seals lying out of the water on rocks about an hundred yards from the waterside, they took no notice of any noise I made to frighten 'em, but when I whistled their whole body was in agitation, as if sensibly affected by it, we saw the heads of others in the water near them which I took to be young ones. In another mile we came to Balihiar & at the same distance to Ballygeny, in half a mile near Kilroan Castle & saw in land Brinikan Houli, & Kilstoran Church in repair & Hil Castle & so came to Roslaer, where I dined in a Cabin on what I had brought with me;— Having travelled on a bank over the sea for about three miles the Coast here making such a turn that we had the sea to the North of St. Ellin's point, we passed to the South making a great shallow bay with the land of Wells in the way to Gory. I came some part of the way on the Strand, as I might have come all along but as I had no view of the country I chose to ride on the Cliffs over the sea which are a kind of blew Clay with herbage on them, the Sand to the Southward as well as here being all white, & there is a great variety of Granite among the pebbles on the beach. I rid a mile & half farther northward on the point to Whitehouse Mr. Boyd's, where in the waren on the Sandbanks I saw the dwarf withy. I observed them making ropes with rushes twisted with the same kind of instrument I described before, which is here call'd a Crook: At the end of this point is what they call the Fort, where a Custom house Officer resides. We passed again near Roslaer Castle & in about a mile passed by Grange; in about two miles we come to Clonck where there was a pattern or rood, & I saw the young men playing at hand tennis: I observed the women were dressed extremely neat with short[147] Cloaks of Cloth. In a mile we had Kileny Castle at a litle distance, Mr. Harvey's, & in another we came to Kilau, where there is a rivlet, & here they dig very good Limestone in quarries: I was told also that they are in search of a rich mine in this place: we had gone since we turn'd our faces to the East under the mountain or hill of Forth, which extends westward for seven or eight miles, the foot of it this way is rocky & I observed from this place to Wexford it consists of a reddish stone; we came in another mile to Wexford. The common people of the Barony of Forth are mostly Roman Catholicks, & I shall conclude this Barony with some account of their language, which is the English of the time of Henry IId & comes pretty near to Chaucers. They now indeed almost all affect to speak good english, & do speak it with a very good accent, & I met but one who did not speak tolerable modern english, but they make use of some particular expressions, & many of them talk very broad. I took down some of the words & expressions.

Right well	very well	Ichas our ladies I lone last yere or Vorn yere
Broad way	High way	Wast ere in Divline? Dublin
Ichas	I was	Ichas nere in my lieve. But if Ish live shall go to it piste March
Cal	Horse	How old art thou? fourscore going on five God Almighty keep thee saf upon zee & Lone
Cales	Horses	Keep you your health & send you well abrode & better home.
Kine	Cows	Just before the downing.
Kew	Cow	I had a good friend going along with me & I did not heed it.
Well e new	Well enough	

When they come in old age what kin is then upon 'em. This last I cannot explain tho' I writ it down.

Wast ere upon Montain a Forth? this is the hill I mentioned near Wexford of which they tell a story of a person who was going to it & had never been out of the Barony & finding it a great way, return'd, & said that such a one had been in France & Spain, but was nere so far off. And of another who seeing the prospect from the top of it was struck with astonishment & said what a wcid worn this is. What a wide world is this. & tho' the difference is so litle, yet when I heard it spoken I could understand very litle by reason of the different pronunciation.

Between Grenon point I have mentioned & Rane point north of it, is the entrance to the bay of Wexford, which extends Southward like a great lake, just opposite to the entrance is an Island called [   ] with a Castle on it; the town of Wexford is situated on the southside of the bay on the angle where the land turns from the north to the west, & a Cape extending towards it from the north, it is there only a mile over, opening to the west in a large bason, which appears like a fine lake, with high ground round it beautifully improved with plantations of wood, & particularly Sr Arthur Gore's Kilpatrick to the north west, & Athtraman Mr. Stevensons. Wexford consists chiefly of two Streets, one on the flat, the court & gardens behind the houses extending to the see, so that there are only two piers built out as keys, the other Street is over it on the side of the hill: The Streets are very narrow, & there is a wall built round the town which is near a mile in length & the town may be about a furlong broad, the houses are mostly mean buildings, for it is a town of no great trade, by reason that there is a dangerous barr at the entrance of the harbour: The chief trade is an export of corn & an import of deal boards & some wine, it is the nearest land to England, being about eighteen leagues from St. David's head, Wicklow is about the same distance from the head of Carnarvonshire which is seen very plainly from Bray head & from the mountains of Wicklow, whereas Holy head is about twenty leagues from the hill of Howth near Dublin, so that there have been thoughts of having packet boats from St David's to Wexford: This is the market town of the

South west part of the County & especially of the Barony of Forth & Bargie: There is one Church in service St [   ] the other old churches within the walls are St Oulaks, St Patricks & St Maries. Out of the town St Peters, St Michael & St John, I saw also in the principal Street St Ivers a Sort of Chapel with a Saxon door to it. Besides there there is a Church call'd Selster with a very large tower in the middle of it, which I suppose is that of the Priory of St Peter & St Paul, de Selster for canons regular of St Austin. St. John is probably the Priory of St John & St Bridget founded by Wm. Marescall Earl of Pembroke for Knights of the Hospital, of this there are hardly any remains. A Fryery of Mendicants is also mention'd as founded in the time of Henry IIId. There is a good Courthouse here for the Assizes which are always held at this place, it is esteemed one of the Cheapest places in Ireland, & they have great plenty of wildfowl in the season, especially widgeons & that kind of them call'd wyniard which are thought to exceed the wild duck; they have also Barnacles: The reason why the market is so cheap, is that it is a nook of Ireland, & by its Situation & rivers is cut off from a Convenient Communication with other places. The South Supplies'em with barley & oats, beans & Pease, the North with Wheat, & all the Country round with tame fowl; the see with plenty of fish especially Oysters for which they are famous. There is a very good Chalybeat Spaw here which purges by urine, it is at the West end of the town, & there is a walk & long room, formerly much frequented.

On the 6th I crossed over the broad ferry, there is another higher up across the river Slany which leads to Inniscorthy, & the navigation up that river is very pleasant: there are three roads to Gory, one close by the sea, another on the high land over it, & the third the high road I went in, which is the farthest to the west. In a mile we passed by Tramore Castle Mr. Prestons, & soon after by Castle Bridge, in about three miles we passed over a rivlet called Arbrohan & a little further had Newfort Mr. Kennys to the right: half a mile further we passed Carclough a hamlet & rivlet, & going as much farther came to Ballinemona beg, where about five feet below the Surface they have a good manure of Sand, full of broken pieces of Shells,—& beyond this they find in the fields a sort of Sparr, which is red, blew & white, & make use of it for mending the roads; In another mile we came to Oula, where there is an old Castle, & a rivlet rises here from four or five Streams, which come out of the foot of the hill, & on the side of the hill they have a quarry of rough building Stones; this is nine computed miles from Wexford & half way to Gory, & here I dined. In a mile we came to Killiguian rivlet & a mile farther to Wells, where Mr. Doyne has a large brick house. From this place we had a view of a fine vale to the east having a high ground between it & the sea; & all along this vale is good Marle: in half a mile we passed by Bayley Ray Mr. Boltons, & as much farther through a Hamlet called Bally Edmond, where there is a rivlet also; a litle farther we passed Ballinatra hamlet & river, & saw Mr. Lindons [   ] to the right & several

J.N. Brewer, Ballynastragh, 1825

other Gentlemens houses, & descending into a fine vale which forms a sort of
Amphitheatre, encompassed with hills & all well wooded & finely improved,
we had to the right a wood & house of Lord Anglesea's called Monroe & came
to Balliconon a large village, where there is a Church in repair; I then passed the
river which runs through this vale, & rid over Ballinmenah hill to the vale in
which Gory stands to the South west of the hill Tarah, which like a promontory
is seen from the Barony of Forth: on this hill we passed over I saw many red
Stones like the jasper on which the ancients frequently cut Seals, a piece of which
I took with me, to have it polished & see the Nature of it. Gory is a very small
neat town, consisting of one broad Street about a furlong in length; this with two
other adjoyning parishes belong to the Deanery of Ferns, & there is a neat small
Church here. Ramsfort[148] is not a quarter of a mile from the town, the seat of Mr.
Ram, who is building a grand house of six rooms on a floor, all of it except the
grand front is built of the mountain Stone or Granite brought from the hills about
Agherin on the river of Arklow, it has in it a Sort of Silver mica & looks as well
as fine white freestone; the grand front is of brick with window & door frames
of this Stone; there is a fine avenue & plantations about it & a large park. Six
miles South west of this place is Fernes, which I had formerly seen, there are
great remains there of the Bishops Castle & and other buildings; Branduh King
of Leimster gave Ferns to St. Edan or Moedog the first Bishop of it & made it
an Archbishoprick & the metropolis of Leinster, The Bishop was after this for
some time called Bishop of Wexford, that is probably of the County, & then
without doubt after the Archbishop of Dublin was made the Metropolitan.

On the 7th I set forward & in a mile saw Balinatra to the left Mr. Esmonds's,[149]
& farther on Castletown to the right, Mr. Mastersons; & in four miles from Gory
came to a good village called Coolgrany, & coming into the County of Wicklow,
in three more came to Arklow Charter School for twenty boys & twenty girls on
Lady Allens Estate, which I visited & went on a quarter of a mile to Arklow, a
poor fishing town, without a Custom house, pleasantly situated near the mouth
of the river. They formerly had much fish in the river, but the Coperas of the
mines has corrupted the waters, so as that most of the fish are destroyed. They
have a good hard marle here, which lasts a considerable time. There is a foot
Barrack in this place, & there was a Convent here of Friars preachers founded
by Tibald Butler in 1264. it is said his Statue is in the Church of it, where he is
buryed. up the river is Mr. Howards son of the late Bishop of Elphin, Ballyarklow
Mr. Sims; on the southern branch of the river is Agherim, that to the North rises
near Ballinderry on the next & the principal is Rathdrum which rises in two
Branches, one coming from Glandelough the other from Lough Tee which falls
into Lough Dan & so both of them from this river, & the eastern branch comes
from Glanely: & all this Country is very finely improved & adorned with wood
& even timber in some parts, all the way as far as Rathdrum & along Glanely.
This Country abounds very much in Copper mines & they have found a sort of

Oker which produces lead, out of which they get silver with much gold in it, that is worth ten Shillings an ounce: They have also a water which comes from the mines so strongly impregnated with Copper that finding an old Carr & some tools that were of Iron precipitated into Copper, they now lay bars of iron in it, & in twelve weeks they are turned to Copper, which I was told sometimes weighs heavier than the iron they put in. I Crossed over Red Cross Hill & in five miles come to a village called Red cross in a fine vale, which is divided from another by some low hills, in which vale stands Dungams-town an old ruined Castle belonging to Mr. Hoy, who began to build a large house near it: This is about two miles from the sea, & farther South of Ardaery (The eastern heigth.) A high tower of this Castle & part of the main building is Still Standing, it having been destroyed in the wars of 1641 by order of the Council of Kilkenny, the Lord Deputy having given offence to them. About two miles from Red Cross are some of the chief of the mines & on or near the river of Arklow, they have a Smelting house for the Lead ore. I went to Dr. Wynnes at Dunganstown, who lives there during the minority of his Nephew;

I staid there on the 8th & on the 9th I set out Crossed over the hill five miles to Brinewbridge & passed Captn. Johnsons seat to Newry bridge near Mount Usher a litle to the west of which is Mr. Tighs, a fine finished box & plantations. I come on in the Dublin road & went out of it to the west five miles to Alta Dora[150] to Major Brownings, passing by a village called Newtown Mount Kennedy & near it Mount N[   ]ly which is very beautiful in its plantations chiefly of Firrs, & beyond it is Teny Park, formerly so famous for the beauty of its situation. I passed by Hermitage a pretty box of Mr. Butlers Captn. of the Battle axes & brother to Lord Lanesborough, it is in a beautiful Glyn or narrow vale, at the head of which a fine Cascade tumbles down the hills beautifully adorned with wood; Altadora is on the heighth over it & commands a most delightful view of the rich Country below & of the sea, it is well shelter'd by the eminence above it every way at about the distance of three miles except to the east & south east & north east; It was the retirement of the late General Pearce, who affected to build it as a thatched Cabin, & erected a tower to make it look like a village with a church to it: Major Browning having purchased it, has improved it with great taste; in the middle is a building Consisting of a Hall & beautiful parlor & over them excellent bed-chambers for strangers, with a fine Staircase; on each side a wing is built to it,—in one are the Apartments for the family,—in the other the Kitchen & rooms for servants; Two yards to the South with all Offices, & to the north & west the garden rises with three or four Terraces one over the other, & to the north west are meadows & fields all well planted: In a retired part which commands a view of the fine country below & of the sea there are cut on a piece of white marble these lines over which may be placed the Bust of the Laughing Philosopher.

O Sacred Solitude! Divine retreat!
Choice of the Prudent! Envy of the Great!
Here from the ways of Men, laid safe ashore,
We smile to hear the distant billows roar;
Here blest with health, with business unperplext
This Life we relish & insure the next.

On the 11th I set forward & in three miles came in the road to Wicklow & passing by Wingates, a fine Situation on a height near the sea, we crossed Bray head & passed by Lord Meaths house, where in the gardens are fine hedges & plantations, & going to Bray saw to the left Mr. Odairs, an improvement in very good taste, & at a distance Powers Court,[151] belonging to Lord Powers Court, where there is a large house & great improvements, but the Slopes are rather too Steep & unnatural; In the Park two miles from the House is the famous fall of Water, which is a cascade that falls in one Spot without breaks for [   ] feet[152] the river which makes it falls into Bray river, which rises out of two Loughs up in the side of the mountain, at the west end of Glan Cree: The high ground on each side covered with wood in the way to it is very fine. Below Powers Court the Dargil a hanging ground over the river covered with wood affords a beautiful scene. About three miles from this is ye Glyn of the Downes, which leads from Dublin to a place called the Downs, about two miles from Alta Dora, it is a deep Narrow Valley, with high hills on each side, part of them covered with wood & one of them is called the Sugar loaf. All this country is most exceeding Romantick & beautiful: Near Powers Court, Mr. Monk has a pleasant country house with good plantations about it. The County of Wicklow is remarkable for wood, which grows extremely well in it, they have a Saying that a stick put in the ground will grow: Myrtle thrives in their gardens, & is planted abroad in the natural ground.

Bray is prettily Situated on a height over the river is a very small town, with a Barrack in it. Three miles further is Loughlins town an Inn, & a few houses, near which Mr. Domville has a ruinous seat, very finely Situated, over it is a hill on which Mr. Malpas erected an obelisk, to employ the Poor in the year of famine; at the foot of that hill on the sea are lead mines. I came by Stilorgan[153] Lady Allens seat, where in the Park is a fine Obelisk erected on four arches of rustick Grotesque Arches, in the manner of that in the piazza Navonna at Rome, but much larger. We then came by Mirian the seat of Lord Fitzwilliam, a most glorious Situation commanding a fine view which appears very beautiful from the top of the hill, through the visto's cut in the Grove of firr trees. Butlers town is the same kind of situation where Lord Fitzwilliam has let his land in small parcels for building Country houses. From this place I come by Donibrook to Dublin.[154]

George Petrie, Waterfall at Powerscourt, 1835

Tour the third: the Dublin area, 1753

Pocockeʼs 1753 journal consists of five letters, of which the last remains incomplete. They describe several short trips from Dublin into the surrounding region. Places visited include Tallogh, Holywood, Donard, Athy, Stradbally, Aghaboe, Durrow, Roscrea and Thurles (letter 1); Tara, Ardbraccan and Navan (letter 2); Ballybogan, Athboy, Trim, Laracor, Navan and the region of the Boyne (letter 3); Kells, Monalty, Nobber and the adjoining region (letter 4); Dublin, Rathmore and Kilcullen bridge (letter 5).

The source text is the manuscript copy of Pocockeʼs journal in Trinity College Library, Dublin, which has the 1753 tour appended to it. I have counter-checked this manuscript copy with George Stokesʼs 1891 edition, and in the notes list all textually significant departures made by Stokes from the original. I have not noted his changes in spelling, capitalisation, and punctuation.

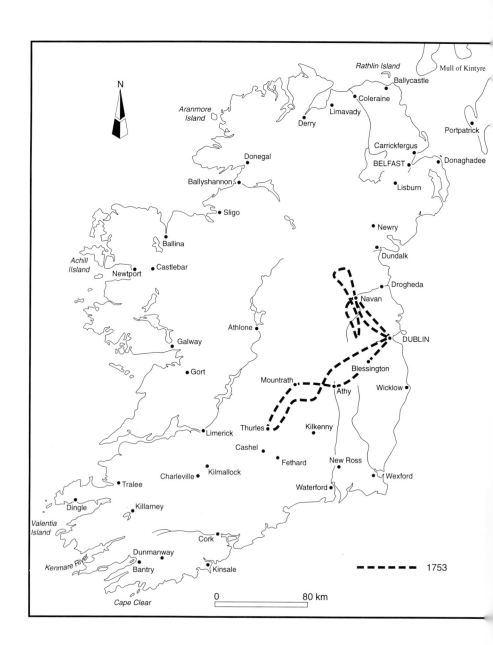

N

Mull of Kintyre

Rathlin Island
Ballycastle
Coleraine
Limavady
Derry
Portpatrick
Carrickfergus
BELFAST Donaghadee
Aranmore Island
Donegal
Lisburn
Ballyshannon
Newry
Sligo
Dundalk
Ballina
Drogheda
Achill Ilsland
Newtport Castlebar
Navan
Athlone
DUBLIN
Galway
Blessington
Gort
Mountrath Wicklow
Athy
Thurles Kilkenny
Limerick
Cashel
New Ross
Fethard
Charleville Kilmallock
Wexford
Tralee
Waterford
Dingle Killarney
Valentia Island
Cork
Dunmanway
Kenmare River
Bantry Kinsale

Cape Clear

0   80 km

- - - - - 1753

Map of 1753 tour

Dublin, July 17th, 1753

Honoured Madam! I left Dublin on the 19th of June & went by Tallogh a mansion house of the Arch bishop of Dublin, repaired by Arch bishop Hoadley; & then coming in between the mountains came by Blessington, a village where Lord Blessington has a seat,[1] & turning to the south I crossed Kings river at Burgage where there is a remarkable old Cross about fifteen feet high of one piece of mountain Stone; Passing by Mr. Leesons fine new built house & offices I came to the Liffy, which we cross'd over Horspeth bridge, near which I sat down & dined by the river, & the poor Children coming about me, I had the pleasure of feeding them. From this place for about half a mile there are several beautifull falls of the river between the rocks; the banks on each side being high & Steep, these falls are called Pooley pucky: We soon came to the small village & church of Holywood, & passed through the Glyn or narrow vale of Holywood, which is very beautifull having on each side steep hills covered with wood, & is something like the Glyn of the downs near Bray: at the entrance of it I saw they had been working for Ore. We came to Donard a poor small town like a Village; with a ruinous Church: About this place three or four rivlets come out of the mountains & form the river Slaney which runs through the Counties of Carlow & Wexford, & falls into the sea at Wexford; the first I crossed is called the litle Slaney, the next is the principal Stream near Donoghmore Church: Here Mr. Howard has an estate, he is son of the late Bishop of Elphin, whose patrimony it was. He has a park here & a hunting house. All this Country on the Slaney is finely improved & planted in most parts of the way which I went to Balkinglass five miles further, coming into the high Dublin road from Ballymore-Eustace, near two miles from Balkinglass, from which the road all the way is through a wood having Mr. [ ] Seat to the right on the river Balinglass is eight computed miles from Ballymore, which is seventeen measured miles from Dublin, eleven Irish measured miles making fourteen English: But the way I came it must be thirty of our measured miles. Baltinglass is a very pleasant village, tho' call'd a Market town, situated in a bottom on the Slaney, & the country round about it is beautifully improved in plantations of Wood: It belongs to Mr. Stratford, who has a small park here on the side of a hill, but lives four miles from this place: He has built houses for weavers, a Spinning School & Bleach yard, but it does not take much. There was an Abbey here of St Mary of Baltinglass or de valle Salutis, the Monks were Cistertians, it was founded by Dermot son of Murchard King of Leinster in 1148.

On the 20th in the afternoon I went through a very fine Country five miles to Castle dermot, I observ'd in the way some ruins of a place call'd Grany & was informed that it had been a Convent; it was an Augustinian Nunnery founded about 1200 by Gualter de Ridelesford: In Castle dermot anciently called Tristledermot is a Priory & Hospital of St John Baptist for Cross bearing Friers founded by Walter de Riddlesford, Lord of the place in King John's time. This town had its name from St. Diarmitius who lived here as a Hermit, from whom it was called the desart of Diarmitius. There is a round tower at the Parish Church of a larger kind than the common towers of that sort in Ireland. They have a Charter School here for forty boys, founded by the encouragement of the late Lord Kildare. I went on towards Athy & in about a mile came to Kilkea hill, which appeared as if it had been anciently fortifyed, & at the foot of it, on a rivlet which falls into the Barrow is a Castle of that name; within a mile of Athy we passed by a remarkable old Rath or fort called Shan rath & arrived at Athy, a small market town well situated on the Barrow, they have a new market house & it is a Burrough, there is a large Stone bridge here over the Barrow. There was a Dominican friery here built in 1257, where several Chapters of the order were held: & on the other side of this bridge was a Priory of St. John for the order of Cross bearers founded in King Johns time by Richard de S. Michael Lord of Reban.

On the 21st I went four miles to Ballykilcavan the seat of the Welsh's where they have pleasant park.[2] I observed in the limestone of this country some of the petrified coral. I came to Stradbally a small market town in a well improved Country. Near it is Mr. Cosby's seat with the finest improvements of high hedges, of White thorn, Horn beam &c: I ever saw round the quarters, which are full of Kitchen Stuff & excellent fruit trees. Mr. Pigot is building an handsom house in a park near the town, the most beautiful part of this garden is a Terrace, over a river & other walks about it, & another river which falls into it: And between these rivers begins that gravelly bank, covered with green Sod, called the Escarp, which I shall have occasion to mention below. This might be made a very beautifull thing, tho' they are carrying part of it away for gravel for the roads, over one of these rivers the County are building a bridge on the Carlow road, which leads to the Charter School: on the other side of the river is a very handsom Charter School for forty or three Score boys & girls, & it is large enough to hold an hundred: it was founded chiefly on the bounty & under the direction of Mr. Cosby. Here was a Convent of Minorites founded by O more, & its thought to be the Convent called Lavasia, for it is called Strallbally in Lese, & this County, Kings-County & some other parts were called the County of Lese.[3] I went along a pleasant road through a fine Country, mostly on this bank of gravel call'd the Escar & in English the ridge, which they say runs almost through the whole Country, it is between the two rivlets above mentioned; it is probable that anciently they were larger rivers than at present & that this was the bank between them: After going about three miles I came to Timohoe, where there is a remarkable round tower, with a door to it of Saxon architecture which is Singular. We came to Bally rowan a large village on a rivlet, which falls into the Nore, & crossing that river came to Spring mount the Seat of Mr. Brereton, near the remains of a fine ruined Castle, on the Nore called Killenny.

On the 24th I went to Abelaix,[4] the seat of Lord Knapton son of Sr. Thomas Vesey late Bishop of Ossory,—Here was an Abbey of Cistertians supplied from the Abbey of Baltinglass in 1183, it is said to be founded by Cochoger O more, buryed there, & in the Street a tomb remains, said to be of Omore in the spot where the Church stood. I went from this place further to Water Castle, Mr. Lyons, a fine Spot of ground, well adorned with plantations, through which the river Nore runs, just as the Willey runs through Wilton, & it might be made a fine thing, commanding a view of a very beautifull Country all round.

On the 26th I crossed on a bridge at Gortineclea an old Castle, a rivlet called the gulley, which rises towards Burres, in Ossory & falls into the Nore below Water Castle, passing most of the way through a morassy ground: Going to the South of this Morass, I came to Aghaboe, a large village where there are remains of a Monastery, & of a singular tower to a building, probably the Refectory now a Church: The tower is five sides of an Octagon, near it is a Mount for defence. This was an Abbey of Dominicans, built by the Lords of upper Ossory: It is said to have been first founded by St. Kenny son of Laidee a famous poet, & that he was the first Abbot: He dyed in 599: 'tis thought the See of Ossory was moved from Saiger now called Seir-Keran to this place about the year 1052 for then a Church was built there, & St. Kennys tomb placed in it; the See was afterwards moved to Kilkenny.

On the 27th I went three miles westward to Reshal on the turn pike road to Limerick & fifty miles from Dublin; this is a ruined seat of Lord Montraths, it was the estate & Mansion house of Costegan the Old proprietor, who was proclaimed as a rebel, & his estate granted to Sr Charles Coote, who in 1641 did great services in Ireland & was made Earl of Montrath in 1660—was one of the Lords justices & died in 1661 & was suceeded by his son Charles who in 1696 was also one of the Lords justices: The small old Mansion remains, to which Sr. Charles made great additions, & the Court & garden are encompassed by walls & defended by Turrets, it is a fine Situation, commanding a view of the Country to the east & of the vale to the west & South west, in which the Nore runs by Burres in Ossory, We returned by Castle town, where are remains of an Old Castle held by Col. FitzPatrick for King Charles the first, who forfeited, & going abroad on the restoration had all returned to him; & Richard FitzPatrick of this family was created Baron of Gowran in the County of Kilkenny: His wife was daughter & heir of Sr. Jno Robinson of Farmingwood in Northampton Shire, which estate his son now enjoys, as well as a large estate in Ireland. He is a branch of this house the head of which in the time of Henry 8th was made Baron of upper Ossory. This title somehow or other was not asserted; & lying dormant the present Lord Gowran was created Viscount of Upper Ossory; tho' it is said there is an heir to that title. A mile beyond this place is Montrath, a small market

town, where Ld. Montrath has a small house. Both these places are on the high
road, one forty eight, the other forty seven from Dublin.

On the 29th I went by Gortineclea & going Southward passed by Cuffs
borough, Mr. Cufs, where I observed Trochi & Entrochi in the lime Stone which
lyes loose in the earth all over this Country; & at Donoghmore, Mr. Morris's,
they have great quarries of this Stone, which is a Coarse black marble, but not
used because the Kilkenny is much better. Going on we saw a small lake to the
East called Lough Ardevin & near it Grantsown an old Castle which is now
inhabited. Coming on a heigth, I saw to the west a Morass, round which are
several places, as near the road Killbredy a ruined Castle; & near that a fortifyed
Mount, called Motchneloiak (The middle mote) from which Mr. Floods seat has
its name; we then came to a small Stream which rises out of the morass: About
two miles farther is Donoughmore, where there is a barrack for one troop of
horse: going about a quarter of a mile farther we crossed over the river Erkin on
a bridge, Near it is Cool cany the house of Mr. Baldwin: We had left the road of
Rathdowny, a small town on the south side of the Morass, belonging to the heir
of Mr. Prior the great patriot of this Kingdom;[5] & going on about two miles came
to an old fort called Rath Philip on a heighth with a burial place near it, 'tho no
Sign of a Church: about a mile farther we came at Whites wall from the Queens
County into the County of Kilkenny, & in about two miles to Farta an old
monastery, where there is an old round tower,[6] twelve feet in diameter & by
measuring the Shadow I found it to be eighty three feet high, but the top point
is much decayed & there is crack down the East side of it. There is a Church in
repair, with some old carved work about it; To the north of it is an old Chapel in
which there is a tomb of the [ ] with an inscription on it, on the tomb is a mezzo
releivo of a man in armour with a dog at his feet, a sword in his hand stretched
on his thigh, & his left hand[7] lying on his other leg; the tomb is adorned with
Sculpture. near it I saw the top of another tomb, which seemed to be of a woman,
with a Singular Head dress, rising up on each side as in two horns. This is I
suppose the Priory of Kiaran of Augustinian Canons said to be at Fert-ne-gerah.
I went a furlong farther to Beggars Inn, on the new turnpike road from Dublin
to Cashel five miles from Longford pass & fifteen from Cashel; near it is a ruin
call'd Baun richen, which they call part of the Old monastery, & probably was
the farm house belonging to it. The Caley hills extend from Darrow beyond this
place to the east of the turn pike road; & from this place is a road to Kilkenny
ten miles off, through a Glyn or Vale between the hills: in the middle of which
is a litle hill, on the top of which there seemed to be a rath or fort: Going on
towards Durrow in our return we came in less than a mile to Aglishhaw Castle,
where is a rivlet that comes out of the Glyn, & a litle farther we had a mile to
the west an Old Monastery called Agha Macart, & nearer a large fort or Rath.
This was a Priory of St. Tigernac for Augustinian Canons. In a mile we passed
Calahil Castle, a large enclosure with two or three buildings like Chapels. A mile

farther we came to Cahil Castle to the west, & a litle beyond saw a very pretty Seat called Newtown. We then passed a Stream, which rises from a Holy well, a litle to the west called Tubberboh; & in about a mile & half, by a pleasant road between the woods of Castle Durrow, we came to Durrow a small market town, & now a great thoroughfare, the Turnpike road from Dublin to Cashel being carried through it. Lord Ashbrook who till lately had the Title of Castle Durrow has a Seat here well situated with a fine Park & Woods. I am &c.

July 3d, 1753. I went from Springmount to Burres in Ossory, a Village pleasantly situated on the north west side of a Chain of beautiful litle Hills finely improved which extend to the south west towards the mountains called Devils bit, out of which the rivers Sure & Nore rise. This is an estate given by King Charles the first to the favourite Duke of Buckingham & is now the estate of one of his family, of the name also of Villers. There is a good Mansion house on it of the Architecture of those times, which seems to have been built to an old Castle, this place is 53 miles from Dublin. A litle beyond it we crossed the Nore, which almost from its rise runs through a morassy ground to Montrath. We passed in sight of Gorvan Castle, on one of those hills to the South, & to the North by Cloncuis Castle, two miles from Borres, it is the estate of Lord Montrath. We came to those hills which divide the Queens County from the Kings County,[8] & in a line from them is the bounds between Queens County & the County of Tiperary, which is marked by a Stone a litle beyond the 56th mile stone on the east side of this hill; just at the end of it is a large Castle called Ballaghmore Castle with a wall & ramparts round it. I saw further on to the South as in the Morass a Church with trees planted round it called Monatinchelieh, We came to Roscrea 58 miles from Dublin, pleasantly situated on a rivlet between the litle hills, which form a Sort of Amphitheater round it, & are bounded by higher hills to the South & North; It is a small town tho' with a litle encouragement in the Woollen Manufacture it might be greatly improved. At the entrance of the town is the front of a very old Church to a Modern building, it consists of a door & two flat Arches on each side of the Saxon Architecture & a Mezzo relievo probably of St Cronan to whom it is dedicated appears over it much defaced. At a litle distance is a Cross in a circle, with the Crucifix on one side & another figure on the other, & adjoyning to it a Stone carved in several figures & at each end a Mezzo relievo of some Saint, they are both of a Sandy Stone with pebbles in it, in which these hills abound, they are both if I mistake not called the Shrine of St Cronan. To the North west is a round tower fifteen feet diameter with two Steps round it at the bottom, about fifteen feet from the ground is a window with a regular arch, & as much higher another with a pointed top: it appeared to be only about fifty feet high, but the height was probably seven diameters, which seems to be the proportion they observed,[9] that is 105 feet high, the top of it having probably fallen to decay. On the river at the north west part of the town, are pretty perfect remains of the Convent of Minorites founded by

Biliana Widow of Meiron O Carol. There is a barrack here for one Company of foot. This estate did belong to the Bishops of Killaloe, who gave it the Crown for the lands of Newcastle in the County of Wicklow & some other lands which the Bishop never got. The Crown granted it to the Earl of Ormond, it was sold by that Duke to Mr. Curtis who sold it to Mr. Daymore. There was a fine old Castle on it, & near it is built a good Mansion house; Some walls appear about the grove to the north, probably the circuit of that Castle: It is no Corporation, nor is there any justice of peace within some miles of it, as I was informed; & most of the inhabitants are Papists. I returned to Springmount by Aghaboe.

I set out from Springmount on the 5th of July & went to Aghaboe, from which place I got into the road to Thurles & passed near the Castle of Kilbredy already mentioned, & going towards Donoghmore, came within a quarter of a mile of it, to a ruin call'd Castle town, it is part of a tower, with foundations of Walls about it extending a Considerable way; & west of it are foundations of another tower; There seems to have been a large village about the Castle which belongs to the Villers, being in the Mannor of Buries. I came to Donoghmore pleasantly situated on a height over the rivlet, which runs by Rathdowny, here is a Church & a barrack. it is the estate of Lord Gowran; crossing over the rivlet on a heighth, is a Rath call'd Donogh more or, the great hill which has given name to this place. After travelling about four miles I saw to the North west two beautiful Hills; at the east end of the eastern hill is Irrin where there is a ruined Church, & I have been informed that there is a monument there like a Cross, to a son of one of the old Lords of Upper Ossory of the Fitzpatrick family; We went across the bog by the pass called Gortahie, near which there is such a round tower as is seen often in Ireland near churches, which is singular. I saw to the right an Old Castle call'd if I mistake not Kinslaney. About this place came into the County of Tiperary, & to a large old Castle with two round towers at the corners, & large apartments joyning to one, now in ruins, the enclosure is about half an acre; it is called Tulleagh McJames.[10] I saw a large enclosure two miles to the east called Baunac-carah, passed through a Village call'd Bally Erle, where I observed there was a large School at the Chapel or Mass-house, where they are taught Latin: Within two miles of Thurles I came to Rahelty Castle, a good building rounded off at the Angles, an excellent regular arch at the entrance; The rooms on each floor about twenty by thirty, there is a very extensive view from the top of it, of the mountains to the west called Devils bit, out of which the Sure & Nore rise very near to each other; hills to the South of them called Kilnemanogh, the Galty mountains on the borders of the County of Tiperary, Limerick, & Cork, Knock-mandown towards Lismore, the mountains of the County of Waterford & to the South east Sleannemane, which is seen plainly from the Key of Waterford & stretches its foot near to Carrick & Clonmell & then to the East the hills on which Killenaul stands which running to the north east are joyned by Cully hill which extends to Darrow. I arrived at Thurles situated on the river Sure, twelve long miles from Roscrea, seven from Cashel & fifteen from Kilkenny, There is a bridge here over the river, the first being at Loughmore three miles higher. This river abounds in Pike, Eeles & large Touts. The town consists of one short Street, with a market house[11] in the middle, at the end of it is the Old Castle, now the seat of Mr. Mathews in which he has built a handsome modern house, in the garden is a Mount with a winding ascent, which probably was an old Danish fort. On the East side of this river is the Church which is built to the tower of an old Church, the east part of this Church being an Arch under the tower; to the east of that is a Chapel in which there is a Monument of the Archers of Archers Court near, who had contentions with the Lords of Thurles. the head dress of the women is like that at Farta already described, but not so much pointed at each Corner. On the same side are the remains of a Convent, a tower & some part of the Cross Isle to the north; it was founded by the Butlers for the Order of St. Mary of Mount Carmel. There is a large popish Chapel built Chiefly by Mr. Mathews according to an inscription set in a wall near it. They have some tradition I believe without foundation, that this Castle did belong to the Knights Templars: There are two barracks here for three troops of horse—

on the 8th of July I left Thurles came in about nine miles to Burres en Leough, probably Burres on the Lough, being an Island on the bog, which might anciently be a Lough. Here Mr. Mathews has a seat; this is called the bog of Monela, which extends northward near to Roscrea. These Islands consist of a lime Stone gravel & large pebbles of lime stone; five miles from Thurles we came to Longford pass, where there was a barrack[12] for half a company of foot, which is now in ruins, not having been used for near twenty years. Three miles from Thurles, the road to Cashel leaves the road to Thurles, pointing almost directly South. A litle beyond Longford pass, the road goes to the East to Kilkenny, & I turned northward in the road to Durraw, having the hills to the East, which extend along the west side of the river Nore. There is a hill to the west side of these, on the side of which there is a house called Ballispellean; a quarter of a mile above it is a mineral water which runs through a black Slate, which is medicinal, & its said there is a Composition of sulphur in it; it is esteemed good for all kinds of Scrophulous disorders. I came down from this place to Farta already mentioned & continuing two miles along the road to Durrow, I went out of it to the west about half a mile to the monastery of Agha Macarth mentioned before, in which there is nothing remarkable, but a gate at the entrance with a true arch of good workmanship, & there are Stone Sockets for the gate to turn on. This place is on the rivlet called the Goula, which runs near Farta, & a litle below this joyns the river which runs from Rathdowney; I crossed the river about 2 miles above it & came to Grantstown Castle which is oval. Passing by Agha gouran a ruined Church, I came to a litle Mount, which is called the Leap, & so returned by Gorthniclea to Springmount.

On the 13th of July I left Springmount, stop'd at Stradbally & came to the Barrow at Riverstown, where one Mr. Brown has has a pleasant Seat. This a beautifull place, & mostly resembles Old Windsor; the ferry is crossed in a very bad boat, & I was obliged to swim one of my horses.

I came to Kildare on the 14th. I passed over the Curragh & came to Newbridge; here I saw part of the Head & horns of an Elk, dug out of a Neighbouring bog, where they have also found several bones of this animal, & have been informed that they Seldom find a Skeleton together, but the bones dispersed, probably not only by the Current of the water, but where they are found on a descent by the moving of the earth. I Stop'd at Furnace & arrived at Dublin in the evening.

Honoured Madam,   On Monday the 6th of August 1753 I left Dublin to go to Ardbracan which is two miles beyond Navan, in the county of East Meath. I went through the Phoenix Park, & had on the right the rivlet which rises above Dunboyn & falls into the Sea by Bally baw bridge, near Dublin, having passed by Finglass & Glasnevin some parts of it which are planted & are very beautiful. on the top of the hill to the right, is the old ruined Church of Malabilhart, to which the people resort much out of devotion especially on the Patron day. We crossed the river about a mile from Dunboyn, & came from the County of Dublin into the County of East Meath. Near Kileen Castle I saw Dunsany,[13] where Lord Dunsany lives, a Roman Catholick Lord of about £200 a year. We came up to Tarah at the top of the hill of that name, where the Kings of Meath, one of the five divisions of Ireland, are said to have resided; & they have a tradition, that in a field to the west of the Church, the five Kings of the five provinces of Ireland used to meet. I saw five barrows in this Situation on which it is possible the five Kings sat with their people round them, I conjectured also

0 north[14]

0   0

0

0

that they might bear some relation to their respective Situations on the Southern one is a Stone or pillar Set up which might belong to the Emperor or head of them the King of Munster. In the churchyard also there is an ancient Stone set up, on which there is an unshapen short figure, something like Pusterus the German Deity. About a small mile to the South, I had seen the remains of a large Rath, called Erra Meath, probably the place of Residence of the Kings of Meath. Close to Tarah is Brabazon lodge the seat of Mr. Brabazon, brother & heir to the Earl of Meath; it is a large house, & its said to have been a much greater building, probably round a Court. They say it was built by Stopford Secretary to Oliver Cromwell, from whom I am informed the Stopfords of this County are descended. I went a mile across this demeasn to the north to Skreens: on another summit of the hill; here is a good old Church with a high tower; the east end of the Church is in repair. Over the South door is a Mezzo relievo of St. Columb, to whom the Church is dedicated, it is very well executed, in the left hand is a book, in the right, a Staff. A litle below the Church are the remains of the Friary of Augustinian Hermits, to which I was informed 40 acres of land did belong. Descending from Skreens, I observed a point of land which has been fortified & beyond it on the west side of the vale is a large Rath, near this is Lismullen, an estate of the Dillons: From this vale a river runs down to the high road & meets another, which passes through the vale to the East of Bellenter & both of them fall into the Boyne opposite to Ardsallah. I arrived at Ardbracan[15] the Bishop of Meaths, two miles beyond Navan, from which place I made Several excursions, in which & at other times, I made Such observations on the Country about the Boyne, as I shall send you the first opportunity.[16] I am &c.

Honoured Madam,   The Boyn is said to rise out of a Spring at Castle Carbery in the County of Kildare called the Mother Spring of the Boyn; but I observed that the larger Stream rises out of a Bog, near the Charter School, & that this small Stream falls into it. Castle Carbery is an estate belonging to the two Coheiresses Miss Cooleings, & is finely Situated on a heigth improved with plantations which is seen at a great distance. I went farther down the Boyn I see Ballybogan in the County of Meath, a place on the Boyn; which I take to be a Priory dedicated to the Holy Trinity; it was called also Laude Dei & belonged to Canons Regular of St Austin. & I once saw some large ruins this way, which are I suppose the remains of that Monastery: Lower is Clonard the See of an ancient Bishoprick, where I saw some ruins & there was here a Convent of Canonesses, a Priory of St Peter of Canons Regular of St Austin; & another Convent of some Order, founded by St Firmian. About two miles above Trim the river of Trimleston falls into the Blackwater: on this river is Trimleston,[17] the Seat of Lord Trimleston built to an ancient Castle, that was mostly destroyed in Olivers time. The present Lord married young & retired to Paris, where his genius leading him to Botany; he studied Physick, & often gave his advice to the Princes of the Blood & other Nobility: About six years ago he returned on the death of his Father & brought a great Collection of Exotic plants, among 'em the Cinamon-tree & the Hermaphrodite, the latter has on it the leaves of Orange,

Lemon, Citron & Cedra,[18] & each fruit contains in it, the fruit of these four kinds, which caused great Speculation at Paris, but it was determined it could not be done by any inoculation or Art, but that it was a tree of this kind. As his Lordship's Skill in Physick soon became known, people of all conditions resorted to him, & now he allots fridays to hear them all; & he not only hears the poor but gives them drugs, the rich who come to Consult, putting in to a Box for that purpose: He is a Noblemen of excellent sense & of great politeness & address, He has found out near his house thirty six uncommon plants, most of which he has brought into his garden. The River of Trimleston has a large black Trout, exceeding that of the Boyn; & also very good Eeles; I found in it several small Shellfish of different Kinds, & among them I found one about as big as a silver threepence, a most Compleat Ammons horn & alive. They have very good quarries here of Lime Stone, some of which rises as flags or broad stones. & Mr. Barnewall My Lords eldest son has sent me petrifications of Small Nautilus's found in the quarries. Lord Trimleston has a dark avenue to his house, near an English mile long. Three miles beyond it is Ath boy, where was a Convent of Carmelites, & in a Chapel of the Church I saw an ancient Monument: near it is the hill of Ward, from which there is a fine prospect of Skeles, And braccan, Trim & a great tract of Country. Ath boy stands on the river Trimleston, & almost all the way to the west of it, is bog, the further side of which is the bounds between the County of East Meath & West Meath. To the north of the Hill of Ward is Rath more the ruined seat of Lord Darnley, where there is a large wood. We now come to Trim on the Boyn, a small town situated on both sides of the river, it has anciently been walled, & there are remains of the walls & gates; one to the west of the Street from Dangan, another Still in repair called Athboy gate: A high tower remains in part of the Dominican Convent, but one side of it was blown up by Olivers army. There was a Convent of Black friers & Grey Friers one where the barrack is, & the other to the north of the town: But the greatest piece of Antiquity is a very large Castle, called King Johns Castle, which is a building of great Strength, the enclosure extending to the river. About half a mile from Trim on the Boyn, is the Priory of St Peter & St Paul of Newtown near Trim, which was also an ancient Bishops see, of which there were several in the Diocese of Meath, many of them consisting of some one of the present twelve Deaneries of the Diocese. They were here Canons of St Victor, & I was informed that a daughter of King John Iyes buryed here of the name of [   ] & that they show a Stone, said to be over her tomb. Near Trim the Earl of Roscommon had an estate, who was succeeded by his Brother, that Earl's widow who had the estate at her disposal, was afterwards marryed to the Father of Mr. Carter Master of the Rolls, who now enjoys it. At Ardcreagh in the way to Navan was an old Castle called Ardcreagh, to which the Dutchess of Tyrconnel, sister to the Dutchess of Marlborough, retired for three or four years after the battle of Agherim,[19] & then went to London & Paris. Going from Trim towards Dublin on the road is the Charter School for 20 Boys & 20 Girls. About a mile farther is the Church of Laracor which belonged to Dean Swift, & he lived a month or

W.H. Bartlett, Dangan Castle, County Meath, 1842

two in the Summer in a litle house near it.[20] We soon after came to Dangan[21] the seat of Lord Mornington situated on a most beautifull flat, with an Amphitheatre of hills rising round it, one over another, in a most beautifull manner;[22] at the lower end is a very large piece of water, at one corner of which is an Island, it is a regular fortification; there is a Ship a sloop & boats on the water, & a yard for building; the hill beyond it, is improved into a beautifull wilderness; on a round hill near the house is a Temple, & the hills round are adorned with obeliskes; Pillars & some buildings, altogether the most beautifull thing I ever saw. A mile beyond it is Summer hill,[23] Mr. Rowleys a commanding Eminence, the house is like a Grand Palace, but in the Vanbrugh Style;[24] the prospect from it is very fine & there are great plantations about it; the Country behind it does not answer to the other parts in beauty, For it presents to your view a very disagreable Bog. Not far from this is another fine place belonging to Lord Rawdons brother, call'd Bramhall. Returning to the Boyn the next place is the [   ] Corn Mills belonging to Mr. Carter, & below it is [   ] a pleasant seat of Mr. Worthingtons. Near this on the Boyn, are large ruins of the Bernardine Abbey of Bectiffe or de Beatitu-dine founded by Merchand O-Melaghlin Prince of Meath about the year 1150. the Cloyster is almost entire with a tower. At this place there is a bridge over the Boyn, which is the Shortest road from Athboy to Dublin: Below this near the road from Dublin to Navan is Belenter, Mr. Prestons a very handsom new built house of six rooms a floor, with convenient offices, joyned by a Corridore, & a Court of offices on each side; there is a fine view of the Boyn from it, which is at the distance of a furlong from the house. After the Boyn has run to the east all the way from its rise it here takes a turn a litle to the north, & at the angle is

Ardsallagh Mr. Ludlows seat, lately married to the present Earl of Scarboroughs sister, the house is just over the Boyn, the garden laid out in the old way, has the Boyn on two sides, & there is a Shady walk near the river, having the rock on the other side, which appears in several Strata, & is a most singular & beautiful thing; At the mill beyond it there is a rough ford across the river. Below this is a Bridge over the Boyn & a litle beyond it Athumley lately the seat of Mr. Coddingon, from which there is a beautiful hanging ground over the river, partly planted with wood, it extends much in the same manner all the way to the mouth of the river on both sides; & half a mile further is the Old house of Athlumley, very large, & they say never finished; it is the estate of Sr Quaile Sommerville: This house was built by Sr Luke Dowdle one of the principal fomenters of the Massacre in 1641.[25] The river then runs to Navan & very near it turns to the East. Navan is well situated on an eminence, at the Confluence of the Blackwater & the Boyn, & there is a beautifull hanging ground from the town covered with trees. Passing over the Blackwater, I rid on the north side of the Boyn & in a mile came to the Church of Doneghmore, near which[26] which is an ancient round tower fifteen feet in diameter, the three lower tiers of Stone set out about half a foot & make three Steps round it, the door is about fifteen feet from the ground, there are three members round it,[27] which is not Common, & a head on each side of the spring of the arch, & what is Singular a Crucifix over the arch, cut in a barbarous manner, as they are usually cut on old Crosses. A litle below this is the Castle of Dunmow. In two miles we came to Stackallen, first passing by the road which leads to a bridge over the Boyn. Stackelleon[28] is the Seat of the late Lord Boyn & now of Mr. Hamilton brother to the present Lord. near opposite to this, on the other side are the Seats of Mr. Meredith & Mr. Lambert, the former has a large new built house: Mr. Lambert is building a very good house on an eminence over the Boyn where it makes a Short turn, so that this Situation commands a fine view of the river. near it are some Copper Mines: Going further on the north side of the river I came to Barstown Cross, on which there is an inscription, & down to the Castle of Slane[29] a large house of Mr. Cunninghams, since who I saw this place has been created Lord Mount Charles, it is very finely situated on the river: A litle above it on the other side is a small rocky hill, from which a perpendicular rock extends down the river for a quarter of a mile, appearing like a wall with trees & shrubs growing out of it, & has a most beautifull effect. Above this about a furlong from the river is the poor town of Slane. They were in search of Coal about a mile from this town, & it is said there is certainly Coal there, of the kind of Kilkenny Coal, but that they cannot get it worked by the obstinacy of the Proprietors. From this place to the mouth of the Boyn, I gave you an Account in a letter I writ last May of a tour I made into that Country. I am &c.

Honoured Madam,   I mentioned in my last that the Blackwater falls into the Boyn at Navan. This river rises out of the Lough Ramor in the County of Cavan

& passes by Kells a small market town situated on an eminence; about three miles below Kells, the river Monalty falls into it, which rises likewise in the County of Cavan near Ballyborow: on it about six miles from its Source is Monalty a poor village finely situated, there are remains of the enclosure of a Castle, which belongs to the Beta's the old proprietors; & there is an old Mount in Mr. Maxwells garden to whom the place belongs. The river then runs near Ardbraccon & by Liscartan,[30] the family estate of Lord Cadogan, which is set in lives for ever at £200 a year; his ancestor was a Colonel in Olivers Army & governor of Trim, had great estates & Considerable influence in this Country.

I made an excursion northward from Ardbraccan, & cross'd the river a mile above Lord Cadogens at Dunogh Patrick bridge: We had a flat morassy country to the west, all the rest hilly rising to the east towards Navan & Slane; the Castle of which we saw, & in about three miles came to the high road from Navan to Nobber to Coote Hill & to the middle parts of the Kingdom: Here is a large Rath commanding an extensive view of a very fine Country. I went northward a mile & half in the road to Atherdee & within a mile of Suddan near the borders of the County of Lowth in order to observe the Course of the rivers & the Geography of this Country, in which I found the Maps very far from being correct. I turned along a rivlet, which falls into the river call'd Owen More (the great river) a little below Nobber, which is a very poor town, pleasantly situated on that river. The family of the Balfs were formerly in some Condition here, & they show their ancient Monuments. A mile above Nobber on the river is Brittes[31] the seat of General Blithe brother of Lord Darnley, a neat box & fine plantation, with some ornamental buildings: A litle above it the river forms a Lough called Kilmainham about a mile in circumference; here I suppose was the Preceptory of the Knights of Jerusalem, said to be at Kilmainham near the Nobber. The country about Nobber & for three miles beyond it is covered with loose free stone of a reddish & yellow Colour; they told me that Carrickeleg at about that distance is a rock of free Stone, so that these Stones have probably rolled down from this rock. It is on the eminence which must command a view of that valley, in which the river Lagan runs & falls into the sea at Garlandstown between Dunleer & Dundalk, & in some parts the County of Monaghan from the Counties of Cavan & Lowth. In sinking a well at Nobber near forty feet they found it a gravel mostly consisting of the free Stone & with it large pebbles of Limestone. I went two miles in the high road & turn'd out of it a quarter of a mile to White wood Lord Gorman-stowns: This is a fine eminence over the vale between Kilmainham Lough & Lough Carr about a mile[32] above it made by the same river & it commands a view of both. The house is new built of the free Stone found over the fields. I returned to the road & soon left it, going down near Lough Carr to the river above it, & came to a very beautifull narrow vale, in which the river runs between two hanging rocky grounds covered with tress. We went through this for half a mile & came to a hilly Country & in about half a mile to Everch Lough, out of which they say the river Owen-more rises, but a river falls into it from Lough Muff about a mile higher, which must be the rise of the Owen More. On the South side of the Lough there is a Meeting-house. We then passed a Skirt of the County of Cavan, & came again into the County of Meath, & had to the right a ruin'd Castle called Faun Breehan & to the left the river Carig which falls into Monalty river. There is marle along this Valley with Shells in it, & so it is in most parts of the country I passed through; in the bottoms it is mostly in patches in different parts. I saw here a long hill called Shribogh, on which I observed several litle barrows, as if there had been niches sunk in it, but I could not be informed of any such thing. We had travelled along the foot of the hills which are the bounds between this County & that of Cavan, but towards Monalty we came into a fine well improved hilly Country. I come to Monalty & returned to Ard braccon & to Dublin. I am &c.

Honoured Madam,   On Monday the 27th of August 1753 I went by Cromlin into the road to Naas, turned out of it in about six miles from Dublin up to Sagart on the foot of the mountain & in a mile came to Coolmine Castle, on the side of the mountain, & a litle farther at Newtown, saw three Stones set up an end in a field, they are about five or six feet high, & seem to be part of some piece of Antiquity: in all the Streams about these hills are fine Stones, which are a Composition of pebbles & would polish. We had a fine view of the Country to the west on each side of the Liffy, & came to Rathmore, a very large Rath or fortress, said to have been the place of Residence of the Kings of Leinster, it is about twelve miles from Dublin. After travelling about three miles farther we came into a beautifull plain Country extending to the Liffy, in which there are some good houses of Gentlemen Farmers, which have a fine effect in the prospect, & came to Loughlantown an old Castle belonging to the late Mr. Calvin who owned the estate we pass'd through. Half a mile brought us to Hamitown the estate of Mr. Eustace, situated on a rising ground & commanding an extensive view every way, particularly of the Course of the Liffy. The park is a remarkable fine Spot well planted, & below it a Command of water, which might be improved into a beautifull serpentine river. I went two miles further to Kilcullen bridge; over the Liffy a quarter of a mile below it, is Castle Martyn.[33] a pleasant seat of Mr. Carter Master of the Rolls, especially the meadows on the river afford most delightfull walks; on the opposite Northern side there are high Cliffs over the Liffy. Half a mile above the bridge is the new Abbey, of which the Church remains, & there is a fine old monument in it of Rowland Eustace & his wife, who are represented in in Mezzo relievo, the former in armour & the woman with a very—

Tour the fourth: south west Ireland, 1758

In mid-July, 1758 Pococke set out from Kilkenny and travelled through Fetherd and Cashel to Cork, then turned westwards to Kingsale, Timoleague, Clonikilty and Dunheedy Head. He took a boat to Ross Carbery, then went to Skibbereen, Cree, and Baltimore, and took another boat to Iniskertain and Cape Clear islands and Crookhaven. He rode around Missen Head then went on to Baltimore, Skull, Roaring Water Bay, Castlehaven and Bantry. He sailed outwards down Bantry Bay, crossed the headland and once again sailed over the mouth of the Kenmare river. After a visit to Kenmare town he set out by road for Valentia Island, travelled northward to Milltown and Castlemain and circuited the Dingle peninsula, He arrived in Tralee and toured the region northwards to the mouth of the Shannon before making for Killarney. From here he returned to Kilkenny via Dunmanway, Mallow, Kilworth and Clonmell.

The source text used here is the copy of Pococke's journal kept in the Bodleian Library, Oxford (Ms Top, Ireland d. 1 [30,722]). I have counter-checked against it the edition published by Padráig Ó Maidín in 1958–60, and have listed in the notes any textually significant departures from the original made in that edition. I have not noted Ó Maidín's modernization of spellings and of punctuation.

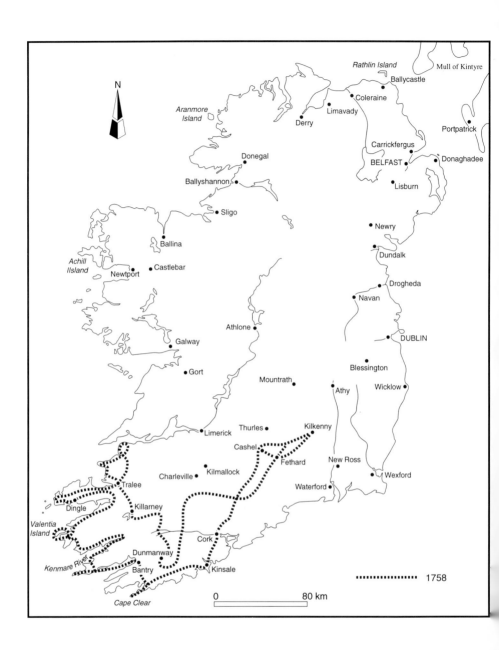

Map of the 1758 Tour

Barry's Hall near [   ] in the County of Cork
July 17th 1758

Dear Madam,   On the 10th I left Kilkenny & came to Fetherd in the County of Tipperary, it is a poor small wall'd town, much improv'd of late in buildings by Mr. Barton a Bourdeaux Merchant, who out of an old house, has built for himself a very large handsome dwelling; but could not succeed in being chose a member of Parliament, as the Voters are mostly outlyers.[1] They have a small manufacture in Rateens, Half Clothes & Serges. There is a monastery here.

This they call the Abbey;[2] in it are burial places & monuments of the Dunboyn family, who are Romans: I saw also monuments of the Wales of Rathkyyran & of St Johns & Nugents. There are remains of a large house in the town with fine chimneys of Hewn Stone, it was an Almshouse, on it are the Arms of the Founder, as I suppose, & a Crucifix, with an Inscription.

Two hours brought us from this place to Cashel, through a fine Country, mostly sheepwalks & Gentlemen's seats very thick, the whole diversifyed by rising grounds. I visited the charter school, & had a most glorious prospect of a beautiful country from the rock & Cathedral of Cashel, of which I have formerly given you an Account.[3]

Archbishop Goodwin[4] began a fine house here, finish'd by Bolton,[5] who left his Library to it; He also brought water to the Town, but the people were stirr'd up by some in a contrary interest to destroy the work, & now they are in great want of water. An hour brought us to Golding Bridge over the Sure. A mile beyond it is Mr Mathews fine place of Thomastown[6] 1500 acres within a wall; the great beauty of which is the Hernery & Duckoy. A litle beyond Mr Brombery has a beautiful place. The road fine Hedgerows & a country highly improv'd on each side, are most exceeding fine. A heigth to the left has been improv'd into a fort with an entrance to it, built of stone, it is call'd Mote Kilkety. We soon came to Tiperary, call'd five, but it is eight miles from Cashel, it is a small town with a remarkable Danish fort & a keep with half a mile to the north. There is a fine Spring here, which they say, flows in such a mañer as to turn a mill. The great Mr Daymour has built a fine house[7] & offices 2 miles from this town, & lives in the latter, the house not being finish'd. They have here only a small manufacture of combing Wool. We turn'd our faces southward towards Cork & cross'd a small stream close to the town call'd the Aaron, famous for its Trouts. I a [*sic*] mile we cross'd over low hills cover'd with wood, & came into the fine vale of Aerta, in which the river of that vale runs which rises in the County of Limerick & falls into the Sure near Caher, the valley inclines to the East, & is bounded by the Galty mountains to the south, which are high, & extend in length from this place about ten miles near to the Sure, & may be about 5 miles broad; they abound in red Deer: At the head of this vale, in its western direction, is new forest[8] which belongs to Massey Dawson Esq.[re], a beautiful retirem[t] a fine well timber'd Park & Rideings, cut through the wood, up the hills to the South. There a plant of an Oak of which so many stories have been told, tho' it is only 3 feet 7 inches broad:

The house is now neglected, not being inhabited by the owner. The river from this place runs pretty much from South to North, but then turns to the east. We soon cross'd over it, as I take it into the County of Limerick, & pass'd by Sr Oliver Cursons seat; about his estate is a new Model for ornamental state [   ] with a Chimney in ye middle; & a pediment in front. We soon saw a village call'd Gulbaty situated on an eminence to the west of Aerla, with a fine old ruin'd house, built like a Square Castle near it; & before the house the remains of an Abbey St Francis, in a romantick situation over the river. We approached near the foot of the Galties & going over two hills, cross'd the river Puncheon on a bridge & came into the County of Cork & soon to Mitchelstown. This river rises in the County of Limerick & falls into the Black water a litle below Ferney: Mitchelstown is situated on a rising ground, is a proper place, in the turn pike road from Dublin to Mallow, being 18 miles from Clonmell, and 8 from Mallow. It belongs to Lord Kingston, who has a tolerable house[9] here, and a litle Library in a round Tower. They have in this Country a Grey & white Marble.

on the 12, we came over the hills, in about an hour & half to Kilworth, passing by a tower on a hill, which is call'd CaraGrihurst; Kilworth is in a fine vale, & in the Turnpike road from Dublin to Cork; near the town we passed the Puncheon again over a Bridge & came in two miles to Fernoy, on the Blackwater, about 8 miles from Lismore, 3 more brought us to Rathcormuck. We raw about a mile to the East Castle Lyons,[10] a small town pleasantly situated, where Ld Barryimore has a seat on an estate which the first Earl of Cork gave to his Daughter married into this family.

On the 13th we came 12 miles to Cork, of which place I have formerly given you an Account.[11] The tower of Christchurch[12] is remarkable for its having settled in a very extraordinary manner; part of it was taken down & built perpendicular; but as it still settled, they took it down & now it overhangs, I think as much as the Tower of Pisa. I went through the town & in about a mile in the way passage road came to Douglass, where there is a great linnen Manufacture; here we turn'd to the south & went over the hill four miles to Carigaline, leaving Shannon Park to the right, which has given Title to the Earl of that name. I saw the ruin'd Castle of Carigaline[13] which is situated over the river call'd OenBoy, it is in ruins, but consisted of a Square Tower pretty entire & its enclosure. Here the river widens & opposite to the Castle on the same side of it, a large basin being form'd, here is Coolmore[14] Mr [Newidian's?] seat, most charmingly situated on a Peninsula, not unlike the Boromean Islands,[15] but I think more beautiful in wood Buildings &c.: below this is deep water in which large ships can ride, & the river falling into the harbour of Cork near the mouth of it, & is so litle to be observ'd, that Sr Francis Drake came into this river, pursued by a Spanish Fleet, who coming into this harbour, & not seeing him, Ships went out again, probably supposing they were gone up higher towards Cork, where they might not think it prudent to go.[16] I cross'd this river on a bridge, & going to an heigth, had a fine view of Halboling & the whole cove of Cork & crossing a creek & rivlet at Browns Milles at Kingsale came to that town in all seven long miles from Carigilane: This Town I have also formerly given an Account of, & particularly seen of it in Governor Foliots Acc[t] of the place lately printed,[17] & observe that there are a Colony of English fishermen at one end of the town, of whom I could get no information but that they comonly marry among themselves; the other that they keep unmixt ever since Queen Elizabeth's time, & the present is call'd Filly. This town is chiefly under the influence of Mr. Southwell & S[r] Jn[o]. Mead.

On the 14th I went to Innishanon of which before.[16] I saw here the French colony of weavers of Linnen & cotten, & some of them are famous. I cross'd over the Ferry on the 15th, & went four miles to the Old Head, which is joyn'd to the land by a flat Ishtmus; on which Ld. Kingsale has an indifferent house, the seat of the family; who are descended from the Earl of Ulster, call'd to the first Parliam[t]. in Ireland under Henry II & K. John, & having defeated an enemy of the kings in single combat, had the priviledge of being covered in the kings presence, which the family enjoy to this day, & are the first Barons of Ireland; the present Lord is melancholy & has no male Issue; but has found out a relation, whom he is educating for his Estate & Title; they have about £700 a year. About a mile further on the high road, there is a large old Fortification, by which a narrow neck of Land is enclos'd, except to the west, on which side it [sic] secured by high cliffs—on a Head to the South east of this, is a Lighthouse: In this narrow head there are several passages worn by the sea through the ground & rocks, to w[ch] a great number of Seals resort. We pass'd by some pleasant Seats in this fine uneven corn country, which is very beautiful tho' there are but few trees in it. We came down to the river Arigadun & to Timoleague, on that river we went half a mile further to Bary's Hall the town of the Honourable & Revd Mr Bligh brother to Lord Darnley & the General who is now to command our Horse. It is most pleasantly situated, commands a view of the river & part of the Bay, of several seats adorn'd with Plantations, of the Abbey of Timoleague[19] & of the low hills rising one above another & cover'd with corn.

On the 16th I went to the church of Leslee, to the south east of Don worthy head; a litle beyond it are very high Cliffs, famous for Airyes[20] of Hawks. We return'd by the bay of Timoleague, by Court Mac Shery, an estate of the Earl of Shanon Ballenemona; this house from whence the Travers are sprung, & by Abbey Mahon a mean building, which belong'd to the Bernardines. Timoleague is a poor place, like a village, with one short street of very indifferent buildings; at the east end of it are the ruins of a Castle: There was a monastery of Franciscans near it, of which there are great remains. It was the burial place of the Macarty

Reaghs, O'Hea's, [O Cutluins?] & O'Donovans. This bay is famous for fish, especially a large Plaice which is prefer'd to Turbut.

on the 17th I rid out to one of the seven Heads, which make the Curve to the west of the Bay, that Head is call'd Dunwurta. On one side are remains of an old Fort on a Peninsula, & at the South end is a Peninsula call'd the Island, the narrow neck of which is defended by a tower & a wall on each side of it, not being above fifty feet broad; it is a very fine Head & produces a good herbage. We here saw a fleet of between 50 & 60 Sail, as we suppos'd from America, a very fine Sight, I am, &c:

Ross Carbary
July 21ˢᵗ 1758

Dear Madam,   On the 19ᵗʰ I went two miles to the north-west to Temple Brian,²¹ where about two hundred yards to the east of the church is a remarkable circle of Stones 33 feet in Diameter & from five feet to six feet high of irregular figures, the sides being from two to four feet; to the south & north are two Stones placed as for the entrance from 3 to 4 feet apart; there is a stone from the east & west, the former eighteen feet from the stone on each side, that to the west is twenty one feet from the Northern entrance, & only 13 from the southern. In the middle is an irregular stone 2ᶠᵗ 6ⁱⁿ high, two feet on three sides & 5ᵗʰ 6ⁱⁿ broad on the fourth side; directly west of it is a stone near the church about 7ᶠᵗ high, & there was another directly east on another eminence. I went a mile to the south west to the best market town to the west of Kingsale, call'd Clonikilty; tho' it is but small it is tolerably built, & is a Borough that sends Members to Parliament, & is situated on a rivlet, which falls into a Bay, which has its name from the town. From this place we went towards Dendeedy head & pass'd by the indifferent seat of the Moores Coheiresses & sisters of the late Sr. Charles Moore. A litle beyond it we came to the Lead & Copper mines of Duncan; they are chiefly lead, but they do not at present work 'em. I went on about three miles further to what is call'd the Island Dundeedy, which is the point of the head, it is a Peninsula, & the neck of it is defended by a castle with walls on every side; except to the west, where there is a steep cliff: The Island consists of 36 acres of fine pasturage, which lets for 6ˢ–8ᵈ an acre, the measure being the English Statute measure in all this County. A litle without the Island to the east are Dr. Barry's copper mines. They see the veins on the Cliffs & follow it commonly when they see Sparr in a Stratum there is ore; they have work'd it four or five years at the Dʳˢ. expence & have got very litle ore. I was told that there is a dark colour'd free Stone in the Cliffs. There is no limestone to the west or south of the Sumit which falls down to Badon river; but here they abound in Chrystals, found in the fields & on stones: And where there is limestone or marble there is sparr. There are also sparr & Chrystals where these are. I would suppose that Chrystals & Spars both are found in the ores, Spars only with freestone & Limestone. From which I would conclude, that the waters which impregnate the earth & form limestone or marble, are charg'd with such juyces as form Marble of which sparr is always ye concomitant—there being[22] in water spar & chrystal & a fine sand; for sand is commonly compos'd of fine chrystal probably when spar prevails, it is a limestone; where chrystal prevails which is not easily calcin'd it is a Lime Stone; & I believe there is no limestone where there are ores & no petrification of Shells &c.: but in the limestone, this may preserve the shells— the juyces of the freestone[23] may corrode & destroy the shells.

We took boat at Dundady & came two leagues to the river of Clomkilty & came to Ring on that river where we din'd with M^r. Brereton.

on the 20th I left Berry's Hall, & pass'd through Clankilty & in about three miles, came to a chapel rebuilt by a Protestant, who made a vow on recovery from sickness according to an inscription there, concerning which chapel they have a legend relating to S^t. Fackman as built about his time.[24] We came down to Ross Carbry pleasantly situated on a rising ground under a hill on the harbour, which is a bad one; Ships of 30 or forty tun only can come up when the tyde is in, & that not near the town, which is small & ill built. It is a Bishops See, founded as they say by St. Fackmã about the Sixth Century. S^t. Finchard disciple of St. Barr was the second Bishop. Thomas O Hirliby in 1570 was the last Bishop who enjoy'd this see without any other: It afterwards went with Cork & Cloyne till after the time of Edward [   ] in 1678 when Whittenhall was made Bishop of Cork & Ross, & so it has continu'd ever since. The Cathedral is a small modern building, with a body & a choir & a small tower & steeple; There is an old plain Saxon doorcase placed in the south side of it. There are remains of a very old small Church of the Priory of Ross founded by S^t. Fackman, they were Canons of St. Austin. About eight years agoe digging near the Churchyard, they found a difficult entrance into several caves, as they inform'd me, the first about ten feet by 8, the next ten by 6. The larger were about 6 feet high, the other five; & cut in the white clay, Archwise, in one was a stone, on which there seem'd to have been fire, they suppose they might be made to preserve corn: & they say, they have dug in on such caves in the gardens to the South. There is a barrack in the town: The soil here in digging a well, was found for three feet common earth, then five feet white clay & lower exceeding hard rock like a flint, in which they sunk two feet: In the bay they soon come to turf, which is about five feet deep; it does not burn to ashes, but turns hard & red: Under this is the white clay, with roots of trees in it, as there are in the turf. This place is s^d. to have been anciently a famous university, in which S^t. Brendon was a Professor. I went up to the Hill over it, on which there is what they call a Danish Fort: & there are others on the heigths round in view. They sow much flax here, & have a great market for linnen yarn, as well as at Clonekilty & Skibereen. I am &c:

Cree near Skibereen
July 22ᵈ 1758

Dear Madam,   On the 22ᵈ I left Ross & went over a hill to a valley in which
there was a rivlet, call'd the Rory, & on it are the entire walls of a large house,[25]
built about the time of King James the 1ˢᵗ by Sʳ Walter Coppinger;[26] He had
design'd to have built a town here, the harbour call'd Milk Cove being much
better than that of Ross or Glendon, as they told me; we went over two hills to
Glendon harbour, which at first appear'd most beautifull, like a large Lake, the
land looking in & round it ['are' *deleted*] on the sides of the hills are two or three
Gentlemens seats with plantations about them; on the east side of it is an old
castle[27] which belongs to the Donohoes. As we came to the North end of this part
of the harbour, the entrance about half a league in length open'd, which is full
of rocks insomuch that it is with difficulty a Ship of 30 or or 40 ton, can enter;
we then came to a narrow part above this where the sides of the hills of each side
are finely cover'd with wood & some Gentlemen's seats appear. The west side
is the parish of Miros. We came to the head of the bay, where a small rivlet falls
into it at the Mills, it first falls down a rock about 10 feet and rushes through the
rocks with litle falls till it comes between the rocks, in which it has wore away
about fifteen feet over & sixty deep, into which the water tumbles & being kept
up, one sees the still water at the bottom of this Chasm, which with the wood
hanging over it, has a beautiful effect. This is the Leap beyond which it was said
formerly there was no law.[28] Going along by the head of the Bay we came to
what they call the Leap Hill, which is nothing but a steep pav'd ascent for above
two hundred yards. I turn'd out of the road to see an ordinary house, & a great
plantation of wood of Mʳ. Jervais's,[29] behind the house are hanging Gardens all
gone to ruin, & no prospect from it; several lakes are form'd by the Stream which
falls in at Glandour, in which there is a short thick red Trout that is most excellent.
Sᵗ. Mary's Abbey of Maur or de Sancto Mauro, call'd also Fonte vivo, is said to
have been in the parish of Miros. They were Cistertians founded by Dermot
Macarmark; Smith supposes it to have been about Carigiliky, & what is call'd
the Abbey Stowrey,[30] was a cell to it; but as there is no tradition of its being at
Carigiliky, it is most probable that it was somewhere in the parish call'd Abbey.
When we ascended this hill we saw the country very rough & rocky round about
for about a mile; This is the rocky country which forms the craggy head to the
west of Castlehaven harbor, opposite to which are rocks in the sea call'd the
Stags: We had small lakes to the north & came to the road that leads to the harbour
of Castlehaven, at which there was a sea fight between Sʳ. Richard Levison &
the Spaniards in 1602.[31] We found the country improv'd upon us, & descended
to Skibereen, the last market town this way, situated on the river Islan, which
falls in at Baltimore. Here is a Custom house, & about two miles above the town
on the river Mʳ. Beecher has a handsome House & Offices: Nothing can be
imagined than in a fine evening the ride of three miles to Cree. Mr. Durham the
Minister.[32] The river is beautiful when the tyde is in & the country on both sides

is well cultivated—under corn between the rocks cover'd with Furze, & the uneveness [*sic*] of it adds to its beauty, Mr. Hutchinsons summer house on an eminence three miles to the west & Mount Gabriel have a very fine effect. I went up to the top of Mount Knockoumah to the east of Cree about two miles & had a view of the harbour of Baltimore, of the Islands of the harbours all the way to Crookhaven, & more particularly of Lough Hine at the foot of the hill, with a Promontory in it from the South, on which there is an old ruin'd Chapel[33] & an inlet on one side from the sea by which the water falls when the tyde goes out like London bridge: There is an Island in it, with the remains of a Castle. Here is great plenty of fish at all times & of oysters always in season; & it is a remarkable place for swimming, here is a well near for sprinkling the cows that have the murrain, & there is an Altar at it where they say Mass for them. To the west of this Lake we saw the Castle of Ardegh.[34] To the east[35] we saw Denis Cove & Angetun Cove[36] beyond which is Castle haven harbour. On the hill we observed a Boundary with Stones set up an end, probably between the territories of different clans. It was curious to see from this hill every spot of ground under corn or cultivated herbage not only such as where a plough could go, but where there is any ground to dig.[37]

Another day I took a ride to Lough Hyne & pass'd by the fountain call'd Skeuer, over which an arch'd room is built with an altar in it mention'd above.

We rode to Baltimore & saw the ruins of the old Castle.[38] The houses of the town seem to have extended from it to a creek to the South with the gardens to them, probably on the rocks toward the water. The rocky Isles to the west of the Island of Donnegal[39] afforded an uncomon View. Here I saw pill corn,[40] a sort of oats that boyl without grinding like rice for eating, have no husks & are us'd only for that purpose. They have on this coast the round Echinus[41] & about Kingsale the broad short Pirna[42] as in the north. I am &c:

Cape Clear
July 24th 1758

Dear Madam, On the 24th I set out in a row boat, went down the river & passing by the Island of Inibeg & Donegal, we came in a league opposite to Baltimore, where are remains of an Old Castle, & only a few Cabins the Fort having been burnt by the Algerines in 1631.[43] It is a Corporation & sends Members to Parliament; & there is a church a litle to the north of the Castle. We went a mile further to the Island of Iniskertain which is in the parish of Baltimore, & defends the harbour against the South west winds; There was formerly a Barrack with 19 guns, & a Fort with 17 guns. The Island is about two miles long & ½ a mile broad containing 90 ploughlands & about 100 families eight of which are Protestants with Captn Becher the proprietor of the Island at the head of them, who lives here. We went ashore to see what they call the Abbey, which was a Friory of Minorites of observance, founded by Florence O'Driscol in 1460.

The Church is a good building, with a Tower rais'd on an Arch & there are large pillars in a south Isle. There is a greenish freestone in this Island & Cape Clear as well as about Crookhaven: They are all fishermen both in this Island & Cape Clear; & they have on the coast, places for curing fish, comonly call'd fish palaces,[44] & come to these parts from Cork & Kingsale, & especially about Crookhaven, which abounds in fish, & make up litle huts in which they live during the summer; & in time of peace the French come over here to fish: When the Pilchards came great fortunes were made by them: now they get chiefly Mackrel during the month of July & August Herrings also come in at that time, they catch likewise Hake, Ling & Cod, all which they salt, & barrel up the Macreel & Herrings. The Mackrel sell well, as they give only half a mackrel to the Negroes, which they call a fish with one eye. In Crookhaven they are out in the evening, & as soon as they see the sholes by the motion in the water they draw their Sein nets across & enclose 'em, they take also, Breme, Turbot, Plaice, John Dory: & in the season the people live on fish. They have great plenty of Salmon, but it does not sell under a peny a p^d, Lobsters, Crayfish & Crabs sell for pence apiec & are very good. Wild fowl are sold by the couple,—Plover 2^d, Partridge 3^d, Teal 4^d. Duck 8^d. They have small black[45] cattle, which at 3 years old sell for10^s, & when fat weigh about 300. We went to Cape Clear, the most Southern Island, & the Old Head of Kingsale is reckon'd the most Southern land; it is about half a league to the South of Iniskerham, is 3 miles long & a mile & half broad, We went into the North CoveX,—X[46] over which is a a [*sic*] ruin'd Church dedicated to St. Kieran, Founder of the See of Ossory; who according to Archbp Usher was born in this Island, & a litle beyond it is an old Castle on a rock,[47] which is a Peninsula, with a narrow passage to it. The Island consists of twelve plough lands, & there are about 200 families in it, all Romans.[48] It is a parish which commonly goes with Affadown—on this bay is a Stone on which two Crosses are cut, as its s^d by S^t. Kieran & in another part of the Island are two Stones near one another about 8 feet high, & half way up a hole cut in the middle of each of them, probably for fixing a stone across in order it may be to form a Greek Cross, they keep S^t. Kiaren's & S^t. Clara's days as their Patrons the original of the name being the Isle of St Clara. The great vice here is drinking Spirits, which they do excessively even some of them, they say, to a gallon a day.[49] They were alarm'd at seing our boats, thinking it was the Kings, as they had laid in great Store of Rum from the West India fleet which had lately pass'd. They were glad to be undeceiv'd, tho' when the officers not long ago made a seizure, the women rescued it. They brought in a bottle of rum by way of civility & dealt it round, & we return'd this civility by a piece of mony. They have here very fine flags. There is a lake in this Island, with a particular kind of soft worm in it,[50] which 'tis supposed cleanses all vessels put into it of whatever filth they have contracted; the water is very soft, occasioned probably by the saltness[51] of the soil from the sea spray. I am &c:

Crookhaven
July 25 1758

Dear Madam, We sail'd & rowed three leagues to Crookhaven, the Fastnet rock to the South west is about the same distance from Cape Clear. It is the most western harbour on the head of Land call'd West Carberry. It is a very fine haven opening to North east, & is made by a head of land extending to that point which ends in a rock head call'd the Alderman, through which there is a passage for a boat, a point of land comes from the north west & defends it against the easterly winds: It is a very fine bason about a league in Length & half a mile broad: The poor town of Crook stands about the middle of the long head of land, with the ruins of a fort & of a Barack & there is a church built in it, by the late famous Bishp Brown.

The West India fleet often puts in here, by contrary winds going or coming. When an East India fleet or indeed any other puts in here, it raises all provisions to an exorbitant price. The whole county from the western point to Skull is very rocky & every Spot sown with oats, English Barley or Potatoes which they are forced to cultivate for their Support. I took horse in the afternoon & first saw Spanish Cove, & then came to Barley Cove, which form the bays, one coming within a quarter of a mile of Crookhaven, the space between being partly sand & partly rock; if ever the sea should break in here it would entirely destroy the harbour. We cross'd over the Strand of the other part of the Cove & pass'd by the ruined Church of Kilmore, from which the site of the parish church was remov'd to Crook about ten miles in length of the head being the district of that parish, we were then very near to Missen head the notitium of Ptolemy,[52] there are two points at the end of it which have either faln down, as the tradition is, or the sea has almost separated from the land; there is a hillock on the heigth of this head, which is seen a great way like a Pyramid. We went on to the Promontory of the three Castles about 2 leagues from Crook haven. There is a fresh water lake at the entrance of it, about half a mile long. At the north end of this entrance & just over the end of the lake, a wall is built so as to defend the head of land against any invaders; & this wall is carried along the side of the lake, to a high wall defended by two towers & a Castle with one room on a floor & three stories, the lower room is cover'd by narrow arches from which large Stones are laid across so as to make the floor of this Story over it. At the end of this wall is a perpendicular sea cliff which seems to be above 300 feet high. From the three Castles we ascended up to the Head & had a fine view from it of Dunmanny & Bantry Bays & of the Dursey Island off Bally bagg head, which is the most western part of Ireland. We saw also the rocks near it, call'd the Bull, cow & calf.

We had a distinct view of the entrance to Beerhaven which is form'd by Beer Island. We also saw the remarkable Hills call'd Hungry, famous for the remarkable Water fall. This was altogether a most glorious View. On this head there grows a very small Shrub, about six inches long, it has a leaf like firr, bears a black berry with 5 or 6 hard seeds in it Shap'd like beans, & has a sweetish taste, they call it Monoduna.[53] I saw Elecampane grow wild near the haven, & they told me they have also Marshmallows. It is a great Misfortune that there is no law nor justice in this Country. For they cannot execute the last form of it a Caption.[54] And some one or two men generally govern the Country & are often in opposition to one another & so kirb each other. It is not difficult to get Affidavids; & a Custom house officer can hardly live amongst them. The surveyors are soon weary & desire to be remov'd, & in all these parts hereabouts to the west of Kingsale, they have a term of hiding an officer, which is knocking in the head & putting him under a turf: There have been many instances of Officers never heard of. But they are the most hospitable generous people in the world in their own houses, & extremely ready to show any civility, & to give all kind of assistance to strangers. In all these countries[55] they manure with sea sand & sea weed. I am &c:

Baltimore
July 27ʰ 1758

Dear Madam,   On the 25ᵗʰ. I set out on my return on horseback to go ten miles to Skull; we found the Country very rocky & the road but indifferent: We cross'd the [five?][56] narrow Strands of Ballidivlin Bay: & over the eastern bay, I saw an Antiquity call'd the Altar being an ancient burial place, as I suppose, of which I have seen several. Three broad flat Stones are set up an end in a line, about six feet apart, & three or four feet high, & form a wall of about ten feet in length, & then two very large Stones about 8 inches thick, were, I suppose laid each of 'em about eight feet broad & ten feet long lay in a cross one of them remains in that State, the other appears as if it had slid down to the west. I did not observe any Stones at each end: They are all of a greenish thick flag, We pass'd in Sight of a small Island, which consists of only 3 or 4 acres, in which one Mr Hull & his family live retir'd. We came down to Skull, where there is a Church & a very good Parsonage house on a pleasant bay call'd Skull harbour. From this place I ascended Mount Gabriel, which is a hill abounding with a coarse herbage; we had a view from it of Missen head Carbery Isle in L—maur bay, of part of Bantry bay, & of the Islands & country to the East & South east, On one Sumit of it they say, there is a small Lough: I here met with a very small Shrub, something like Myrtle, but the leaves smaller then any myrtle,—on the back of the leaves were small red berries, but whether Seeds or Galls I cannot say,[57] I could not perceive any Seed within 'em. I took Specimens of some other plants I did not know; & they told me that London-pride grows wild on this mountain.

I set out from Skull & soon came to the Bay call'd Roaring Water, observed a Danish fort, which seem'd to have had a fence round it of Stones put up an end; & in another place I saw a Stone, near as large as those of Stone henge &

set an end: At the north corner Bally dahab river falls into it: This river is one of the most beautiful I ever saw in its litle bays & flat rocky promontories & ground gently rising from it, & there is a publick house on an eminence over the end of that part which is made pretty broad by the coming in of the tyde, & is one of the most Romantic situations I ever saw. We soon came to the other rivlet which falls into it call'd Roaring water, where a mill forms a beautiful cascade & a deep creek comes near to it, where Hoys load with Turf for Cork & Kingsale, which they pile up 6 or 7 feet above Gunnel, & can be navigated. This bay is very beautifull in the many Islands which are on it & before it in very fine weather.

We went on to Affadown where M^r. Hutchinson has a house & estate of the Bishops, finely situated on an eminence & lately in the possession of the Beachers, a Summer house on an eminence commands a fine view all round & more especially of roaring water bay: we descended to Affadown church, in which parish at a place call'd [   ] is a large Stone, laid on three Stones set upright. We cross'd over to Cree M^r. Durhams house, having been absent from it only six & thirty hours,

on the 27th I rode through Skibereen, & went four miles from it to Castle-haven; I saw in the way a chalybeat spaw on each side of the road call'd from the rivlet near it Gustine Cloky Spaa; it is not very strong, but on a tryal it has been judg'd to be a good water. To the east part of Skibereen which is in Cree parish & far from the church they have a burial place for the Protestants. The other part is in Abbey Shorey, which is a parish & Impropriation; The Church is half a mile below Skibereen, just beyond the Bridge, it is a very old small Church, the Chapel to it is in the town, in this parish the Impropriator has a Glebe of 500 acres; & it is supposed there might be a Cell here to Abbey St Maur or de Fonte Vivo, concerning the Site of this Abbey, I cannot find that anything is known, tho' it is positively said, I know not on what Authority, to have been in the parish of Neiros:

Castlehaven harbour is one of the most beautifull I have seen, but then it is not safe in strong southerly winds tho' it appears to common observers to be well defended by hope Island at the mouth of it, but there are two entrances by which a great Sea rolls in when the wind grows Strong from any of the Southerly points. I row'd round it in a boat from Castle town: At the north end of it, is a litle promontory, making out to the east & forming it safe litle basin[56] for small Craft, just beyond which the bay ends, where the river falls into it, which rises from the Loughs we saw in the way to Skibereen from the Leap.

Going out on the west side in a sort of Bay is Castlehaven where Ld Castlehaven has a small Castle & house adjoyning to it, which has formerly been inhabited by that family, in this bay is the Church, which is to be remov'd to Castle town. Going on to the South, I saw a small cave to the west, with beautiful grotesque rocks making the arch of it like some Gothic carvings, the Western passage is not safe but for boats in good weather, the Eastern passage is open.

Horse Island so call'd for being remarkable on account of its fattening horses, consists of very fine rich pasture, on it are the remains of a round tower, for a sea mark of no great antiquity: This Island is mostly of a brownish freestone but there is better at Carrigiliky. There is a fine prospect from this Island of the coast to Dundeady head; but to the west all view intercepted by Fee head. M^r. Townsends plantations at the bottom of the bay, which grow very well add a great beauty to the prospect, & with Castletown forms a beautiful landskip. The gardens are in winding walks up the Side of the hill & upon the top, where I observ'd that Mulberry trees & Standard figs thrive exceedingly, & produce ripe fruit. They observe the Sicamore grows very near the sea better than any tree. The bowling green on the summit towards the bay, commands a fine view of the harbour of the Island & of the openings of the bay on each side which have a beautiful effect. In my return I saw on a heigth to the south west not far from Castle town four Stones set an end, probably an ancient place of worship. I am &c:

Bantre
July 30th 1758

Dear Madam,   On the 28th I left Cree & cross'd the ford at Abbey Shoury & in about a mile came into the high road from Skibereen to Bantre & to Dunmanway, there is a shorter way to the former, but it is not so good. We cross'd the river Islan several times, & came to a church on a heigth call'd Drimoleague, six miles from Bantre, where the road turns off to Dunmanway, we went on in the Bantre road & soon descended to a beautiful woody Glin, in which ruine[d] bridge crosses the four mile-water rivlet, that falls in at Dunmanway bay four miles from Bantre. We had an exceeding fine road, & passing to murdering Glyn, we came in between a gloomy amphitheatre of hills, almost entirely cover'd with heath, & had a fine Lough to the right of about four or five acres, & in so regular an oblong Square figure, that it appear'd like a work of art. I saw in this road some Stones set an end, as the remains of a Druid Temple; & at the entrance into this place, a Romantic confusion of rocks which had tumbled down from the hill. Coming from this unusual dark scene, to the heigth where Bantre bay open'd to us, we were most agreably surpriz'd by the finest sight of the kind I ever saw in my life. The bay as far as we could see it, lock'd in by the land, appear'd like a long lake, with beautiful Islands in it, fine small bays which they call coves & well cultivated heads of land making into it, & within them, small hills under corn; & all bounded by very high rocky mountains, at a proper distance, altogether making the most pleasing & with that the most awfull sight that can be imagin'd. At the bottom of the South east Cove of this bay of Bantre, the town of Bantre is situated, which tho' small is the best on the coast to the west of Kingsale. There was a barrack of foot here, now in ruins; & they have a small church & pretty good markets. The Chief support of the town is fish & a clandestine import of French Brandy & rum. They import grain for their own use & have no sort of manufacture. We row'd out to see the Islands. Whiddy belonging to M[r] White a very worthy gentlemen of considerable estate, who lives in the town; it is two miles long & a quarter of a mile broad, & has in it three eminences, it is finely divided into arable & pasture fields; there is a part of it well stock'd & a great number of hares; & it is altogether a most delightful place: The passage to it at low water, if I mistake not, is about two hundred yards. Near the South east side is the rabbit Island; & near the north east point, is Chapel Island, which at high tyde is over flow'd in the middle & forms two, & is the estate of Lady Burlington. To the North of this is Hog Island & horse Island. I went a small mile to the north of the town to Donemark waterfall; It is a rivlet which falls down in two places from the rock near twenty feet, & has worn a channel in the rock; one in such a manner in shelves, as to form three sheets, one below the other, the which extends four hundred yards, & when there is a flood, the water falls down to that breadth, except under the rock in two or three places is a litle[59] higher than the rest & beautifully adorn'd with small trees growing out of it, as they do out of the rock which continues some way to south behind the fall: This is one of the most beautiful things I ever saw. There are no less then six Coves at this end of the bay; & the largest Ships ride at the north east end of Whiddy; but not with safety to the west of that Island, except in Beerhaven; & small Vessels in [   ] harbour; they have here in this bay great plenty of Scollops & pectens,[60] the latter have two hollow Shells & one [   ] at the joynt, the other one flat Shell & two [   ].

The pectens polish to different Shades of yellow, & many in most beautiful reds & white of all Shades: They have also plenty of oysters & of most kind of sea fish, Pilchards they had about 20 years ago, & forty years before that, so the comon people have a notion, that they will come twenty years hence; whenever they come their ruinous fish palaces will be repair'd. There is a most extraordinary singular thing in this bay, they have banks of what they call coral sand, there is a bed stretches from the south west point of Whiddy, & another northward from the north east part of it, & there is one in Beerhave. They scoup for it, as they do when they would clean harbours it is almost all a very small white coral, in litle trees about 2 inches long or 3 at most, & in branches about 1/16 of an inch in diameter; some of it, but a very litle, is of a purplish colour. This is most excellent Manure for land, & they use it as sand[61] for many purposes; Tho' they take it all away, yet in no long time the bank forms it self again. There are seaweeds about this place which exactly resemble it in shape. An Iron foundry was carried on to the north of this bay by Mr White; they had the ore near the surface in these parts & smelted it with the Lancashire ore, nothing but Charcoal will smelt the ore; but sea coal & even turf burnt to a coal will serve to make it from pigs into barrs & they were oblig'd to leave off the work for went of Wood. However there is one still carried on at Counshouler, to the North of the bay, between water green sail & Bantre. A litle to the west of Bantre on the south side of the bay where it sets out to the north, was what they call the Abbey.[62] The church yard is about 100 yards up the side of this hill, there are no sort of remains of the building, it is a most charming situation, commanding a most extensive view of the bay. It was a Friery of Minorites founded by Dermot Sulivan in 1460. I am &c:

Beerhaven
Aug. 2ᵈ 1758

Dear Madam,   About eight miles from this place is the Sound between the land & Durray Island, which is about 200 fathoms over, but a boat cannot cross except it is very Calm weather & when there is no great swell. This Island is about three miles long & a mile wide; the Cliffs are high to the north & there is a descent to the South: it is a fine pasturage, & consists of nine small plough lands & belongs to [   ] who have property on the adjoyning continent; in the 3 parishes are 800 families, & only about 8 of them Protestants, & notwithstanding the laws can be executed here better then in other parts of Kerry. In the heigth of the Island are fine Springs of water which never fail. They begin to fill to prevent Moss; they keep here Sheep & black Cattle, but they often fall off the Cliffs; they swim 'em over tyed to boats: They have a small berry, not seen any where near & is probably the same I saw at 3 Castle head, I observ'd London pride growing about Beerhaven. There are near twenty Roman families in this Island, some of them natives of it. The Privateers kept this Island in Queen Annes wars & water'd there, & the Government the Proprietors £50 a year for the rent of it, & all the people fled from it. On the Continent Privateers made contracts with the inhabitants who left their Cattle to be taken away by them, which they might otherwise have easily drove off; & they had such possession of Barhaven as to come & clean their Ships there. In the Island they draw up small boats at the place when they land, for there is no Creek or harbour. The large fishing boats harbour in Kilcuchine Bay, if I mistake not in the cove call'd Lough Ian cove to the South east. About 7 or 8 leagues to the South west of Dursey, is a rock call'd Lae rock, about 30 fathom under water, here the fishing boats fix with a stone in summer in fair weather, & fish with lines for Hake, Cod & Ling which lay on the rocks: the Proprietors of the boats give 'em seven shillings for the first, & twenty for the others: Maiden Ling are about four feet long & Ling grow to seven feet in length; maiden ray are the small Skeat, & here they throw away this last kind both young & old: A small whale came ashore dead on this Coast some years agoe, the whale bone was about four feet long. Whey they can't fish off the rock they come & fish in the Sound or somewhere under the Shelter of this Dursey; but the fish caught off the rock is greatly preferable to it. They can legaly send no fish to France but Salmon, all the rest goes to Spain, or is run into France. It is to encourage their own fishery. People live here to a great age, notwithstanding they drink drams imoderately, living on fish & potatoes & the sea air may make this custom less pernicious, especially to some particular constitutions. They sit & drink Spirits as others drink wine: But the smallpox is very mortal among them; supposed to be owing to the first diet. A sort of scurvey also which sometimes comes near to a Leprosie is frequent among them. They have great notions of Fairies in all these parts, which take place of Witches in other places. Instead of laying a dead body tyed up in a sheet or blanket in which they are buryed without a Coffin. They lay the body on a form under a table & throw a Sheet over it. All workmen, tho' only making ditch or threshing & all Sorts of Handicrafts in a private house or fields have the Shameful custom in these parts more than in any other, of holding a String or something a cross the way & begging money, more than in any other parts of Ireland, tho' it is pretty frequently done in the Country places. I am &c:

Beerhaven
Aug. 15ᵗʰ 1758

Dear Madam, On the 31st we set out in a sail & row boat from Bantre & came in three leagues to Adragile harbor into which several streams fall from the high rocky mountains. We came here to see the famous Waterfall wᶜʰ has been so much spoken of & is to the west. When we first saw it, it appear'd like a vein of Sparr in the rocky mountains; we walk'd about 2 miles to it. The whole mountain is call'd Hungry Hill, the top of which is computed to be 700 yards above the sea, but I do not think it so much, the upper part is very steep, it may be about one third of the heigth; at the foot of this eminence is a lake on that part of the mountain call'd Coumgira (the crooked clog)[63] the water comes from the lake first in a gentle declivity; it may be two hundred & fifty feet perpendicular, it may then fall down the rock which is very steep about as much more to a Shelf, which may be 100 feet broad, from this it may fall down about 450 feet down the rocks near perpendicular & after that it may be 100 feet in a gentle descent, & is not seen; it divides into several very narrow Streams close to each other, but when there is much water, it seems to have spread to the south it may be ten yards or more most part of the way down. The rock is beautiful on each side cover'd with Shrubs & particularly to the South, where it forms four or five hillocks all down the side of the hill with shallow valleys between 'em: Men went up to the Shelf to throw down Stones, which made a great noise, & in speaking to them we observ'd an Eccho, which I think repeated six syllables & one syllable four or five times, like the Eccho near Milan: They call the waterfall Mounlare (Mares stale.) There is a fall to the north after rain, which they call Eskimileen ([Poets?] hillock) & another to the South which now Flow'd, it is a gentle declivity & is call'd (Geravilen) Rough Island. On an eminence above the rivlet to the South I saw four or five Stones, which they told me form'd a circle, the place is call'd Gustinereha, & was doubtless an ancient Druid Temple. We saw also some Strong Chalybeat Springs, which seem'd in taste to have a mixture of Sulphur. Camomile grows here: We had civilities shown us by a widow, the daughter of an old Proprietor, so we thought proper to take our provisions to her house, & accept of whatever civilities she could show us. We took boat & soon came up with the east point of Beerhaven Island which is two leagues long & about a mile broad, (there are many families in it; here are houses & no foxes, & a great number of foxes & no houses on the Continent, being destroy'd all by the foxes) forms the harbour of Beer haven, which is of that length & about half a league broad, & would hold all the fleet of England; the passage in at the west end of it is about half a mile broad & is rocky & unsafe without a Pilot. There is no Village at this harbour, only small houses; they have a small Stone bridge here of red Coral, of which I could not get a Specimen. I went to see the remains of the Shores Castle of Dunboy to the south of the harbour,[64] to which the Irish fled as their last resort in 1602, & when they were attack'd by S[r] George Carew[65] who planted 3 batteries against it, one on an eminence near it, & the two others on eminences to the north side of the harbour; here he took twenty five of the heads in the rebellion, who were all hang'd. I went to see the Creek of Poleen two miles to the south west, where a rivlet call'd Copel rising out of several lakes abounding in trouts, forms a beautifull Cascade, falling down an easy descent in several Streams, for about 30 feet perpendicular heigth. On the west side of this Creek is some free stone in an hill over which the road leads to the Dorteep Island; on the east side of the Creek is a Cave, into which they can go only at Spring tydes, when there is no swell in the sea; it is said to be 50 yards long, forty feet broad & 20 high. This Creek is a good fishing place; they draw the Sein[66] to a litle Island in it, the harbour being rocky all round. The Mountains have good pasturage on them, & they make huts & keep their cattle on the mountain in summer & live on new churn butter & milk. They marry very young, the women at 13, the men at 16, & those of condition are call'd Gentlemen of good families, chiefly the Sulivans, have a way of portioning their daughers by what they call Coleprits; they go round all their relations & friends who give each family an Head of black Cattle, they call it lending; for the compliment is return'd as occasion offers; but if they take of their inferiors it is only understood to be purchasing their protection & friendship & no return is made: the mother & sisters go about to get Sheep & this goes for the fortune of the Daughter, & they make up from 40 to 200 head of Cattle in this way. These Gentlemen have about ['500' *corrected*] 300 acres each, most of it let out, & the Tenants are entirely at their command, & are heads of these litle Clans; which have been of late reduc'd to great poverty. For one of the Principal of them, Martogh Oge O Sulivan who had been a forreign officer & outlaw'd & proclaimed for a rescue for a seizure, & returning was told, that one Puxley the Surveyor (by whose widow I was entertain'd) had said he would take him: On which about five years agoe he & two more shot him from a smith's forge, as he was going to Church, he liv'd about three hours. Part of the army were sent to take the assasins but miscarried & went off; & return'd upon them in a wet night, where 20 of 'em were asleep in a house, they set fire to the house & all of 'em escap'd except the true Martogh being kill'd on the spot, & the two others taken & quarter'd at Cork, & the three heads were set up publick place. This broke the Combination, & they have been since kept under by the excessive high rents they are oblig'd to pay. The three Parishes united here, which make up the whole County of Cork, consist of a hundred Plough lands which may be about 1000 acres each; the land is let for about one Shilling an acre; Twelve Geneva's make plough land & four Cusses[67] a Geneve. Another told me that 36 acres make a Geneve, which is about 250 acres to a plough land;[68] but there are plough lands of 1500 acres, so that the quantity may probably make up 250 acres. They have a Custom of Shooleing or corstuming about,[69] the former is rather an expression of Spunging, the latter of visiting those you entertain again,—that is those of a family who are very poor, go from house to house, & must have the best of every thing, which is a great oppression on the poor people. I am &c:

Milltown in the County of Kerry
Aug 12 1758

Dear Madam,   On the 2^d I set out on horseback from Beerhaven, to cross the head of land northwards. In the way to the Church we pass'd a narrow defilee between rocks, over which are the ruins of a smiths forge, from which Martogh oge Sulivan shot Mr Puxley, he first saw blood on his hands when he was wounded & thought his own pistols had gone off; the second volley came on him as soon as he pass'd the rock & twenty balls were found in him. As soon as it was over Maclogh & his two bravoes went & stood behind the rocks near in sight of every body, & drank a bottle of Brandy, he then went to Mass, & said, if any one was sorry for Puxley death they might [*sic*] go & cry over him, concerning which I am thus particular, because it was the most villanous, audacious & extraordinary act, that probably was ever committed. Passing on I saw on an eminence a circle of stones, & near us to the right, two stones near each other & about twelve feet high, being larger than any I had seen, except the single stone near Roaring water. I was inform'd of one about 15 feet high, a mile from Roaring water in the way to Bantry. They say there are many of these circles in these western parts, as there are in Cornwall; which is a proof that the Druid worship provail'd more to the west than in other parts of these Islands. We came to a rivlet call'd the Inches near the sea on the north side of the land. This rivlet forms a beautiful cascade, in three or 4 falls thro' the rocks, the whole making a cascade about 30 feet perpendicular. I observ'd several very strong chalybeat springs, not far from the sea; & at Beer they have found Lead ore, of which I have a specimen, but they do not pursue it: To the north of this river are the ruins of Martogh Oge's house, which was never repair'd, after it was burn't. when the army first came, he was always on the neighbouring mountains & saw them looking after him, & with his companions made a jest of them, but the last affair was very well conducted by Mr FitzSimmonds, the nephew of Mr Puxley & is now in the same office; They came by water, landed near the house & surrounded it, & the besieg'd fir'd upon them, so were forc'd to burn the house. We came to

Coolagh bay where a row boat & sail met me, & I embark'd for Kerry. We sail'd
to the north east about a league, & were between Goats point & Inisfernan Island.
I stood & came into the bay call'd ['Kilimare' *deleted*] Kenmare river. We saw
to the north west a high Island call Hog Island off the South west point of Kerry.
We came about two leagues into Sneem harbour which is form'd by some small
Island, & we went by mistake up to the north west part of the bay, into which
two rivlets fall, between which Dr Bland did formerly live:[70] here we saw a great
number of seels some of them lying on the rocks, We return'd to the other part
of the bay, & came to the house where the D^r now resides, where he comes fir a
short time twice a year to see his Estate, but he was not here. At this place my
horses met me & I rid to the east as I shall relate to you. Near Hog Island I
mention'd to the west of the South west part of Kerry are the Isles of Seelig on
one of which call'd Abbey Island are the ruins of an Abbey, now famous for
pilgrimage's to it. Ware saies that the Friery Bali-ni-seelig[71] was an Abbey in
one of the Isles of Seelig remove'd to this piece; after which only some Chapels
remain'd on the Island, the friery of Bali-ni-seelig on the continent so close to
the sea, that some part of it has been wash'd away by the see. This Island is now
only a high rock difficult of access. Ormet in the parish of Kilcrohan is a circle
of stones seven feet high. Sneam is a very good harbour, the outer part of it for
Men of war, the inner for vessels of 100 tons. Near opposite to it, but a litle more
to the west is Kilmakaloge harbour, a very good one. Near Lough Quinlan in
which are floating Islands form'd by the sedge matting[72] together as in sol farare
between Tivoli & Rome. To the east I saw a waterfall, which seem'd to be form'd
by a rivlet which falls into the cove of Ardea Castle; the first fall I concluded to
be at least 100 feet & almost perpendicular; it then runs on a Shelf & falls as I
conjectured 50 feet, & must be a fine object after rain, I set out to the East, we
had small Loughs mostly to the north, mostly to the north [*sic*] of the road, &
observ'd several waters in the way; & crossing over a hill, we came to a small
Stream, which runs beautifully winding through the rocks down the hills in
several falls, comunicating one with another by gentle descents for at least 100
yards perpendicular. We went over another hill & descended to a most romantick
narrow valley, beautiful in its rocks, woods & waterfalls, particularly just above
the Bridge there are three or four falls, of about 10 feet each between the rocks,
in which it has worn several passages. The bridge consists of two arches, one
built on a rock, twenty feet higher than the rock, which supports the other arch
on the opposite side; in very great floods, tho' very rarely the water falls down
from the upper rock below the bridge, it is a still water in a deep bed, with high
rocks & wood on each side of it. I am thus particular, in the face of the Country,
as there is nothing else worthy of curiosity of a stranger, the acc^t of the old
Castles, the seats of the heads of Clans here, can afford very litle amusement to
those, who do not live in this country. We pass'd by a very high ruin'd Castle,
call'd if I mistake not Cappana Cushy,[73] & about a mile further the ruin'd Church
of Temple noe, which is large: We then came to the high Castle call'd Dunkeron,[74]
this is the Barony of that name, which gave title to the late Lord Shelburnes eldest

son.[75] And crossing by a rivlet over which a high bridge & one arch is built on the rock we came to Needen a small village, where there was a barrack, & a mile futher to Killowen to the house of Mr Orpin minister of several extensive parishes in those parts to the Western point. In the middle of the mouth of Kenmaire river they catch among many other sea fish abundance of Cod, they find prawns in their bellies, which might be caught for the table, but at present they catch only Shrimps, They have very large Lobsters, one of which was caught measuring three quarters of a yard, from the end of the tail stretch'd out to the end of the claw. Pennyroyal grows wild about the Blackwater. The Islands at the upper end of the river about half way over are litle Stones: & so is the country to the north, for about four miles in length along the river. They talk much of a small rock of limestone, on the hill on the south side, & another of fire-stone, on a hill on the north side of the limestone, which must have been owing to a Stratum on each side on the top of those hills, the earthy & loose Stones have been wash'd away, The river Roughty falls into the bay at the head of it, & from the south falls in a rivlet call'd the Shene, which after rain comes tumbling down the hills in a gentle descent, with several small falls & affords a very agreable & uncommon prospect. This part is call'd the Salmon fishery, which is perform'd in a very curious manner, down on the Shelf to which this water falls about 15 feet, two men stand in front, with flood gates, one made with net, another with lattice, to stop the fish, then on the side men stand with bagnets, one holds two, & one on each side, niches cut in the rock to let 'em in,—a man goes in naked & beats with a Stick, the hole of the Shelf & Nich about the waterfall [   ] looking like a Triton;[76] when the fish goes into the net, they breack his neck & hold for another, we saw two taken immediately; they watch to see the fish go up & go in again.

On the 4th I rid out 3 miles to the east to Ardilla, where there was a Castle, now entirely ruin'd, belonging to Mac Finan over the [   ] the wood & water points out that it might be made to resemble the lower part of Leixlip, being beautiful in rock, wood & water when the river is full, We had the great Mangarton to the north & saw the old way up to it. I saw in my return, the firestone on the top of the limestone, & observ'd several others near it; just beyond it to the north the limestone ends, at the bottom of a Shallow Valley, extends about a mile beyond Ardfilly, a little beyond Dunheron Castle to the ['west' *deleted*] river extending northward, only about half a mile from the river of Kenmare & the Roughty & is in the Island along the river rather further to the west. near Needen is the red & white slaty marble which cannot polish well, it seems to be of a dark or grey kind. I am &c:

Dingle
Aug. 14ᵗʰ. 1758

Dear Madam,   We set out on the 5th & in two miles came to Dunkeron castle,
a quarter of a mile from the river are foundations of a wall in the wood, which
they say is circular enclosing two acres. It seems some notes on Wallis's
Geography mention Dunkeron, as the Ierne of Ptolemy call'd by him the Capital,
I think of Munster: We went on & I took a view of Temple no Church, which is
not very old. We came to the Blackwater, where the fall appead [sic] better than
before, & we went down it to a rock near which we saw them fish for Salmon
& take 32 at one draft in a Sein net. We had two of them roasted & din'd on the
rock, in this Romantic place, in the middle of fine wood & rock. We came on to
Dʳ Blands house at Sneim harbor, & saw the great waterfall but litle better than
before.

We perform'd the Divine office on the 6ᵗʰ & cross'd the river Sneim & over
two mountains to that part of Kilcrohan parish call'd Poolansbay. On the top of
the first mountain, I observ'd a circular fort with a stone wall round it; & the
second to have been another on the rampart about 3 yards from it. It was about
40 feet in Diameter; as I conjecture, as well as another I saw in the valley to the
right at the foot of the second hill: here the wall was entire & there is a set in
about six feet from the ground, this part might have a flat covering on it, but
what is singular, the wall is about 8 feet higher, & round within
are eight figures of steps to the top of the wall in this manner as to go
up to annoy the enemy, & by 'em to be supplied with Stones it may be or other
materials for that purpose. We came on near to St Crohans Cave over us towards
the top of the hill, & turning to the South, we pass'd by another round fort entirely
ruin'd, & at the Castle of Bonaneer came to the east side of Poleen ragh bay, this
castle was made with a set out on every side, so as to receive the gabel end of a
roof. We came to Mʳ Orpins litle cabin; a most beautiful situation, in view of the
litle Islands in the bay, with hills rocks also cover'd with such Shrubs, & wood
as one would plant on them in a garden. A litle beyond is an eminence with a
circle of Stones & to the South a pretty Strand of white Sand, very rich in broken
Shells; here we saw many of the litle yellow periwinkles; nothing can be
imagin'd more Romantic then this situation having the sea to the South & rocky
mountains every other way at about five miles distance; & one beautiful hill near
like a Pyramid.

On the 7th we cross'd to the same Castle & ascended up the hill to the North
& coming to a Stream, we ascended near to the top of the mountain to St Crohan's
Cave, which is about ten feet long & six broad & five high; it is in a Vein of red,
brown & green Stone, with a great mixture of Sparr, & the people by their

devotions have worn it so smooth as to give it a polish. They hold a pattern here on the 1ˢᵗ of August Sᵗ Crohans day.[77] They say St Keran founded the see of Ossory liv'd for some time in this Cave; & some say that he composed his rules here, for the monastick life. Near this I was shown a Wolf trap fill'd up; it was a round hole about six feet diameter, & on this they put a hurdle, with a Swivel in the middle & a bait on it, laying a litle fern on, the wolf coming to the bait the hurdle turn'd & let him down. They say a Fox pursued a Sheep into this hole & fell in it & got out, being not so deep as formerly, that an Eagle descended to the Sheep & was caught not being able to get on the wing. We had a fine view from the mountain & saw the Dursey Island in its whole length & very plainly Baley dungan bay no secure harbor to the west of Colagh bay where we embark'd after we left Beer haven. We saw what we took to be a small circle of Stones lower down & came to the foot of the hill to Kilcrohan church, a very old good building, near which is his well & an ash tree, which they say is alway green, concerning wᶜʰ I doubt, The Church has the narrow window with the true arch & that to the east is divided in two, by a Stone across the middle of it. We came on & cross'd over a hill, to Baley Carney Castle, & soon came to a white Strand over which we cross'd half a mile to Mr Connels house so well shelter'd by the hills & sand tho' very near the bay, that trees grow well about it, & especially orchards. We walk'd along the Strand to the Peninsula call'd Abbey Island, where there is an ancient church a sort of Hall & Dormitory & two other buildings adjoyning to it: they say this land was given to two Monks of the Abbey of [   ] on a vow.[78] It is a charming spot of ground producing fine herbage & Elecampane. On the green sod near the strand, I saw a plant very common in Hamps.ʳᵉ[79] with stalks of yellow flowers on it in clusters, the flowers not so big as a pin's head, they call it Dah divell (sand bank dye) the root of it dying a fine red & is used by the common people for dying stockins &c: on this herbage are most beautiful streak'd snails. Juniper also crawls on the ground & so it does in Hog Island. I here also saw the Cornish Daw, which they likewise have at Beerhaven. This Strand is call'd Aghamore (the great Eddy). In these parts they manure for potatoes with dry fern. I was inform'd that at Argroure bay & at Cloheen, they have a coral sand of a brownish colour, & a gentlemen assur'd me he had seen it grow to a shell about two inches long & of a reddish colour. The Kites here are white & their wings tip't with black. They have the large Eagle in great plenty, & the rock Eagle which are smaller. The Sea Pye is a beautiful bird the head & wings black the belly & neck white, & the back grey, the long bill & legs red, about as big as a Pheasant. They have another extraordinary sea Bird the Ganett[80] as large as a Goose, it is grey the first year, the wings all black the next year, & afterwards the tip of the wings only black, they have a brown bill something like that of a gull, like them they fly over the skulls of fish & dart down with such force into the water, as to throw up a spout about six feet high; if the prey is near the surface they do not go with such force, when they rise they shake their wings to dry'em & then soon in again, to take another; 'tis said, sometimes when they are gorg'd they cant rise, & may be easily knock'd down with an oar: They also put a prey on a board on the end of a boat, a litle under water on which they come with such force as to kill themselves: they brood on the litle Skelig, &'tis s^d are so bold, as like geese to come & fly at the oars & bite'em, as people land. They take the young ones & sell 'em dear for their fat, which the people use to make rush lights. On Puffin Island they take Puffins when young & sell 'em dear salted, & they are allow'd to be eat in Lent as fish, as all other sorts of birds are that live altogether on fish. The Great Hog Island which we saw belongs to Lord Orrery, & there is a vein of Ore in it, Lead & Copper as I was inform'd; & they find large pieces & lumps of Chrystal in that Vein.

I must give you some Idea of a Milesian feast & manner of living. We had a dram offer'd before dinner, & had at the upper end Bacon & fowls & cabbage, at the lower a large roasted Turkey, on one side a leg & Loyn of mutton boyl'd & cabbage, on the other a boyl'd Cod, pease on one side, Lobsters on the other & 2 dishes of Potatoes on each side below, & a large dish of Stew'd apples in the middle, all succeeded by a large bowl of punch & wines. The Breakfast the remnants of the day before, Cold Turkey, chickens minc'd Turkey, a dish of fryed Mutton & of Boyl'd Salmon, a large wooden bowl of potatoes at a side table, cover'd with a cloth to keep 'em warm, boy'd eggs at the tea table, & a dram before they sat down, I am &c.

Tralley
Aug. 15th 1758

Dear Madam,   We went on the 8th & saw a round fort on the hill, & a litle further one Stone laid on Stones set on end, they have a notion that they were altars, & some that they serv'd as houses. The Stones set up an end they call Goulanes,[81] some of them are certainly burial places, others set up in honour; as where a body was rested in the way to the Church of one of the name of Dermoud, it is call'd Goulane Dermode in Glam roughty. We pass'd over another hill & descended to the river Currane, which runs about a quarter of a mile out of Lough Leagh into the see. This is a fine Cane[82] of an irregular Shape, there are high mountains to the north & east & about a dozen Islands in it, on one of which there is a church, it is about four miles long & two broad, & is computed to be twelve miles round, it abounds with good Trouts, Salmon & Eel: The river Curraine is very full of Trouts & also of Salmon; we drew a net & enclos'd so many that the net broke, but we caught near fifty; & they said that almost as many escap'd. This Stream falls into the bay of Bally seeligs; we rid along the Strand of that bay, the Cliffs being about thirty feet high, we cross'd the river Ennah which is deep, a fine Bridge of one Arch was turn'd over it a litle higher up, but they suffer'd it to go to decay. We came to the South west corner of the bay & leaving our road went along the west side of the bay to Baley Seeligs Abbey. It was curious to see the Gannets diving for fish: But the Landskip we had in sight was still more curious. The two Scelig high Islands or rather rocks to the South west, the Island at the mouth of the harbour, the Hog Islands to the

South east, the ranges of mountains extending from the eastern head & two or three more rising higher & higher, the top only of the most distant being seen, form'd altogether one of the most extraordinary Grand Stupendous views I ever beheld, the Sun shining most cheerfully on all the mountains. We went & pass'd by the well of St Michael to which they pay much devotions & came to the Abbey of Baley Sceligs, call'd also St Michaels Mount, first to a Chapel & a building to the west of it, which might be the apartments of the Superior, then to the Church; to the South of which is the Cloyster, consisting only of plain arches, over which probably was the Dormitory; there are two other buildings to the South of the Church which seem'd to be seem'd to be [*sic*] the kitchen & Refectory, all very mean buildings. This was a Friary remov'd from the great seelig Island; they were Augustinian Canons founded by Flan Mac-Cellach in 885. It is mention'd by Giraldus Cambrensis.[83] The great seelig from which it was removed is a most beautiful rock with a high point & several smaller down the east side which is rather steep & some on the west, these points appear like Gothic [   ] ing about half a furlong below, the top of it sets out to the west, & makes a platform on which there are twelve cells, & the church near them, probably this was the number of the monks. There is a fine fresh water spring on it which never fails. It is lett for ten Shillings a year for the liberty to go & take seafowls on it for the feathers. The litle Scelig is to the north west of it, & is likewise a fine Spiral rock almost perpendicular to the west. Before the bay of Baley Scelig is a small Island to the west of it, is a very narrow, rocky passage, which if fill'd up they say would be a very good harbour, whereas now it is no harbour at all, but this Island adds greatly to the beauty of the prospect. We return'd & saw a small circle of stones, to the west of the bay. We went on had the parish of Kilernly towards Valentia to the west, it is all fine improv'd mountain or Bog every way cover'd with heath as far as to the harbour of Castlemain. We pass'd by a Castle call'd, if I do not mistake, Agha tubrid,[84] & afterwards passing a bog on a Cause way, we had the Castle of Cappagh I think to the right, & a most glorious prospect of the Island & harbour of Valentia, the former making three or four beautiful bays from so many Capes, with their pointed heads extending out so as to afford a most agreable prospect; the Isle of Valentia is six miles long & two broad, consists of two hills, the skirts of which were all under corn, two Islands towards the north west mouth of the harbour, high mountains to the north & the high Blasquet rocky Islands to the west, altogether form a most extraordinary beautifull prospect. We descended to Cahir to the Rectors house Mr Ferny on the river Farten which falls into the north east corner of the bay: near the church is a small round Fort on the hill & a small village to the south. They talk much of this being a Sanctuary or Asylum, but I fear it was only an Association of honest people to defend one another. On the opposite side are the ruines of a large old Castle call'd Baley Carbery,[85] the O Connels drove by the Strong [   ] out of Connaught were tenants to it formerly, who now live more to the South: & from this place that family in the county of Kilkenny came about Olivers time.

We sail'd about the bay on the 9th first by Church Island on which there is a Chapel & they told me also one of the altar monuments. We then came to Begnish Island or Beg-Inish (the small Island) & to the west of it, to the northern point of the Island of Valentia, which is a rock & on it a small Fort of one Bastion six guns with a Barrack of one room & a closet & two floors on each side & which were built by Cromwell,[86] two of the Iron Cannon still remain; the fort defends the entrance of the harbour this way. Many of the large rocks here appear in the figure of Cornishes, insomuch that at first we thought we saw hewn stone exactly in the same manner as I show'd you a small one from Lough Foyl in the County of Derry,—We had here a fine view of the Basquet Islands some leagues to sea, which have a fine appearance. We saw also the large Island to the west of Dunmore head near Dingle, which they told me was the Ferreter Island. In the rocks to the north we saw the entrance to a cave, said to be 50 yards long, 20 broad & 30 high. There are red Deer on the mountains. They have in this harbour plenty of Oysters [   ] & Scollops; & I am inform'd that in Ardrom harbour in the river of Kenmure they have oysters 8 inches over, which are larger than those of Tenby in Wales. We sail'd along the north east side of the Island & came to Port Magre, where the Chanel winds which on the east side is not above half a mile over: Here are high rocky Cliffs on this Island as well as on the other side & on an eminence in the Island are the ruines of a small Fort built like wise by Cromwell to defend this entrance. We went to the very mouth of the harbour to fish for Whiten & Haddock with a hook: & here the Scelig Islands appear'd most beautifully, as describ'd. We saw also the Puffin Island mention'd before & return'd. We had seen 'em here & in other parts fishing for Conner, with rods on the rocks, & a fish beautifully spotted with brown & yellow & about 18 inches long. I am &c:

Kilarney
Augt. 21ˢᵗ, 1758

Dear Madam,   On the 10th we set out to the South east & cross'd the river Farten several times; we ascended the Glyn to the north between the mountains & pass'd by a round Fort encompass'd with wells, & soon after saw another. When we gain'd the heigth, we had a view not only of Valentia harbour, but of the west part of the harbour of Castlemain, with the harbours of Denyck & of Vantry which are in it, & of the Islands to the west of Dunmore head, & turning to the east we ascended a heigth, from which we had a view of the harbour within those heads, which they call Islands within these it is much like the harbour of Chester, & the sea seems to have gain'd on the land. We had a long descent on the inside of the mountain over the see, & soon ascended another hill & came down over & came down over [*sic*] a perpendicular Cliff, to that sandy Country which is at the neck of the Southern head, & crossing the river Carra we came to the Strand & travell'd partly on or near it to a small town call'd Killorglin on the river Lane, which rises out of the lake of Kilarney, & produced good Trout & Salmon. Here lives one of the Hassets. We cross'd the river in a boat, which is fordable at low water. We now found our selves in a better country & tho this place is call'd but twelve miles from Cahir, yet it is double the number of miles of 2200 yards; we had a distinguishing view of the mountain call'd Mac Gulley Cuddy's Reeks, about ten miles in length, with about a dozen Summits, we saw two basins in which are loughs, out of one of them falls a fine Cascade, mostly on a gentle declivity; from the other a water fall descends after rain: We saw the hills where the Lake of Shillanny begins, with Turk and Manderton beyond it, altogether making a very grand appearance. Having now left the Barony of Iveragh, I take leave of it, with observing that all the Cattle & fowls are very small in it, some hens eggs litle bigger than pidgeons, & Turkeys no larger than Hens. Sheep sell for 4^s each, & a bullock 3 years old for 30^s; & if they bring larger kinds into the country, they soon become small. It is remarkable that there are no jacks[87] in the rivers of Kerry.

In two miles we came to Mill town, & went to Mr Godfreys at Buslefield[88] just at the end of the town, which is situated about half a mile from the river Mang or Mayn, that rises near Castle Island not far from the Black water, which falls in at Youghal & forms a fine deep river, which is navigable to Castlemain & abounds in Eels, Salmon, Trouts, Mullets & flat fish, which last are taken five miles higher, but are not good above Castlem^n—. Eeles, Lampre's & flat fish, the river Lain abounds in & trouts & salmon Mr Godfrey has lately built Mill town for Tradesmen of all sorts, & is endeavouring to establish some trade here for butter & fish for Cork. Not far from the town & near the river, are the ruins of the old Parish Church of Kilcolman, which seems to be very ancient, is built of a fine Stone, probably brought frō the mountain, X a vein of which begins at the river Lean X on the other side by water before they knew of the Limestone quarry is from 100 to 400 yards wide; in these parts & further on from a mile to four miles in breadth, extends to the north east to Castle Island & from that to Trally, as I shall hereafter describe; it is probable the same kind of black-marble as that at Trally, & saw that it is full of Shells, chiefly the cockle kind: Whenever they find it & would drein the lands, they bank against it to keep the water from the bed of stone, otherwise it gets up through it & destroys the effect of their drein. For the sea has gain'd on the land between the rwo rivers & the tyde goes up to Castlemain a mile higher; this is seen by two feet of Slab[89] over the bog made by the tyde, between the two rivers which meet about two miles lower, & by all that Sand down to the Islands, call'd the Peninsula, I have mention'd. Most of this is drein'd by Mr Godfrey & his tenants by making Dykes as in Holland, with double ditches that produce fine oziers & where the soil is not too salt, all sorts of trees; for they grow about this place very fast, indeed beyond any thing I ever saw; but apples, plums, mulberries & Walnuts are much inclin'd to shoot out below, & to dye at top if pruned so as to make them shoot upwards, probably owing to the sea air, but cherries in shelter have grown to a great heigth & thickness in a very short time, spreading below. In the orchard there is a round hole about 50 feet deep & 100 yards over, it has often water at the bottom, & probably was made by a water course underground which has wasted[90] away the earth they might lay between the bed of Stone. This is work'd into a winding walk down & planted with flowering Shrubs. At the other side of this estate at an eminence, is a round Fort with a double fossee, one fifteen the other about ten feet deep; under it are some passages under ground, wall'd on each side & cover'd with flat Stones,—probably to conceal goods in time of danger: & on the north side of it, is a deep hole fifty feet, which seems to have a mine work'd in this burrowing way, it was lately tried, & they went down twelve fathom, & found only an oare which [   ]

All this place is cover'd with young oaks. A quarter of a mile to the west of Bushfield is the Abbey of Shellahah[91] dedicated also to St Colman, nothing remains but the Church which is about 150 long & 30 with a fine Gothic east window: In this building they have made great use of the Limestone. There is a pill[92] to it from the river: Near it Mr Godfrey found a brass bason, which had been gilt, is adorn'd with emboss'd work, & there is an inscription round the bottom in Saxon letters, which I have not yet writ out. A hand bell was also found at the Abbey, about 15 inches long, made of iron rivetted together & a Copper handle, but almost all destroy'd with rust, which I have in my possession; both these Mr Godfrey presented to me, & the latter doubtless serv'd to ring the monks to their several duties. They also found a large old Brass spur: & in making the shaft above mention'd, they [   ] with some leaden Mendick cubes,[93] about /16 of an inch; and in some other part, an earth much like the soapy rock, but in small pieces, a specimen of which I have in my Collection. I am &c:

Macroom
Aug. 22^d, 1758

Dear Madam,   I set out on the 12th & in a mile to the north east[94] came to Castlemain a very poor village, the Castle was a tower built over an arch on the east side of the bridge, which is now ruin'd, & there was a gate at each end to the bridge, & it was a very important pass; the river being deep, to the west is a rising ground, from which they batter'd down the Castle. We had a very good road near the hills & travelling westward we pass'd by Castle Drum & a Glyn to the north call'd Comen rack dery. On account of the great number of wolves that were in it they had Gin traps to catch 'em, as well by holes mention'd before. A litle beyond the Islands or rather heads of land before mention'd, on which there are plenty of Hares; about ten miles from Castlemain we ascended the hill & stop'd to take some refreshment. We went on & came to the mile-Stones seven miles from Dingle, a mile further we pass'd by Castle menard & had a fine Water fall in view, which in about eight falls, I conjecture, might descend 8 or 900 feet in a gentle descent, Three miles from Dingle, we pass'd by Ardemore, where there is a rivlet, & the tyde comes in & forms a Lough. Dingle is a town of one

Street, situated on an eminence over the north east corner of the Bay. It is a Burrough & the Knights of Kerry[95] to whom it belongs have a house here. The Parish Church was a Chapel to a larger, the ruins of which are in the town & now seen & particularly the Grand East window: There are many old houses in the town, which has lately receiv'd a great Shock by loosing 8 Ships chiefly concern'd in the Smuggling trade; which will force'em to the more usefull employments of either Husbandry or Fishing. The harbour is about two miles in length & half a mile broad; the entrance to the South east is narrow but safe, except that there is a rock near the entrance; it is sufficient for ships of 300 tons; Men of War commonly go to Vantry bay, tho not a safe harbour from the north west Dingle harbour appears land lock'd & has all the beauty of a river & a Lough, & the Situations are most delightfull, something like those near Limington in Hampshire.

On the 14th we took a ride out & came in two miles to Vantry bay, it is s^d that there is an Old fort on the western head of it. About half a mile from the bottom of it, we went to the Castle of Rathnam, where the Knights of Kerry formerly liv'd, & to whom it now belongs; there is a deep fossee & double rampart round it, & remains of a large enclosure as well as of a wall built on the rampart. There is a passage under ground from the fossee, which they say goes a great way, & of which they tell strange stories. We went over the hill & had a view of the Islands, & pass'd near Dernmore held by some to be the most Western land of Europe on the Continent; here they find the Chrystals call'd Kerry Stones, & in the cliffs just north of it they work for them between the Strata of Stones, with Chissles & such instruments as are fit to draw out the earth & chrystals together; they find also some in the Cliffs to the north. The great Blasquet Island consists of two hills is about half a mile broad & three miles long to the south west, beyond it is Inchvilane. Another to the north is the Isle call'd Inish-Turhuf & there is a fine rock with two heads to the west. We ascended to a rock on the hill to the north, where a sort of a dry Well is made, & there is a heap of Stones which is call'd Kil-Gubbo net, as if that Holy Lady was buryed & a litle below it is a well sacred to her name. We cross'd over the hill to another bay full of rocks, against which the waves roll in most beautifully, there is notwithstanding a Custom house-boat here as well as at Smoriwick bay, tho' here it can seldom go out, on the north side of the bay is a neck of land defended by a rampart & old Castle in ruins: It is said one of the Fenchers got the watch word, surpriz'd the garrison by night & put'em all to the sword. We came to Inuriwick a very fine bay, but not entirely safe; to the south of it, is a fresh water Lough, full of Trouts & Eeles; & near the South East corner of the bay is Galerus Castle;[96] & a litle beyond is a most curious building, it is within about fifteen feet high, six of which are upright, the rest in a Curve like so as to meet within about eight inches of the top which is cover'd with flat Stones; on the outside the whole is in a curve line from a base I saw of one tier of stones. The door is two feet wide & 5 feet six inches high, & the wall at the bottom of the door 3–9 & at top 3ft–4in the window at the east end is 2^f & 3 high & the Stones are plac'd against one another in curve lines the arch consisting of only two stones, & diminishes to the outside to about half the dimensions. I number'd 27 tiers of stone within, they are not hewn, but level'd with small Stones in every tier, the stones on the outside at top do not end in a point & here is only one Stone in breadth, except there are two stones at the end. The door seems to have been double, for there is a Gudgeon Stone at each side at top, so that each leaf probably consisted of one plank, or it may be of a Stone; in the east end are small Stones setting out beyond the others as to rest a scaffold on. This building seems not to have been built on a center, but probably a frame inside out, at each end from whence they draw a line to direct the workmen. Near this building they show a grave with a head at the cross of it, & call it the tomb of the Giant; the tradition is that Griffith More was buryed there, & as they call'd a Chapel, so probably it was built either by him or his family at their burial place. As we return'd we were shown a hill to the north east, from which they say there is a fine prospect all round this head of Land of the several bays. On the estate of Ballibeg a mile from Dingle is a spaw which consists of Sulphur & Steel & they have found some lead near Durain, of which I have a specimen, I am &c:

Dunmanway
Aug, 24th 1758

Dear Madam,   I set out on the 15th & return'd seven miles in the same way I came, passing by the park of the Knight of Kerry three or four miles from the Town: soon after we turn'd into the Tralley road from that leading to Castlemain. We had a view into that Romantick Glyn, in which was the water fall I observ'd, of which we could nee nothing now, as the waters had faln there on the high rocky mountain on each side of this vale. I observ'd in the road some fragments of a white freestone so that probably there is a quarry of it near. We' ascended up between the mountains of Inch to the west & Brioskehah to the east, & had a glorious view of Tracey bay & of the Coast to the mouth of the Shanon; We had seen all along in the mountains torrents many on perfect chrystals on a sort of Stratura or Spar & there some small ones which are perfect & clear, but the greatest part are in appearance like Spar, tho' Hexagons; they seem to be wasted from their beds toward the top of the mountains. It is to supposed that Sparry Strata are form'd by the running of water full of Sparry particles; that when the water brings with it Chrystallne particles, the Chrystal is form'd upon it, that on these there are again Sparry Strata from the same cause. As we descended on the other side, I observ'd the walls full of these Stones in a ma[   ] built with Chrystal.

We came down to Skibobban at the entrance of the Strand where we staid some time, & went along the Strand at the foot of a very fine high mountain

John P. Neale, Crotto House, 1818–23

call'd Cahir Conré. I imagin'd I saw the remains of a Pier or Causeway from one part of the Shoar, which abounds in a Sort of brown gritt Stone, & there are many very fine large Stones, compos'd of pebbles cemented together in the brown Stone, & if they had the art of sawing them would make very fine tables.

Having cross'd this part of the bay, we went a mile across a marsh, & came to a wet Strand on which we rid for three miles, over to the other side, crossing the Tralee river which runs through the Strand, & in a mile came to Traley; (the Strand of the Ly or Leigh) which is the name of the river that falls in here. It is a poor irregular town. S[r] Thomas Denny lives in the Castle; There is a plain market house in the Square, & a neat new built Church on one side of the town. There are hardly any remains of the Friery of Predicants founded in 1243 by John Son of Thomas Giraldine; except one neat[97] arch'd building, which probably was the Chapel for the burial of the Desmond family, for near it are several pieces of a fine old monument it may be of that family.

On the 16th we went through a fine Country five miles to Crotto,[98] Mr Ponsonby's descended from a younger branch of the Ponsonby the Besborough family being the elder. There are fine plantations about: we travell'd near two miles to Lixnaw[99] to the left of the road, scituated on the river Brick; it is the seat of the Earl of Skerry; the house is very indifferent, but there are large plantations about it, & Canals cut through the bog to the west of it, which might be turn'd into serpentine-rivers, & the bog drain'd; at the north end, is a small round tower, built by the late Lords father, for a monument over a Burial place; but he alter'd his mind, & the body only of his son is deposited in the vault under it: The whole is a large field for improvement, & might be made a fine place in its self. Near the house is a large Village. We return'd to the road & saw Ennismore to the left, an ancient seat of the Knights of Kerry, & came six miles further to Listowel a Castle[100] & Village on the river Feal, over which there is a fine eight bridge of twelve arches. The Castle here held for L[d] Kerry was taken by S[r] Charles Wilmot[101] in 1600, after the infant Lord had been convey'd from it, but he being discovered was educated by the Queens direction. It consists of two ancient high small towers joyn'd by an arch, built with large Spise[102] holes, probably soon after the English came over, an oblong Square building was joyn'd to it there, like a Castle, altogether it is improv'd into a a tolerable house, & is a very pleasant Situation. There are two fine roads from this place, one to Limerick by Newcastle, the other westward to the Ferry over the river Cashiri which is the name of Feal, the Galy & the Brick after this all meet. This river falls a litle below into the great mouth of the Shanon, which they call four leagues over, I am &c:

Iniskein
Aug. 26th 1758

Dear Madam,   We set out on the 17th came near to Corlin Ferry & cross'd the Strand towards Bally burnian Castle,[103] we saw up the Brick on the west side of it, is the round tower of Ratoe.

We went a mile to Ballyunian Castle, & a litle beyond it came to a Head of Land pointing to the north, which was defended by a wall & a tower at each end: here the Cliffs are very fine; & on each side of the head of land is a small creek; in the eastern creek which is the longer are several caves, that which made the report of a Canon when the waves roll into them: & in this Cove is a high small Island in which an Eagle breeds every year. There is also another thin rock in a triangular figure; but the great curiosity of this place is a hole about 30 yards over, at the bottom of which the sea comes in under arch it has worn in the rock & is a very singular sight. This place which is a fine green sod, it may be of four or five acres is call'd the Dune (the hill) a litle further is the ruin'd Castle, & we saw a semicircular Danish fort on another cliff & another head defended by a wall made across the neck of it, this is near the burning cliff & from this head one sees a fine view of a waterfall down the Cliff, which comes in two Sheets, joyn'd by a thin leaf of water, one falls down on a litle Strand in a plain Sheet, the other is broken in several places by the rock in its fall, which may be about 50 or 60 feet. What they call the burning rock or cliff may be about 40 yards in breadth & ten deep it is faln down it may be 30 feet below the Cliff, & when it fell the fire went out; it burnt for five or six years about twenty years agoe, it alway smoak'd, & in wet weather they could see a flame, especially by night: The poor people used to go to it to warm themselves, as they do to a Lime kiln. They find Pyrites about it below when the tyde is out, & there is also much burnt earth & stone. In a litle bay to the South of this are very fine Cliffs, & one rock is less, like a beautiful Square Obelisk in a Gothic taste.

On the 18th we set out & went by Lixnaw & crossing about two miles to the west, & then turning a mile & half to the north we came to Ratoe, where there is an exceeding well built round tower, consisting of about 100 tiers of Stone, besides the point. About 15 feet probably from the old ground & ten from the present is an arch entrance into it with a plain moulding cut round it in the Stone; at the door is the set cut[104] for the first floor, where it is six feet in diameter within, & the walls 3^{ft} 10^{in} thick, the entrance is 1^f 10^{in} wide & 5^f 2^{in} high; there were 3 floors over this laid on Stones which set out the lower & upper floor seem to have been laid on the solid wall & made by the setting in of the wall, the upper one being very near the point. There are four windows near the point as usual, & only one more which is over a good distance over the door in this shape Δ near this is the Parish Church, patch'd up out of the old buildings, they say near it were seven churches. Some distance lower is the ancient Church, which appears

J. P. Neale, Balleyheigh, 1818–23

to have been in a ruinous Condition & afterwards repair'd, the Cornish within consists of two plain members with a drop at certain distances. The tradition is that it was a Franciscan Friery. The Patron day is call'd the Apostles, & is kept on the 18th of December, probably in honour of some of the first planters of Christianity in this land. Mr Gunne who lives here has made a pretty improvement of a garden, into which he has taken the round tower. This Priory is call'd Rathery it was dedicated to St Peter & St Paul they were Aroasian Canons of St Austin founded by Frier William & confirm'd by K. John.

We went on Northward near to the ferry of Castine we had been near in our way to the burning Cliff, & turning to the west we soon pass'd near Castle Shannon over the sea cliffs at the mouth of the Shannon; about a mile the west of this is such a hole as describ'd near the burning Cliff. It is call'd Poulionneget. A litle beyond it, is a silver mine which is not at present work'd, it is on the land of Lord Bellamont & is a hundred fathom deep. From this I cross'd over to Peninsula of about ½ an acre of ground call'd Pierce's fort, there are Signs of building in it. We went on & saw several oblong Square rocks at a litle distance from the Cliff, over which the white waves rise, it may be fifteen feet & falling down as soon as the rocks appear'd form'd most beautiful cascades beyond any artificial wall rocks in the world: which is an extraordinary effect I never saw before in such beauty. We came on to another Peninsula & Fort call'd Balurigany, it seems to have been entirely cut off from the Cliffs, & there was a drawbridge to it; it consists of above an acre of ground, & there are remains of buildings on it, two fossees are drawn from the cliff to the tower to the South, & another head of land to the east of it has been strongly fortifyed as one sees all along the coast, these were only to drive their cattle by night to preserve 'em from men & beasts, & those are call'd Bauns as all places are which are enclosed for keeping Cattle. Mr Crosby's ancestor of Baley heigh[105] maintained himself against the enemy for some time in this fort in king William's time. We went to the hill over Baley heigh, & from that two miles bad road to the Amethurst Cliff which is to the north, just within the mouth of the Shanon, whereas we ought to have continued along the sea cliff, near which I was inform'd there is a curious small old chapel. A wall is built across over the sea cliff & when a company were pursuing these works till within this twelve month there was a door to them was kept lock'd: It is sd that on blowing to loosen the rocks the Amethust became flawy: but whatever is the reason they yeild no price; & the Chrystals sell only for 3^s-6^d. a pound. they are found chiefly in a white Clay between the rocks to the South of this cliff. At the Amethist Cliff the descent is difficult, winding down the Cliff, which is almost perpendicular & leads to a Shelf about six feet broad, the rock below being perpendicular, here the stratum of reddish earth is seen between the rocks, in which they find the Amethysts; in some of yellow earth they find Topazes or rather yellow Chrystals; & so they form Caves to work in; 38 feet below this is another Shelf, to which they descended by a ladder to the bottom of this it is 108 feet frõ the top, & the descent to the sea is computed to be about

40 feet, in all about 150 feet; there are also several strata of sparrs with Chrystals on them but the Chrystals on these are small. Mr. Crosby hearing of us, very politely came & invited us to his house, which was a very seasonable piece of hospitality, the sun being near sett, & tho' call'd but six yet it was ten long miles to Tralee: This Gentlemens Mother Lady Margaret Crosby lives with him, she was the Daughter of Lord Barrymore & Grandaughter of the first Earl of Cork & is 88 years old, enjoying all her senses in great perfection, except her hearing, & goes abroad into all companies. We soon pass'd by Kerry head, wch is made into a Beacen: & we went near the Chrystal rock, & sent for some of the white clay: We saw also the rock not quite separated from the land, against which a ship was drove In the night, & the crew jump'd on this rock, & lay still all night, thinking they were oncompass'd by the see, & when it grew light, found they were on dry land. The next wave broke the ship to pieces, & her Iron Canon lay on the Shoar. There are a great number of Hares here: & in hunting Deer they will leap into the Sea from the Cliffs & perish; sometimes they swim in from the Strand, & one was drove back as they say, three times by Porpusses & come ashore & suffer'd himself to be taken. Near a house built by Sr Thomas Denny we Pass'd by the old Chapel of Macada; & there is a Holy well near it, the Romans pay great devotion to this place. 1800 acres were bounded by these Cliffs, & a wall built across by Mr. Crosby's Father for a Park. Mr. Crosby has begun a large design for a house, in this pleasant summer situation over the north side of the Bay. Trees will grow only under the shelter of the walls; he has above twenty acres enclos'd for gardens & orchards, & the trees planted against one wall being exposed, they grow over the wall, spread, thrive & bear fruit. I am, &c

Mallow
Augt 30th. 1758

Dear Madam,   On the 18th I set out & rid along the Strand; to the north of it is a lake in which they have Eels & trouts. Between it & the bay are sand banks; if the sea should grow on them it would lay a great deal of the Country under water. About the middle of the bay are some rocky Islands of Limestone here, the limestone begins begins [*sic*] & continues toward Castle Island & beyond Tralee near to the mountain, & so as describ'd across the flat country to Castlemain & to the river Lun, & some suppose that the Strata goes along under the mountain near Traley are the famous quarries like the Kilkenny black marble, but most white from large Shells & some veins are beautiful in coraline spots. From the Strand we cross'd to the South east to Ardfert. There is a Strand way all round to Traley & near it a mile beyond Ardfert, is a Spaw which has been much frequented. Ardfert is the see of the Bishoprick of that name, which is united to Limerick; it is call'd also Aldart, that is the Heigth of of Ert, probably the first Bishop of it. St Brandon[106] to whom the Church is dedicated was his

Disciple, & was Abbot of Clonfert: The see of Aghadoe was sometimes held to
it. And Bishop Singe in 1660 had it with Limerick, it is a poor village & so it
has continued: The old Cathedral is in ruins, the front of it is Saxon architecture
with three doors. There are Narrow windows at the east end, & [   ] close
together on the Southside. To the north west of it is a small church entirely Saxon,
& seems to have been the first Cathedral; near that is a Gothick chapel. There is
a high round tower, which does not seems to have been well built, that is not by
a line, & it is much shatter'd by some Settlements at the bottom, & is by no
means good Masonry. In the town is the ruin of a large house which did belong
to the Earl of Kerry. A quarter of a mile to the east of the town, we waited on S^r
Maurice Crosby, since made Lord Branden, who lives on the site of the Abby,
as it is call'd, of Ardfert,[107] which was a Friery founded by the Ancestors of the
Fitzmaurices. The Church a Chapel & part of a handsom small Cloyster & some
other buildings are remaining. The Church is in the same taste as the east end of
the Cathedral. There is an inscription on a pillar of the church, relating to a
Donation, which I shall send you.

Sr Maurice has a fine lawn behind his house & beautifull hedges of Elm &
Lime, of different heigth's to fifty feet like those at Kensington. Three or four
miles to the north East is Abbey O Dorney,[108] call'd also Kyrie Eleison it was
dedicated to the Blessed Virgin; they were Cistercians founded in the year 1154
as some say by the Fitzmaurices. We came three miles to Traley: On the east
side of the bay beyond Ardfurt are great remains of old ruines, & they find a
great quantity of small burnt stones, of which kind also are found in round heaps
in the County of Kilkenny, they are of a Firestone & are supposed to be used in
smelting Ore, as a flux to make it run, for as they did not make shafts but
burroughs, so neither had they furnaces but only small bloomeries.[109] I set out
from Tralley & in half a mile turn'd out of the road to the left & went ½ a mile
to Ballybeggan: Mr Morris's has here a great natural Curiosity, a rivlet rises in
the mountain to the East, & runs under ground at Knockavadra about a mile off,
in Mr Morris's orchard are three caves, down into which one descends & can see
the river running through them, in the meadow west of it, are three more, where
the river also is seen, & in the nearest it forms a pool at the west end without any
visible outlet, but from this it goes to another & then about two miles to Braley
Mullen Catstre & then falls into the river at Tralley; I have been since told, that
it appears two or three times, & goes under again in the way from the last Cave.
These Caves are cover'd with fine Stalactites; & in one I ascended by a ladder
to a Grotto which is most beautiful in those works of nature: In the lowest are
Strata of marble, some of a brownish black with red large Spots of white Spar,
& make most beautiful chimney pieces: some is mark'd with oval spots of white
about an inch long & pretty thick of this Mr Morris has two tables 8^f long & 3^f
& 6^{in} wide. They have gone underground from the entrance above throug a litle
cave except the two lower ones. In Mr Morris his house is a small portico with
a pediment supported by two Corinthian pillars, the whole is most beautifully
form'd with Chrystals of different colours & a very few of the Stalactites are

mix'd with them. We pass'd by some fine plantations of Mr Hasnets & cross'd over a foot of the mountain call'd Sleamish & came to Bush field again near Mill town. From that place we went 9 miles to Killany, leaving the Limestone Country; which they find about Killarney only in patches up & down. I am &c:

Kilwerty
Aug 31ˢᵗ 1758

Dear Madam, The Lake of Kilarney is most beautifull 'tis computed ten miles long 3 broad in some places, in the west end of it are no Islands but about the middle & towards the east end, are several Isles cover'd with wood, & some high rocks interspere'd; & at the South east corner it forms a beautiful bay call'd Glenar; almost the whole length to that bay, it is bounded to the South by a plain mountain call'd Tonerih, this is bounded to the west by a most Romantick rugged glin compar'd to Glenar mountain; the surface of Tonerigh is rather smooth, & the foot of it is adorn'd with wood: the end of Glenar mountain faces to the north & extends along the west side & south end of that bay, it is very uneven in its surface, is divided into several parts by Shallow Glyns or Vales, & is cover'd with wood, on the other side is an Island likewise cover'd with wood, & so is the eastern side, on which stands Muscruss,[110] Mʳ Herberts a most delightful Situation, & on the north Side is Cahername another seat belonging to a Gentlemen of the same name, which is finely diversified by rock & wood near it are Lord Kenmary's house & gardens,[111] & then the Town house of Kilarney, there being low ground to the north, with a rising ground at a litle distance, on which stands the round church of Aghadoe another small Bishoprick united with Limerick, where there are very litle remains of a round tower. But how beautifull soever this lake is, it is exceeded by the upper Lake, & the passage to it, which is by a winding river for about a mile, on each side of which are high rocks, some of them perpendicular, with trees growing out of them, & over an high mountain. The Ecchoes of this place are wonderful; Canon make a report toss'd from one side to the other, like long peals of thunder, the sound of musical instruments is return'd like a concert of a great number of Instruments; & what is beyond all, is the hunting the Stag on the bay of Glenar, in which diversion the Eccho of the huntsmen & the dogs, is something beyond Conception unless it is heard—& the Sport is commonly ended by the Stags taking the water & the hounds following, & he either Swims to an Island or crosses the bay. When you come into the upper lake, which may be about four miles round, you see a number of litle Islands rising high above the water & cover'd with wood, I formerly took an Eagles nest on one of them: & in both Lakes the trees are mostly evergreen, the Holly, the yew & the Arbutus with a veriety,of other trees & particularly the mountain Ash with its red berries, & after rain you see a great variety of waterfalls, but one near the North east corner of the upper Lough is in its beauty as to trees rocks & the division of the waters beuond any thing I ever saw; it soon

J.N. Brewer, Ross Castle, Killarney, 1825

divides into two Streams running down all the way pretty Steep, it then unites & falls down through the Stones, in the whole I believe near 200 feet, beautiful wood, rock & water appearing in every part. The lower lake appears best near from the eminency of Cahernane & between that & the Park, in which situation the different greens of the trees being distinguished adds greatly to its beauty. Ross Island is entirely cover'd with wood, & a causeway is made to it: There is an old Castle[112] in it & a Barrack for a company of foot; & there are very considerable Copper mines, which have brought in great profit, but the vein is grown very small, there are other mines[113] near Mu cruss, & on Cahernane they have found silver ore & a red ocre.[114] Lord Shannons gardens are laid out in Lawn, Gravel walk, parterre & Canal in the middle, which by flood Gates might be carried near a mile to the South west to this Lake & would joyn a rivlet, which was work'd into a kind of Canal by the late Lord, but they found that the lake was much lower than the ground about his Ldships house. It is wonderment to see what the Lord Kenmary has done in about nine years. He has made a walk round the Isle of Innisphalen at a mile distance on the lake & built a house there for company to dine in. He has built a Tower & Steeple to the Church, & a market house, caus'd many roads to be made, & some at his own expence, allotting the profits of a Salmon fishery to public works; he has encouraged tenants to build three or four Streets by giving them long leases; he has variety of boats to attend all Strangers, & what is more extraordinary, he has raised such a town without any manufacture; in a word, he is a pattern for a most noble public Spirit, conducted by an excellent understanding & an unprejudiced judgement. The Park chiefly hanging grounds to the north east is finely wooded, there are beautiful ridings in it, & it commands a charming tho' I think, too distant a view of the Lake. I saw this place ten years ago, a miserable village, & now there are good Inns, Lodgings & accomodations for Strangers who come to see this place, mostly during the month of July & August. Mu cruss is a most charming situation commanding a view of the Lakes & the bay & is a design for [   ] but all is neglected from this one sees Turk mountain, on the side of the passage to the upper lake and Mangerton to the west of it, the highest of all the mountains, in it is a Bason call'd the Devils Punch Bowl, out of which there is a fine Cascade of water after rain that falls down a great way; it is sd. this hill is a thousand yards above the Lake.[115] Near Mucruss is what they call the Abbey of Prialogh,[116] it was a Friary of Minorets dedicated to the Holy Trinity & founded in 1440, by Donald Son of Thady Macarty, within in the walls of the ruin'd Church, there was a remarkable large yew tree, this wood was so common that most of their houses were built of it, & the rooms floored with yew plank. In the Isle of Inisfallon was a Friery founded by St Finian about the middle of the 6th Century, of which I saw some remains. When I was last here, I saw the ruins of the Church of Aghadoe,[117] that Bishoprick is worth but £2 a year, but there is some patronage in the Diocese. We went also to the mouth of the river Lane, by which the Lake empties itself into the harbour of Castlemain. Here we were entertained by O Suliven More who is since dead & the family extinct. I am &c:

Jonathan Fisher, View of the Upper Lake, Killarney, 1789

Jonathan Fisher, View from the park, Killarney, 1789

Callen
Septr 1st 1758

Dear Madam, I Left Killarney on the 22^d & going through the Park went in the fine turn pike road to Cork. I saw up Glanflesk in which the Flesk runs & falls near Shilanney into the Culn. To the west of this Glyn there is an opening near Mongertin & a most romantic rough pyramidical hill appears between this opening. We went on & came near the two mountains call'd the Paps which are very remarkable in the resemblance; we went mostly through a heathy, boggy Country abounding in Grous; we came to five mile water where is a Salmon Leap. We went on & near an Inn call'd Stalaris at a riylet we come into the County of Cork, & were near the Blackwater, which falls into the sea at youghall; after travelling 12 computed & eighteen measur'd miles, we came to a small village call'd Mill Street where there is a barrack for foot: We saw Drishave to the north Mr Wallis's. Going on we come into a very rocky hilly Country between the Blackwater & the river Shillane, on which the Town Macroom stands, some of the rocks appear'd at a distance like towns. We saw Kilmady Castle to the right, & the ruins of another barrack near it. Further on I saw a circle at Glantaur like those at seven burrows in Hampshire: & at Cariginency pass'd by the ruin'd Church of Clondrohid. We then pass'd by Caherhaven the house of Mr Townsend, near which we saw fires made to split the Stones in order to clear the ground of them & make fences, it is a sort of a red Gritt. In two miles we came to Macroom & from this rocky Country were most agreeably surpriz'd to see the fine river Shillan kept up like a Canal under Mr Eyre's gardens, & the populous town on a litle eminence over it, with a large Square & a face of business. It belongs to Mr Eyres & Mr Bernard, & they have a manufacture of Spinning woollen yarn for the blanket Manufacture at Bandon, as well as for making here flannel & also Frieze from 8^d to 2^s-4^d a yard. the Square leads to two or three litle streets which are ill built; the Church is pleasantly situated, over the river as well as the Castle,[118] two large towers of which remain, & between'em is a building in which there is a fine room; the meadows over the river are planted with firr & are most delightfully Situated with a hanging ground to the river: There are about 300 families in this town & fifty of them Protestants. It is 16 miles from Cork, about 12 from Dunmanway & Smalloe.

On the 24th I went on toward Dunmanway & in less than a mile cross'd the river Lee (which falls in at Cork) on a bridge. I saw to the left the Castle Mashaneglas,[119] & Drumcarn to the left, & saw a Bank on the road 2 Stones about seven feet high, which were ancient monuments. We pass'd by a pleasant Situation & improvements of Mr Warrens, & cross'd the river Bounich about nine miles north of Inishan we turn'd to the right & going South west we came in two miles to the village of Castletown & a litle beyond it to the Church of Kineigh, near which is a very singular tower[120] built on a rock; It is hexagon below of ten feet six inches on each side on a plinth nine inches deep & setting out four inches: ten feet six inches from the basement is a window 4^{ft}–8^{in} high, 2^{ft}–4^{in} broad, & the wall is there 4^{ft}–2^{in} thick. The height is not in proportion to the Size of it, being only about 80ft high, over the window are four tiers of Stone in the hexagon & the work is carried up from each angle about three feet so as to end in a point; in different parts there are small windows so as that they seem to have been one window to each Story. Over the Story which is about half a foot below the door; the floor is made with flags a hole being left a cross in the middle, below which I was told it is hexagon within, & above it is round. The whole is very fine masonry & a stone projects round at top, but the point is faln down. The church, excepting the Chancel, seems to have been of the same time; there is a Singular door to it 3^{ft}–3^{in} broad at bottom 2^{ft}–7^{in} at top & 5^{ft}–11^{in} high. There is a large Stone over it & another over that, & the Gudgeons in which the door turn'd remain with a quarter circle for the door to turn in, There is a large Stone likewise over the door within, in which the upper gudgion is practic'd. From the round tower there seems to have been two fences drawn, as of a fortification for the enclosure of the churchyard. This Church is said to be dedicated to three saints, of which Keneigh was the principal, there is a Holy Well near; they have no pattern day, but the women & Children come to the church every Saturday. This place is not only encompass'd with an Amphitheatre of rock, but the bottom also full of [   ] & furze growing out of them, it forms a very romantic & uncommon appearance. I came on to the fine road from Iniskeen to Dumanoway at [   ] Mr Connors & pass'd over a small stream on a bridge, which runs into the Bandon river very near. I am &c:

Septr 2^d. 1758

Dear Madam,   Sr Richard Cox's house at Dunmanway situated to the north of two rivlets, which joyn a litle below it & form the Bandon river, the stream to the South being call'd the Bandon river to its source. Sr Richard Cox's house is to the east of the town & is ornamented with large plantations up the hill behind the house: & at some distance in the front is a fine piece of water, which through a Visto appears like a river. The town consists of one Street of small houses[121] built for weavers by Sr Richard, & of a return to the bridge over the river, which leads to a Green beautifully planted, on each side of which are the houses of Labourers & others; & a quarter of a mile to the east, a bleach yard. This Manufacture was begun in the year 1746,[122] & now there are about 60 Looms constantly employ'd, & spinning goes on sufficient for them, which with ['at' *inserted above line*] ten wheels to a loom is 600 wheels; it is a most agreable Sight to see Children employ'd in reeling even from four years old & such a general face of industry. Wheels are distributed to them, & they pass bonds to produce 'em once a year in repair, & if they do not they are taken away from them. But Sr Richard Cox has writ a treatise concerning the management of this

Manufacture; which has been reprinted at Boston in New England & translated into Italian & publish'd in Italy: & he is about to print a new Edition of it with several further remarks. The country near this place is well cultivated & bounded to the north & west by fine rocks; & there are low mountains at some distance to the west. We went three miles east to see the Castle of Balliacarig,[123] which tho' it belong'd to the Hurleys, yet I saw these figures & letters in the North window 1585 R.M.C C. It is one of the finest Castles I have seen, is situated on a rocky hill over a rivlet, which about half a furlong off comes out of a litle Lough & forms a beautiful Cascade just under the Castle. The entrance to it is defended by a wall & two round Towers which encompass a small Court. It consists of a long room of 32^{ft} by 24 & a narrow apartment at the end, which in most of the stories is divided into two; there was an Arch over the 2^{d} floor, which is now broken down, this was probably the apartment of the great man, as the servants might live below. The State room was over this, in which there are two windows of very good workmanship, being arch'd over & the whole [   ] off & adorn'd with Sculpture, in one are the Instruments of our Saviours Sufferings on one side & the Salutation on the other, in the opposite window is the Crucifixion with the Virgin Mary & St John very rude figures; the other parts are adorn'd with trees & other ornamental Sculpture; the room at the end of this was the Kitchen, in which there is an Oven. There are Stone seats at the end & on part of one side, to which without doubt their long tables were plac'd. There is also a passage practiced in the north side to the 2^{d} floor, wch led to a water closet. The Coins of the building are excellent workmanship, it appears to have been roof'd at top. On the east side of the entrance there is an extraordinary figure with short legs & the hands fix'd on the thighs, & is very like the German God Puiterus, a figure which I saw abroad & have engrav'd in a treatise of it. This might be a figure proserv'd in the family from the time of Paganism & brought here out of some old Superstition. I went also to Iniskeen, which is a good village; & a mile beyond it to Palace Anne,[124] which belongs to the descendants of a brother of Judge Bernards. It is a showy house, & there are great plantations, much money haying been laid out on the whole. I went to see the Charity School at Dunmanway, which is very well regulated, & there are large convenient buildings for forty boys & girls, with an Infirmary. They have a quarry of Slates here, in which they have found a Copper Mundik, & on Mr Fenwicks estate near, there are also Slate Quarries. They have no limestone nearer than Dr Barrys estate between the Lee & the Toon about 2 miles from Macroom & ten miles from this place. To the north of Sr Richard Cox's house about a mile, are perpendicular rocks at the side of a hill & under those rocks is a yew tree about 15 feet in circumference. From this hill over this there is a fine view of the Country, & in fair weather they have a prospect of the sea beyond Clonekilty: A Wall is carrying along on the east side by the Bandon river is to enclose this hill, which with the lands below is to be form'd into a Park & Demesne.

Kilkenny
Septr. 4th 1758

Dear Madam,   I left Dunmanway on the 29th & a litle beyond Iniskeen turn'd
to the north, & came to the place where we turn'd out of the Iniskeen road to go
to Kineigh & we turn'd to the North east in the road towards Iniscarra, &
descending went over a long hill came in sight of the valley in which the river
Bride runsfalls into the Sea. When we came in to this valley we came on the
Limestone vein, which is known by the name of Kilcrea marble being grey &
which it begins about a mile above, which we saw on the Bride above Castle
more & near Kilcrea Castle:[125] we came to Lodge, Mr Orpins to whom I paid a
visit & he set out with me. The freestone vein was along to the South of the Bride
till it falls into the Lee, & then continues along the Lee to Cork for about 400
yards in breadth, as I was Inform'd. We saw the Abbey of Kilcrea,[126] in which
there is a Tower built to the Church on arches, & the several buildings round the
Site of the old Cloyster, which is destroy'd. We came to the parish call'd the
Ovens, where they have lately built a tower to the Church, which they are doing
in other parishes in the neighbourhood, particularly at Iniscara. There is a fine
quarry of marble near the Church & from it you go into those caves, call'd the
ovens, they are low mostly with a sort of natural arch in the middle in this
Shape ⋀ from which probably works of nature in other places this kind of
Gothic arch was taken; in several places just under the middle of the arch one
can walk upright. There is a thick coat of the Stalactites kind form'd over the
rock & some few that are pendent, one passage they affirm goes to the church,
but without an outlet, another they say goes to Carigrohan Church two miles
off, a fine situation towards Cork on the Lee, & there are several other short
passages. I dined here & cross'd the Bride & then the Lee on a Bridge near
Iniscarra where my friend Dr Philips lives who was not at home. Iniscarra is to
the north of the Lee; in a Romantic Glyn or short vale, with high ground on each
side cover'd with wood being open to the south. The Parsonage house & Glebe
is the prettiest Hermitage I ever saw, & near it to the south is the Church, with
an handsome tower crown'd with a Cupola. We ascended to the north & coming
into the Turn pike road from Cork to Macroom, & from it went through the fields
& woods to Castle Blarney,[127] which is a fine old Castle with projections,
battlements to annoy the enemy, it is situated over the Arbeg, & there are large
buildings added to it; near it tho' not seen from the road, is a small Lake which
they say is very beautiful; here is a patch of Limestone. This Castle did belong
to the Earle of Clankarty, who forfeited it by following King J. It is but 3 miles
from Cork. We went on 3 miles further & lay at Mr Williamsons. We cross'd
the Country & came into the high road from Cork to Mallow; two miles from
the latter at Ballenemona, where to the left is a house & fine improvement of S^r
Robert Dean's. A litle beyond it are ruins on each side of the road, a Preceptory
of the Knights of St John Baptist of Jerusalem, call'd Morne, Mora or Balle ne
mony, founded & endow'd founded or endow'd [*sic*] by Alexander of St Helens.

W.H. Bartlett, St Canice, Kilkenny, 1842

On a large building, which did not seem to be a church, & on the other side are other ruins of no great consequence. I came in two miles to Mallow where the Canal in the way to the Hot Well has been improv'd, as well as the walk on each side; & above the well is a grotto form'd of large Stones in which the Campany may sit. This water is of the nature is of the nature of the Bristol Hot well & is much esteem'd. I went from Mallow directly to Kilworth, a road I had never gone before, 12 computed & I suppose 18 measur'd miles; about half way we came to Castle Rochl over the Awbegg, which flows if I mistake not on three Sides of it, 'tis situated on a hanging,[128] & is a large enclosure, two or three walls being built across within: It belongs to Lord Roches family who were attainted in the rebellion in 1641. They are now in the King of Sardinia's service, & Lord Roche was Governor of the Castle of Milan if I mistake not, when I pass'd through that place in 1734. The River Awbeg rises towards Charetvila, Boutevant & Done rail are on it & it falls into the Blackwater a litle below Castle roch. This river is call'd by Spenser the Medea, & about two miles north west of Donerail that Poet liv'd in a Castle on the fine Lake of Kil colemen.[129] We afterward pass'd the Funcheon, which rises in the hills near Mitchels town & runs not far from that Town; Glanworth or Glanore stands on it, which I saw coming from that town, where there is a large Castle which belong'd to the Roches, where they founded a Dominican Convent.

We came to Kilworth & on the 31st went on in the Dublin road from Cork over Kilworth mountain & saw Mitchels town in the vale to the North west coming into the county of Tiperary through Baliporen & Cloheen & to Ardfinnan

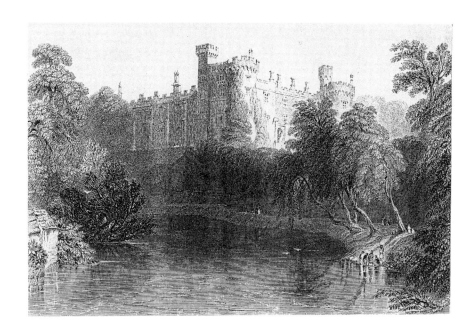

W.H. Bartlett, Kilkenny Castle, 1842

on the Sure, where there is fine hanging on both sides of the river, the rocks to the South being very beautifull. To the north is the Old Castle of Ardfinnen, belonging to the See of Lismore, two towers remain & the walls of the grand Hall. We went through this beautifull Country, & saw to the South [   ] the late Mr Hutchinsons which forms a fine Landskip & so does Marlfield,[130] the Abbey Clonmell & all the vale to Carrick.

On the first of September we went on & cross'd over the foot of Sleaneman near Kilkash; the sides of this hill are of late greatly improv'd. At the ruin'd Church of Grampmoder there is a fine Gothick door case & to the east of the Church a hollow Ash tree which measures at bottom about twelve feet in diameter & higher up eight. I descended the hill to the east into the County of Kilkenny, which as I take it is bounded by the top of the hill we came down, for at the top of it is the first parish Church this way in the Diocese of Ossory, that of Killanny dedicated to St Nicholas, where there is also a Saxon door case. This Parish belongs to a Prebend of the Cathedral of [   ] in Kilkenny. At Callan I saw an ancient Square Mount, which had been encompassed with a wall & is call'd the Castle.[131] From this place I arriv'd at Kilkeny having been absent eight weeks within three days. I am &c:

Tour the fifth: Dublin to Donaghadee, 1760

Pococke set out on 23 April from Dublin and reached Donaghadee on 29 April after a leisurely journey through Newry, Banbridge, Hillsborough, Castlereagh and Comber.

The text is taken from the copy of Pococke's journal of his 1760 Scottish tour kept in the British Library. Dr C.J. Woods edited this Irish section of the Scottish tour in the Ulster Journal of Archaeology *in 1985, 1 have adopted some of Dr Woods's notes, but whereas he modernized some spellings, capitalization and punctuation marks I have kept to the style of the eighteenth-century copyist. Textually significant differences between Dr Woods's reading of the tour and mine are listed in the notes.*

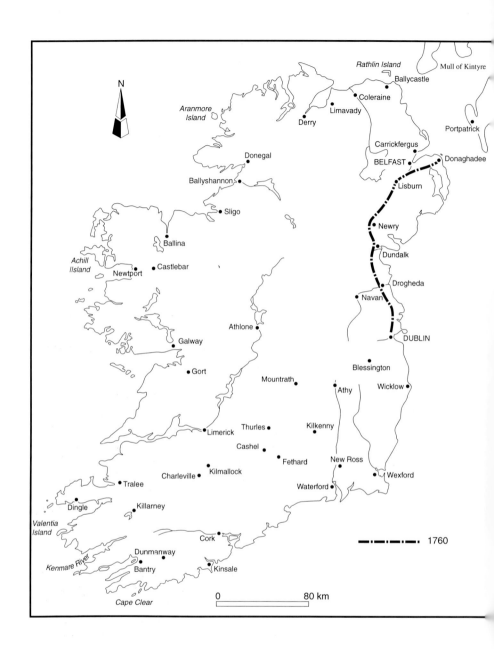

Map of the 1760 tour

A Journey
Round Scotland
To The Orkneys
and
Through Part of England and Ireland
By Dr Richard Pococke Lord Bishop of Ossory
Volume The First

Port Patrick in Scotland
April 30th 1760[1]

Dear Madam, On the 23[d] of April I left Dublin for Donaghadee to Embark for Scotland:[2] On the 25th we Crossed the Mountains, which Extend to the west from Carling ford: As well as I cou'd observe, the Mountain Stone which is a granite begins from a stream to the North of Dundalk and Extends beyond Newry to Bannon Bridge;[3] further to the North there is a Coarse fire Stone, and about Lisburn a red fire Stone; the land on the County of Down Side having a great Mixture of red Sand in it.

Newry is situated between the hills and Mountains (something like Inspruck in the Tirol) upon the river Newry, which is Made navigable from the Collieries; but by Some Mismanagement the Collieries doe not Succeed. It is a town well built, the Houses Mostly fronted[4] with the rough Mountain Stone, & Some of them with their hewn Stone; the Streets are well paved, and there is a great face of Business in Manufacturing linnen, in a Salt & Sugar House, & a Pottery of Coarse Ware, besides a considerable import: they have a large Custom house, and near it are Ware Houses for goods imported; & above at the Navigable Canal are Store houses for the Export.

On the the [*sic*] 26th we Went Eight miles to Lough bricken, a Small town on a lake which abounds in Pike eels and Roch;[5] two Miles further brought us to Bannon Bridge a very Small New town[6] with a fine inn built by the Hilsborough family: Here are two bleach yards.[7] Seven miles more brought us to Drommore, a poor market town, where the Cathedral is like a parish Church, but the Bishop lives three miles from it at Marling, and is happy in his Situation, for he can dine in Any part of his Diocese and return home in the Evening.

Three miles further we came to Hilsborough, a Village very pleasantly Situated over a lake, in which there are two or three Islands, beautifully improved by Lord Hilsborough, who has a large House not well Situated to the Lake, & he is therefore making all his improvements for building a new house in a better

Situation, & proposes to Sell his old house to the Bishop of Down for the use of the See. This nobleman has likewise planted Clumps of trees on all the Eminences in which this Country abounds, the County[8] being in general Hilly so these platations have a very fine Effect. They have great Scarcity in this Country of good Springs, the Loughs & rivulets being mostly Supplied from Boggs: There is a Slight fortress here, built by an Ancestor of the Hillsbro' family for a Barrack, with a handsome Gothick Building in the middle.

I Came in three miles to Lisburn a very neat, well built town on the ridge of a rising ground which falls beautifully down to the fine river Laggan on One Side, & to a sweet Vale on the Other; the houses are built of Brick: they have a handsome Church and Market house, & drive a great linnen trade, there being several Bleach yards all over the Country. The trade of raising flax and spiñing &c is Carried on by all the farmers in the Country: The Merchants buy the green cloath, & give it to be bleach'd, and send it to Chester & London Markets: This place is near Equally Distant from Belfast & Lurgan, both of them great Linnen towns, that is about 7 miles. Three Miles from it is Moira a fine Situation on the Side of the Hills, the Seat of Lord Rawdon.[9] Ld. Hertford is the Proprietor of Lisburn & has an Estate in this Country, as I was told, of £12,000 a year and had formerly a Castle here but it is destroyed.

On the 28th I went on towards Donaghadee: Crossing the river, in a mile I passed by an Old Inclosure called Hillhall,[10] w[ch.] was the Ancient Seat of the Hills, who now Enjoy the Title[11] of Hilsborough. I then passed by a house finely Situated of Arthur Hill, Esqr. brother to the late Lord Hilsborough, who has now assumed the Name of Trevor, & leaving the road to Belfast, I came by Castle Reagh, & afterwards by Comber, a small Village & Seat of one of the Name of Bayley, Situated near a bay of the sea called the Lough of Strangford; and in three Miles More to Newtown at the End of this bay; To the West of it is a fine high rocky hill, which produces good freestone, now they have got deep into the Quarry; tho it was not so good or not dug at a proper time when the Stone was raised out of it for the College Library. I passed through this place in my tour round Ireland in 1752, It belongs to Mr. Stewart, who has made a fine Collection of pictures in Dublin.

I passed by a Colliery[12] near to Donaghadee, which is 7 Miles from Newton and is a poor fishing town Chiefly Supported by this business, & the packett Boats; and lately, by an Export of Horses and black Cattle to Scotland: The Pier was built & put in repair by the Mount Alexander family w[ch.] is now Extinct, and the Estate is in the Widow of the last Lord, the Tenure the Estate being[13] to keep the Pier in repair. Here I embarked on the 29th. for Port Patrick, I am &c

Appendix: Two Accounts of the Giant's Causeway

Reprinted here for the first time are Pococke's two descriptions of his visits to the Giant's Causeway, first published in Philosophical Transactions.

An Account of the Giant's Causeway in Ireland, *in a letter to the* President *from the Rev. Richard Pocooke, LL.D. Archdeacon of Dublin, & F.R.S.*

Dublin, 5 Jan. 1747-9

Read Jan. 28 1747, In my past Passage over to this Kingdom, I saw that very remarkable Curiosity, commonly called the Giants Causeway: the Sea-Cliffs are very high thereabouts, and what is called the Causeway is a low Head, extending from the Foot of the Cliffs into the sea like a Mole. This Head does not appear at first so grand as it is represented in the Views engraved of it; but when one comes to walk upon it, and consider it more attentively, it appears to be a stupendous Production of Nature. The Head ends in two Points: I measured the more Western to the Distance of 360 Feet from the Cliff, and it appeared to me to extend about 60 Feet further; but this part I could not measure, by reason that the Sea was then high, and I was told, that at low Tides it might be seen about 60 Feet yet further upon a Descent losing itself in the Sea. I also measur'd the more Eastern Point 540 Feet from the Cliff, and saw about as much more of it as of the other, where it winds about to the Eastward, and is also lost in the Water. One may walk upon this Head on the tops of the Pillars to the Edge of the Water. These Pillars are of all angular Shapes from three Sides to eight. The Eastern Point, towards that End where it joins the Rocks, terminates it self for some Way in a perpendicular Cliff, formed by the upright Sides of the Pillars, some of which I measured, and found to be 33 Feet and 4 Inches in Height. They say there are in all 74 different Sorts of Figures among them. Each Pillar consists of several Joints or Stones lying one upon another, from 6 Inches to about a Foot in Thickness: Some of these Joints are in the middle so convex, as for those Prominences to be nearly Quarters of Spheres, round each of which is a Ledge, upon which the Stones above them have rested, every Stone being concave on the under Side, and sitting in the exactest manner upon that which lies next below it. The Pillars are from one to two Feet in Diameter, and consist most commonly of about 40 Joints, most of which separate very easily, tho' some others, which are more strongly indented into each other, cohere strongly enough to bear the being taken away in Pairs.

But the Causeway is not I think the most singular Part of this extraordinary Curiosity; the Appearance of the Cliffs themselves being yet to me more surprising; these and their several Strata I examined from the Rocks on the other Side of a little Bay, about half a Mile to the East of the Causeway. I thence observed, that there runs all the Way a *Stratum* from the Bottom of black Stone, to the Height, as well as I could conjecture, of about 60 Feet, divided perpendicularly at unequal Distances by Stripes of a reddish Stone, looking like Cement, and about 4 or 5 Inches in Thickness. Upon this there is another *Stratum* of the some black Stone divided from it by a *Stratum* 5 Inches thick of the red. Over this another *Stratum* of Stone ten Feet thick divided in the same manner; then a *Stratum* of the red Stone twenty Feet deep; and above that a *Stratum* of upright Pillars. Above these Pillars lies another *Stratum of* black Stone 20 Feet high; and above this is again another *stratum* of upright Pillars rising in some Places to the Top of the Cliffs, in others not so high, and in others again above it, where they are called the Chimneys.

This Face of the Cliffs reaches for two computed Miles East from the Causeway, that is about 3 measured *English* miles, to the House of Mr. *John Stewart* two Miles West of *Balintoy.* The upper Pillars seem to end over the Causeway, and, if I mistake not, become shorter and shorter as one goes from it, lying between two Binds of Stone like Seams of Coal, and like those little Pillars found in *Derbyshire.*

These Binds probably meet together all round, and inclose this extraordinary Work of Nature, and if so, the Pillars must be very short towards the Extremities.

I was led to this Conjecture by the following Observations: The lower *Stratum* of Pillars is that which goes by a Descent into the Sea, and which makes what is called the Giants Causeway; and where this Descent approaches the Sea, it seems probable that the Pillars become shorter and shorter, so as to end not much further off. Now the upper Bind of this *Stratum* may have been of so soft a Nature, as by degrees, in Process of Time, to have been washed away by the Sea. And in the Cliff over the Causeway I saw several Pillars lying along in a rude manner almost horizontally, which seemed to me to be some of the Pillars of the upper *Stratum* fallen down by the giving way of the Bind which was under them, and over the lower ones that compose the Causeway. And here most probably the upper Pillars ended, as they are seen no farther in the Cliff. I saw the Tops of Pillars even with the Shore, both on the East and West Sides of the Causeway, and some much lower than the Causeway itself, and it is probable that these are much shorter than those of the Causeway, which I measured above thirty Feet higher than the Tops of them.

When I was upon the Causeway, I saw in the Cliff, to the South-east, what they call the Organs, about a Quarter of a Mile off, and a third part of the Way up the Cliff. They appeared small, and somewhat like a black *Stalactites*: They were not commonly known to be such Pillars as the others; but they are so, and belong to the lower *Stratum.* When with great Difficulty I climbed up the steep Hill to them, I found they were hexagonal, and larger Pillars than most of the others, being about 2 Feet in Diameter; and I measured 5 Sides of one of them, which were of 13, 15, 12, 21 , and 16 Inches respectively. The Joints I could come at were about 9 Inches thick, and each Pillar, as well as I could count, consisted of between 40 or 50 of them: These Joynts are almost flat and plain, the Convexities on their upper faces being so small as to be scarce discernible. I enquired whether any of these Pillars were found in the Quarries within Land, and the People there told me they were not, but since I left the Place, I have been assured by others, that there are some found two or three Miles from the Shore. I am, with the greatest Regard, Sir, *Your most obedient humble Servant,*

Richard Pococke

A Farther Account of the Giant's Causeway *in the county of* Antrim *in* Ireland, *by the Rev.* Richard Pococke, *LL.D. Archdeacon of* Dublin, *and F.R.S.*

Read May 24, 1753. In a letter, which I wrote In 1747 to Martin Folkes, Esq, President of the Royal Society, which was read in January, and printed in the *Philosophical Transactions* for that month, I observed, in relation to the Giant's Causeway, that there appeared in the Sea-cliffs three strata of pillars between thirty and forty feet high, with strata of a black rock between them; that the causeway itself was the lowest of all these, extending in a point into the sea; and that another is seen towards the top of the cliff.

Last summer I took another view of it; I went from Bally-Castle, which is about 10 miles to the east of the Causeway. When I came two miles to the west of Bally-Castle, within less than a mile of Ballintoy, half a mile to the south of the see-cliffs, and about a quarter to the south of the road, I saw the same kind of pillars in a low hill; I observed both hexagons and pentagons.

The rocks towards the sea appeared as if they were formed in the same manner; but when I came to them, I found it was only common rock in several strata, and perpendicular joints.

I went on about two miles to a peninsula called Donseverik, where I saw some tendency in the rock towards this work of nature; and going about half a mile farther, came to the beginning of the pillars in the sea-cliff, as I believe, about five miles from the causeway: and the shore and cliffs being shap'd mostly in little semicircular bays, I had many very beautiful views of the upper and middle strata of pillars: in one, particularly, they had much of the appearance of ruin'd portico's one over the other; and turning the little end of a spy-glass, it appeared something like the ruins of Palmyra, as a view of them is represented in a copper plate, published in the *Philosophical Transactions.*

This wonderful work of nature is continued on in the cliffs for about a quarter of a mile beyond the Giant's Causeway.

I saw it again in the road to Coleraine, five miles to the west of the Causeway, in a low hill a furlong to the south of the road, and two miles to the south of the sea. The pillars here are small; and being about a mile and a half from Ballimagarry, where the earl of Antrim has a ruin'd house, lately burnt down, it serv'd, as I suppose, as a quarry for building part of that house, in which I saw a great number of the stones, and particularly one of nine sides. I saw others near two miles farther, to the south of the road in a low hill, within two miles of

Coleraine; so that the whole extends for about eleven Irish miles, or fourteen English.

Beyond Coleraine, to the east of Magilligan, I saw in the rocks towards the sea-cliffs, the stones in the rocks towards the sea-cliffs, the stones in the [*sic*] hills very regular, appearing at a distance much like these pillars. This is six computed miles beyond Coleraine, and consequently about ten English miles from the last pillars.

At Fairhead also, a high point of land, three miles to the east of Ballycastle, towards the top of it, the rock appears as in grand pillars. They say it is not in joints, but it has something of the appearance of a grand Gothic piece of workmanship.

As I spent a week at the Causeway, and sent away by sea to Dublin as great a variety of the stones as I could conveniently get, particularly a large octagon, with the eight large stones round it; a pair of less, with eight pair, that encompass it; two small pentagon pillars, about fourteen inches over, one of them three feet ten inches and a half high, the other five feet seven inches; one hexagon pillar, about the same size, and five feet five inches high; all which I have placed in my garden; so I have had an opportunity of considering it at leisure.

It is a black stone, weighty and brittle: and I have been informed, that it was tried in a glass-house, and that it melted with kelp, so as to make the black glass bottles; which experiment, I have been told, was made by Mr. Dobbs of this kingdom, who is now in London.

Mr. Drury, whom I shall have occasion to mention, found in a stone of the Causeway a rough pebble in the shape of an egg, about three quarters of an inch long, and above an inch thick; and when it was polish'd, it proved to be a white cornelian. They are from three sides to nine sides, frequently encompassed with as many stones as there are sides, but many of them have a narrow side, which has no stone to it, but is filled up with a piece or pieces of stone, that shall be further explained; which pieces, when the stones are mov'd, commonly separate, and break off. Some stones have two, or three, or more, of these sides: so that it is possible, a stone, that has any number of stones round it, may have double the number of sides: tho' I saw none, that I had reason to think were of this kind, except some, that had probably only three stones round them; being hexagons, with three broad sides, and three very narrow sides.

Whatever the outward figure of the stone is, the concavity or convexity is either circular, or part of a circle; consequently, as the sides of the pillars are plain, the part between the inside circle and the outward figure must either be fill'd up (as it is seen) by stone, which sometimes separates, as mention'd above, and as will be further explain'd, or by the matter pressed up from the sides, as will be more plainly described. In the former case, when the end is convex, this stone often comes off all round at the joint, and leaves the convex end as part of a sphere, and the concave as a mould fitting to it.

I have some stones exactly like a hexagon cut in two, which might be part of a hexagon pillar split; for sometimes a whole pillar appears as split all the way down; of which there is a remarkable one at the Causeway.

In relation to the joints in the pillars, this work of nature seems to be different from any thing yet known: and it must be very difficult to assign any satisfactory causes of it.

I submit to the judgement of persons more experienced in these things what has occurred to me.

I suppose, for reasons, which I shall give, that the several parts of these pillars were at first formed either in the shape of a cylinder, with the upper end in a spherical figure, if not both ends; or that they were either spherical or oblate spheroids.

For, being composed of crystal of six sides, and spar of three, and of a very fine black sand, it may be supposed, that, as the crystals and spars united, and formed an irregular body, the fine black sand fill'd up the interstices, and formed such cylindrical or spherical bodies, as yet soft; but, in thin horizontal laminae or plates like talc, as they mostly appear to be; and, if great force is applied, the stones will separate in such plates between the joints, and those parts of the pillars, which have been exposed to the weather, and corroded by it, appear in such plates. Sometimes indeed there are perpendicular joints; as in the split pillar, there seems to have been such a one all down the pillar.

It is therefore probable, that, when this matter was in a fluid state, and when the stratum of rock was formed, on which it was made, the fluid contiguous to the rock still continued in motion; that, after a time, some of the particles of matter, which compose these pillars, being disengaged from the particles of water, ceas'd to move, and form'd the parts of these pillars, which are next to the rock, in the above-mention'd figures; so much being formed only at once, or in a very short time, as extends to the first joint: that then, either by change of season, or some other accident, so much more water mixed with these particles, as prevented their continuing to form themselves into such a shape, and gave the former motion: that, afterwards, the decrease of the water might again be the cause of the former effect; and so on, till the intire pillars were formed; and the top of the last formed being convex, that, which was formed upon it, would probably be concave, and sit to it, either by its gravity, or by being softer.

All being as yet in some one or other of these figures, we suppose the gravitation of the second stratum above the first joint to operate in such a manner on that which was first formed, and still soft, as to press it down, and so eight stones being round one stone, would naturally press the middle stone into an octagon.

The reason for concluding, that they were at first in some of these figures, are these: That the concavity or convexity are either in an intire circle, or part of a circle: That sometimes the ends of the stones appear to be of a spherical form for some space down, all round the stone, fill'd up only by a matter, that separates from it, as shall be further explain'd.

For it is to be observed, that the pillar is not always so press'd out, as in each stone to form a regular multangular figure; but sometimes there is a narrow side, against which there is no stone, as observed before: sometimes it is pressed out only in part; and this, together with the spherical part, is fill'd up, probably at first with the floating matter; which, I suppose, when the other stone was formed upon it, so united with it, that it remains as a part of the other stone, and breaks off from it, when they are moved: and if this happened to the lower part of the upper stone, this matter, which fills up, might unite with the lower stone; for sometimes this narrow side is seen in the same stone both above and below, the angle being formed in the middle of the stome; and then it is filled up with the matter, which united with the stone above, and the stone below.

It is to be observed, in pursuance of the proof, that the stones were originally round and spherical at the ends; that when the pressure was not sufficient to make out the angles, which I suppose to be the cause of these narrow sides, it is in this case plainly seen, that the original circular shape of the stone is still retain'd; that the silt not being horizontally in a strait line, but appearing plainly to be part of a circle; as may be seen in the three pieces of stone, which I have sent, that separated from those sides, and fitted into them.

I [sic] appears also, that what has been press'd out beyond the circle at the ends is commonly flat, and not concave and convex; as it was probably made; not by the pressure at the ends on the spherical part, but by the pressure on the sides contiguous to it; and when part of the circle is taken off, in that case it is probable, that the pressure on the sides was very great.

In one stone, the matter, which only in part form'd the angle, force being applied to it, came off, and left that part spherical, being one of those stones, in which one part of the same end is flat, and the other convex, swelling like a cushion.

This stone I sent as a single stone. It is a large octagon, twenty three inches over, but after it had been some time in my garden, I perceived a crack in it, and, applying force, it divided. The under stone had been so unequally press'd, that it is not only very thin on one side, but there is a large hole in it, about seven inches diameter, very near the edge of the stone; so that the matter must have been press'd away to the other side of the stone, not equally concave, and the stone above it must have press'd into the stone below this; in which lower stone the convex part, which press'd through the middle stone, must have been left, as it is broken: which I did not observe at the Causeway.

Some stones at the same end are partly concave, and partly convex; probably occasioned by such an unequal pressure; so that I have one, which measures nine inches deep on one side, which is convex, and four and a half on the other, which is concave: another, tho' all convex, yet is six inches clear at one angle, and only four at the opposite angle; so that in these stones the joint appears as indented.

We are to suppose, that, generally, the top of the lower stones is convex, and the bottom, consequently, of the stone, that lies upon it, concave. But as sometimes both ends of a stone are concave, we must suppose, either that the lower part of the stone, which settled on it, was harder, or, being of equal hardness, by its gravitation press'd it down.

Since I left the Causeway, I have been inform'd, that commonly, if the top of the stone in a pillar is found either concave or convex, the top likewise of every stone of that pillar is either concave or convex in the same manner; which may be a subject for future observation.

It seems probable, therefore, that all the ends were originally spherical: some of the stones, it may be exact spheres; others, oblate spheroids; and some longer stones in a cylindrical form, and of a spherical figure, at each end. To which conjecture I have been led, by observing the shape of some I have, and of two models of two stones represented in cork by Mr. Drury, who presented the prospects of the Causeway engraved to the Royal Society, from the drawings of his sister Mrs. Susanna Drury. One of these is convex at both ends; and I have some in the same shape. This sperical figure has been altered by the pressure, in the manner I have observed; for, in the other model, part of the spherical figure is seen round the sides towards the concave end; and I have one exactly of the some kind. In those also, which I have, that are at the some time partly convex and partly concave, the convex part seems to have been the natural figure of the stone, as before described: for, where both ends are concave, that, which was probably press'd by a harder stone form'd before it, is concave, whereas that concavity, which is made by a stone probably form'd after it, is not so perfectly concave as the other; but it commonly remains convex in some part, as observed before; swelling out like a cushion press'd by any weight.

By all that I have been able to observe, the plates seem originally to have been horizontal: in some I have, which are convex, they are apparently so, and, as far as I could remark, in all, where the plates appear. Tho' it is probable, where the end of the stone is concave, the laminae or plates have in some measure been press'd in that form; tho' I could not certainly distinguish it in any of this kind.

Sometimes a joint near perpendicular begins as in a point from the side, and extends into that stone, and into all the stones of the pillar, which are beneath it; so as (when it has run the length of one stone) to take off either two sides of the stones or pillar, or one side, and part of two sides. This indeed sometimes happens to be in the middle of the pillar, and in the same manner all the way down, so as to form two distinct pillars. Thus I have some, which, by this means, have a side less at one end than at the other; and I have one, in which the spherical part takes off at one end two sides of the multangular figure, and makes part of a circle, as in some it takes off all the sides at one end; or, more properly, the stone remains in its original spherical figure. The pieces, which fill up where the stone is not press'd into a multangular figure, sometimes do not break off, as may be seen in the model.

Of the other models made by Mr. Drury, four of them fit to one another, and represent part of a pillar in the Causeway: The seven models not referr'd to, shew a variety of stones; the measures of all of them are marked in inches, and they are made by a scale of a tenth to an inch. The ends, which are cut smooth in the cork, or are marked with a pencil, are such, as he could not see, or neglected to observe.

The fourth stone I have sent, which forms part of a circle, broke off from a stone flat at one end, is the spherical part of a stone, such as it appears towards the concave end of one already mention'd.

From these observations, those, who are well versed in natural philosophy, may possibly form some better judgement, and be more happy in their conjectures in relation to this difficult subject, the cause of the joints in the pillars of this extraordinary work of nature.

Tab. X

Represents the plan and profile of the stones brought to Dublin by the Rev. Archdeacon Pococke.

Explanation of the Figures

Fig. 1. A plan of the pillar, with the measures of the lengths of the sides, A, B, C, D.

Fig. 2. A plan of the pillar, with the lengths of the other four sides, viz. E, F, G, H, and the distances of the circle from the sides of the polygon.

Fig. 3. A profile of the stone, shewing the sides A, B, C, D.

Fig. 4. A profile shewing the sides E, F, G, H.

The black lines shew the deviation of the circles from a plane: and the large prick'd waved lines shew the profile of the swelling and concavity within them.

The upper row of figures in each stone shews the heights of the sides at the angles so far as they are strait.

The under row of figures shews the remainder of the height of the stone at that angle, or it is the height of the angular curved pieces, which, before they fall off, were the complements filling up the prism, and making the sides of the pillar wholly flat, and the edges or angles of the pillar all strait lines.

Fig. 5. Two upper stones of a pillar, as they stood on the Causeway, shewing 4 sides of the pillar.

Diameter of the upper circle of the upper stone 22 inches.

The circle is about half an inch within the polygon at the side D, but is cut off by the side C about three quarters of an inch.

The sides B and b a little broken.

Fig. 6. The two stones turned together upside-down; shewing the other four sides of the pillar.

Diameter of the (now) uppermost circle about twenty-one inches.

The side H much broken. Angle f, rounded off from the circle to the (now) lower end of the stone. Angle G is not rounded off.

Fig. 7. The two stones separated a little to shew the bottom of the upper stone, and top of the under one.

Diameter of the circles, which meet twenty-two inches.

The convex part of the bottom of the upper stone fitting the concave part of the top of the under one; and the concave part of the bottom of the upper stone fitting the convex part of the top of the under stone.

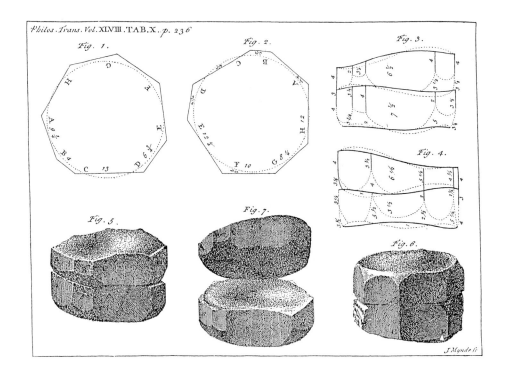

Philos. Trans. Vol. XLVIII. TAB. X. p. 236
Fig. 1.
Fig. 2.
Fig. 3.
Fig. 4.
Fig. 5.
Fig. 6.
Fig. 7.
J. Mynde sc.

Richard Pococke, sketch of stones at the Giant's Causeway, 1753

Notes

Introduction

1 Michael Quane, 'Pococke School, Kilkenny', *Journal of the Royal Society of Antiquaries of Ireland* 80 (1950), pp. 36–72 (p. 36). See also Daniel William Kemp's biographical introduction to *Tours in Scotland, 1747, 1750, 1760, by Richard Pococke* (Edinburgh: Publications of the Scottish History Society, Vol. I, 1887), pp. xxxi–lxx.

2 Quane, 'Pococke School', p. 42.

3 Quane quotes Gibbon's view of the 'superior learning and dignity' of Pococke's account of the countries of the Middle East ('Pococke School', p, 37).

4 C.J. Woods, 'Pococke's Journey through County Down in 1760', *Ulster Journal of Archaeology* 48 (1985), pp. 113–15 (p. 115, note 1).

5 For an account of the development of the fashionable admiration of mountain scenery, see G.B. Parks, 'The Turn to the Romantic in the Travel Literature of the Eighteenth Century', *Modern Language Quarterly* 25 (1964), pp. 22–33, and Barbara Maria Stafford, 'Toward Romantic Landscape Perception: Illustrated Travel Accounts and the Rise of "Singularity" as an Aesthetic Category', *Art Quarterly* new series I (1977), pp. 89–124. On the earlier period see Ray W. Frantz, *The English Traveller and the Movement of Ideas, 1660–1732* (Lincoln, NE: University Studies of the University of Nebraska vols. 32, 33, 1934).

6 See Kemp, *Tours in Scotland*, p. xxxvi.

7 The incident is described by Peter Martel in *An Account of the Glaciers or Ice Alps in Savoy* (London, 1744).

8 Kemp, *Tours in Scotland*, p. xxxix.

9 In his 1752 tour Pococke refers to visits paid in 1747 or 1740 to Gort, Kilmallock, Kilfinane and Charleville. See pp. 93, 98.

10 See p. 60.

11 See p. 64.

12 See p. 85.

13 See above, p. 142.

14 William Petty, *Hiberniae Delineatio, Atlas of Ireland* (London, 1685; repr. Newcastle: Frank Graham, 1968); Walter Harris and Charles Smith, *The antient and present state of the County of Down* (Dublin: P. Edward Exshaw, 1744; repr. Ballynahinch: Arthur Davidson, 1977); Charles Smith, *The antient and present state of the County and City of Cork* (Dublin, 1750).

15 Lady Anne Fanshawe, *The Memoirs of Anne Fanshawe*, ed. by Herbert C. Fanshawe (London: Bodley Head, 1907), pp. 58–62.

16 William Edmundson, *A Journal of the Life . . . of William Edmundson* (Dublin: S. Fairbrother, 1715; second edition London: Printed and sold by M, Hinde, 1774), pp, 125–34.

17 *The Journal of John Stevens Containing a Brief Account of the War in Ireland 1689–1691* ed. by Rev. R.H. Murray (Oxford: Clarendon Press, 1912).

18 See below, p. 64.

19 Sir John Davies, *A Discoverie of the true causes why Irlande was never entirely subdued* (London: Printed for John Jaggard, 1612, repr. Shannon: Irish University Press, 1969).

20 Edmund Spenser, *A View of the Present State of Ireland*, ed. by W.L. Renwick (Oxford: Clarendon Press, 1935; repr. 1970). Spenser's *View* was first published in 1633 but probably written in 1596.

21 Gerald of Wales, *The History and Topography of Ireland*, trans, by J.J. O'Meara (Harmondsworth: Penguin, 1982); *Expugnatio Hibernica. The Conquest of Ireland*, ed. and trans. by A.B. Scott and F.X. Martin (Dublin: Royal Irish Academy, 1978). The *Topography* was first published in 1188, the *Expugnatio* in 1189.

22 *The Journal of the Rev. John Wesley. A.M.*, ed. by Nehemiah Curnock, 8 vols. (London: Culley, 1909–16). See also T.W. Freeman, 'John Wesley in Ireland', *Irish Geography* 8 (1975), pp. 86–96; D. Gregory Van Dussen, 'Methodism and Cultural Imperialism in Eighteenth-Century Ireland', *Éire-Ireland* 23 (1988), pp. 19–37.

23 See H.V. Fackler, 'Wordsworth in Ireland 1829: a survey of his tour', *Éire-Ireland* 6 (1971), pp. 53–64.

24 Thomas Carlyle, *Reminiscences of My Irish Journey in 1849* (London: Sampson, Low, Marston, Searle, & Rivington, 1882).

25 For further discussion of attitudes to Ireland among the writings of English visitors, see John P. Harrington, *The English Traveller in Ireland: Accounts of Ireland and the Irish through five centuries* (Dublin: Wolfhound Press, 1991); *Strangers to that Land: British Perceptions of Ireland from the Reformation to the Famine*, ed. by Andrew Hadfield and John McVeagh (Gerrards Cross, Bucks: Colin Smythe Ltd, 1994).

26 Richard Laurence, *The Interest of England in the Irish Transplantation Stated* (London: printed by Henry Hills, 1655).

27 Vincent Gookin, *The Great Case of Transplantation in Ireland Discussed* (London: for I.C., 1655).

28 Sir William Petty, *The Political Anatomy of Ireland*, ed. by John O'Donovan (Shannon: Irish University Press, 1 970), Petty's book was first published in 1691.

29 Petty, *Political Anatomy*, pp. 25–9, or pp. 93–102.

30 'Extracts from the Journal of Thomas Dinely, giving some account of his Visit to Ireland in the Reign of Charles II', ed. by E.P, Shirley, *Journal of the Royal Society of Antiquaries of Ireland* 4 (1856–57), pp. 143–6, 170–88; 5 (1858), pp, 22–32, 55–6; 7 (1862–3), pp. 38–52, 103–9, 320–38; 8 (1864–6), pp. 40–48, 268–90, 425–46; 9 (1867), pp. 73–91, 176–202; ed. by F.E. Ball, 43 (1913), pp. 275–309.

31 John Dunton, *Teague Land, or A Merry Ramble to the Wild Irish*, ed. by E. MacLysaght (Dublin: Irish Academic Press, 1982). Dunton's book was first published in 1699.

32 At the battle of Aughrim, County Galway on 12 July 1691 William III's army under Ginkel defeated James II's Irish army commanded by the French general St. Ruth, who was killed in the conflict.

33 See note 4 to 1752 tour below, p. 209.

34 See below, pp. 152, 156.

35 Quane, 'Pococke School', p. 39ff.

36 Quane, 'Pococke School', p. 40.

37 See Pococke's comments on St Patrick's Well near Downpatrick, St Terence Marialla's shrine at Malin Head, St Patrick's Purgatory in Lough Derg, St Declan's devotions at Ardmore on pp. 33, 57, 71, 112.

38 *The Letters of Joseph Addison*, ed. by W. Graham (Oxford: Clarendon Press, 1941), pp. 133–85.
39 Philip Luckombe, *A Tour through Ireland in 1779* (London: T. Lowndes, 1780); Richard Twiss, *A Tour in Ireland in 1775* (London: Printed for the Author, 1776).
40 John Wesley, *Journal*, pp. 138–9.
41 Arthur Young, *A Tour in Ireland: with general observations on the present state of that Kingdom: made in the years 1776, 1777 and 1778, and brought down to the end of 1779*, 2 vols. (London: T. Cadell and J. Dodsley, 1780).
42 George Taylor and Andrew Skinner, *Maps of the Roads of Ireland* (London, Published for the Authors, 1778; introduced by Dr J.H. Andrews, Shannon: Irish University Press, 1969). See also, for example, William Wilson, *The Post Chaise Companion: or, Traveller's Directory, through Ireland, Containing a new & accurate description, etc.*, (Dublin: Printed for the author, 1786); J.S. Dodd, *The Travellers' Director through Ireland* (Dublin: Printed by J. Stockdale, 1801); Anon, *The Traveller's New Guide Through Ireland, etc.*, (Dublin: Cumming, 1815).
43 Thomas Sprat, *History of the Royal Society*, (London: J.R., for J. Martyn, 1667), p. 113.

Tour of 1747

1 Ahoghill.
2 Possibly Castle Dillon between Armagh and Rich hill; see Taylor and Skinner, *Maps of the Roads*, p. 26. The house Pococke saw was one of two successive eighteenth-century houses replaced eventually by the present structure built by William Murray in 1845. It is now a hospital. See Mark Bence-Jones, *Burke's Guide to Country Houses, Volume I. Ireland* (London: Burke's Peerage Ltd., 1978), p. 66.

Tour of 1752

1 Gormanston Castle, County Meath originally consisted of a long gabled manor with a chapel attached in which, throughout penal times, Mass was said. It was rebuilt early in the 19th century as a three-storey Gothic Revival castle, and is now a Franciscan school. See Bence-Jones, *Burke's Guide*, p. 142.
2 This was Ballygarth Castle, County Meath, **a** battlemented tower house to which a two-storey wing had been added. See Taylor and Skinner, *Maps of the Roads*, p. 3; Bence-Jones, *Burke's Guide*, p. 22.
3 Possibly Dardistown.
4 A country house built in the 1660s for Sir William Tichborne, and one of the first Irish houses to be built without fortification. Tichborne's father had obtained the estate from the Plunkett family. For an illustration and further details see Bence-Jones, *Burke's Guide*, p, 34.
5 Limestone was quarried in Ardbraccan, County Meath and a particular kind of it, taken from the White Quarry, was used for the bishop's palace. See Samuel Lewis, *A Topographical Dictionary of Ireland*, 2 vols (London: S. Lewis & co., 1837), 1, p. 42.
6 This was William Petty's *Hiberniae Delineatio, Atlas of Ireland* (London, 1685;

reprinted Newcastle: Frank Graham, 1968). Pococke evidently had this map in his baggage and periodically compared it with the regions he visited. His present reference seems to be to 'The County of Lowth' in Petty.

7 Monasterboice, Stokes suggests.

8 Athclare Castle, County Louth was a sixteenth-century tower house with an attached wing; see Bence-Jones, *Burke's Guide*, p. 14.

9 Plunket, perhaps.

10 Stanley, that is.

11 Stokes quotes an account of this industry taken from J.N. Brewer, *The Beauties of Ireland: Being Original Delineations, Topographical, Historical, and Biographical, of each county* (London: Printed for Sherwood, Jones & Co., 1825), 3, p. 323.

12 Stokes reads 'quantity' here.

13 On Dutch enterprise in Ireland see Conrad Gill, *The Rise of the Irish Linen Industry* (Oxford: Clarendon Press, 1925), pp. 14–15 and *passim.*

14 Here a marginal note too cramped to read seems to refer to Brittany and Gascony.

15 This was Bellurgen Park. See Taylor and Skinner, *Maps of the Roads*, p. 11a.

16 See Taylor and Skinner, *Maps of the Roads* p. 11a.

17 Stokes reads 'ascended'.

18 Stokes reads this word as 'roads'.

19 A small sailing vessel for inland navigation (*O.E.D.*).

20 Tollymore Park, County Down was an early eighteenth-century two-storey house with single-storey wings, probably designed by Thomas Wright of Durham. Later in the century the three other sides of the courtyard were built in, and there were also nineteenth-century additions. The Northern Ireland Ministry of Agriculture had bought the house by 1941; in 1952 they demolished it. See illustrations in Bence-Jones, *Burke's Guide*, p. 274.

21 The dominating peak in the Mournes, rising 2,796 feet above the sea.

22 Stokes reads 'fine wooden'.

23 The report of which Pococke is sceptical is found in Walter Harris and Charles Smith, *County of Down*, p. 82.

24 The castle is illustrated in Francis Grose, *Antiquities of Ireland*, 2 vols. (London: Printed for S. Cooper, 1791), 1, County Down Plate 1. The round tower Pococke refers to is the castle's circular keep.

25 Sir Francis Annesley (1585–1660) arrived in Dublin by the year 1606, gathered various Irish estates and clashed famously with Strafford. See *D.N.B.* for further details. If Pococke's 'Francis Annesley of the Inner Temple' was his son, then it was his grandson whom Pococke met.

26 Holes cut above the entrance passage to a castle from which objects could be dropped on intruders. See Peter Harbison, *Guide to the National Monuments of Ireland* (Dublin: Gill and Macmillan, 1970; repr. 1977), p. 263.

27 Stokes reads 'from'.

28 The Holy Wells of Struell are a mile and a half east of Downpatrick and may have been a place of worship in pagan times. St Patrick is said to have landed in Ireland a mile and a half north east of the town at Fiddler's Burn, located at the mouth of the Slaney.

29 Finnebrogue, County Down was a two-storey house over a basement, furnished with attics and projecting wings front and back. It was built in the late seventeenth century and modernised a hundred years later, Some of its internal partition walls were

constructed of turf; see Bence-Jones, *Burke's Guide*, p. 125, who illustrates the house.

30 So suggested by Camden, according to Walter Harris, *A Topographical and Chorographical Survey of the County of Down* (Dublin pr., and repr. London: Tho. Boreman, 1740), p. 25, who denies the statement; Pococke's phrase 'may be questioned' places him between the two authorities. For Ptolemy's speculations concerning Ireland see Liam de Paor, *The Peoples of Ireland from prehistory to modern times* (Notre Dame, Indiana. Hutchinson and University of Notre Dame Press, 1986), p. 35; and *A New History of Ireland. IX Maps, Genealogies, Lists. A Companion to Irish History Part I*, ed. by T.W. Moody, F. X. Martin and F. J. Byrne (Oxford: Clarendon Press, 1984), map 14, p. 16.

31 Castleward, County Down was a three-storey house built between 1760 and 1773 by an unknown architect. Since the owners had divergent tastes, their house was built classical in front and Gothic at the rear. For illustrations, see Bence-Jones, *Burke's Guide*, pp. 78–9.

32 Ground on a slope. See John Richardson, *The Local Historian's Encyclopaedia* (New Barnet: Historical Publications Ltd., 1974; repr. 1985), p. 15.

33 The present Rosemount, County Down, now known as Grey Abbey, was built in 1762 on the site of the house which Pococke saw, which had burned down. There are Georgian Gothic touches in it reminiscent of Castle Ward. See Bence-Jones, *Burke's Guide*, pp. 146–7 for illustrations.

34 These details are taken from Harris, *County of Down*, p. 56.

35 For a summary of Pococke's journeys through Ireland, see Introduction. Donaghadee was linked to Portpatrick by a packet service until the Larne-Stranraer route took over as the normal crossing. Telephone cables connect Ireland with Scotland at this point.

36 Pococke's account is mainly summarized from Harris, *County of Down*, with some details added.

37 Schomberg in 1689 landed here (now Groomsport) with 10,000 men, not 1,000. They camped overnight on the sea-front then invested Carrickfergus, which surrendered when the ammunition ran out.

38 The New Light movement began in 1709 as a revolt against creed-subscription and was held to be responsible for widespread laxity. It was checked in 1750 when orthodox members from Scotland threw their weight against it. See *Encyclopaedia of Religion and Ethics*, ed. by James Hastings with the assistance of John A. Selbie and Louis H. Gray, 12 vols. plus Index (Edinburgh: T. & T. Clark, and New York: Charles Scribner & Sons, 1918; repr. 1963), 10, pp. 255–6.

39 Stokes reads 'Barracks'.

40 Castle Dobbs, County Antrim was a two-storey house over a basement built in 1730; wings were added later. See Bence-Jones, *Burke's Guide*, p. 66.

41 Arthur Dobbs (1689–1765) became high sheriff of Antrim in 1720, M.P. for Carrickfergus in 1727 and in 1730 surveyor-general and engineer-in-chief in Ireland. He instigated Christopher Middleton's 1741 attempt on the north-west passage (Middleton reached 88 degrees in Hudson's Bay), but the men fell out over Middleton's negative report. A second voyage in 1748 led by G. Moor was also unsuccessful, after which Dobbs dropped the subject. In 1754 he became governor of North Carolina. See *D.N.B.* for further details.

42 Stokes reads 'vitch, sticking on'.

43 Ballygally Castle, County Antrim was a Plantation castle built by James Shaw in

1625. In Taylor and Skinner, *Maps of the Roads*, p. 14, it appears as Ballygollah. It now has sash windows but is otherwise intact, and has become a hotel. See illustration in Bence-Jones, *Burke's Guide*, p. 22.

44 Glenarm Castle, County Antrim was built in 1603 by Sir Randal MacDonnell, then rebuilt in the 1750s as a three-storey block joined by curving colonnades to pavilions placed at each side. In the 1820s it received a mock-Tudor facelift from the architect William Vitruvius Morrison. See illustrations in Bence-Jones, *Burke's Guide,* p. 135,

45 Stokes reads 'wood and on both'.

46 Mount Slemish is 1437 feet above sea level. According to legend St Patrick served six years on this mountain as a captive.

47 Petty calls this 'The Apendix of Ardclunis' in his map of County Antrim.

48 Pococke is travelling the route later metalled as the Antrim coast road.

49 Petty places Galbally on the north-facing southern shore of Red Bay, east of the Glasmullen river in his map of County Antrim.

50 Stokes reads 'healthy'.

51 Hugh Boyd (1690–1765) obtained a mining lease from Alexander MacDonnell, fifth Earl of Antrim, in 1736 and a Parliamentary grant of £23,000 towards the construction of a harbour and quay at Ballycastle. In the process he built what was probably Ireland's first tramway, a 310-yard stretch of rail used for carrying stone to the harbour from the quarry. The rails were of oak and fir. See Edward M. Patterson, *The Ballycastle Railway. A History of the Narrow-Gauge Railway of North East Ireland: Part One* (Dawlish: David and Charles, 1965), pp. 11–13.

52 Possibly the Manor House at Ballycastle, built in the mid-eighteenth century and now a Barnardo's Home. Little remains of the original structure. See Bence-Jones, *Burke's Guide*, pp. 19–20.

53 'The most illustrious and noble Lord Randolph McDonnel, Count of Antrim, caused this chapel to be set up in honour of God and the virgin mother of God in the year 1612'. I am grateful to Alan Peacock for help with this note.

54 Dunluce Castle, County Antrim was built for the Earls of Antrim from the fourteenth to the seventeenth centuries. A Jacobean house was built in a courtyard within the walls. It was abandoned in the seventeenth century and is now a ruin. Grose illustrates it in *Antiquities of Ireland*, 2, p. 64.

55 George Villiers (1592–1628), first Duke of Buckingham, was the court favourite of James I. His widow was the Roman Catholic daughter of the Duke of Rutland, Lady Katherine Manners. She became a Protestant in order to marry Buckingham with the king's consent.

56 Pococke's essays were printed in volumes 45 (1748), pp, 124–7 and 48 (1753), pp. 226–37. See p. 233.

57 Stokes reads '5 and ten'.

58 Possibly a copyist's error for grilse: young salmon.

59 The phrase 'as come' has been crossed out after 'people', hence the lapse in grammar.

60 Stokes reads 'beneath'.

61 This is a cross-slab in Fawn churchyard, dated to the seventh century. On one side are two carved figures surrounding an interlaced cross pattern, on the other a similar design without the figures.

62 The modern Buncrane, actually named from Bun Crauncha = Mouth of the river

Cranna. See P.W. Joyce, *Irish Names of Places* (Dublin, Cork, Belfast: Phoenix Publishing Co., 1913).

63 This fortress was built in 1305 by Richard de Burgo, the Red Earl of Ulster, to overawe the O'Donnelis of Tyrconnell and the O'Dohertys of Inishowen. Later it was granted to Sir Arthur Chichester.

64 Rockhill near Letterkenny can be found in Taylor and Skinner, *Maps of the Road*, p. 37b. According to Bence-Jones it was a three-storey Georgian house, added to in the mid-nineteenth century. The architect may have been John Hargrave of Cork, See Bence-Jones, *Burke's Guide*, pp. 243–4. Mr Spaw's house, noted in the same map in Taylor and Skinner, was Ballinacool.

65 The name actually derives from Leítir Ceannainn = hillside of the O'Cannons.

66 What the O'Donnells founded was a fifteenth century friary on the site of St Columba's abbey. Some walls of the friary still stand.

67 Stokes reads 'healthy',

68 Ards, County Donegal, the Wray family seat, was sold in 1781 as a result of the extravagant lifestyle of William Wray, partly described by Pococke. The house was rebuilt in the 1830s and in the 1960s demolished. See Bence-Jones, *Burke's Guide*, p. 11.

69 Since Pococke's day much of the attraction of this phenomenon has been lost.

70 Given the circumstances, Pococke transcribes with accuracy. The grace he probably heard was:

Bail na gcúig arán agus an dá iasc	The blessing of the five loaves and two fishes which
a roinn Dia ar an gcúig whíle fear.	God distributed among the five thousand;
Rath ón Rí a riune an roinn	God made a blessing by which
go dtige sé ar ár gcuid agus ar ár gcomhroinn.	He made the distribution on us, on our food and on our provision.

I am grateful to Seamus MacMathúna for help with this note.

71 Persons living or engaged outside a borough, as distinguished from those of the same class residing within (*O.E.D.*).

72 Brownhall, County Donegal as it now stands is a three-storey late Georgian house built by Robert Woodgate; there are some nineteenth-century additions. See Bence-Jones, *Burke's Guide*, p. 49.

73 Wardton, as Taylor and Skinner call it (*Maps of the Roads*, p. 226b), or Wardstown, County Donegal was a three-storey Georgian house with curved bows at each end and a curved bow at the front. It is now a ruin. See Bence-Jones, *Burke's Guide*, p. 282.

74 Castle Caldwell, County Fermanagh was a two-storey eighteenth-century house over a basement on the shore of Lough Erne with a 'Gothic' front. It was a ruin by 1900. See illustration in Bence-Jones, *Burke's Guide*, p. 64,

75 Castle Hume was Richard Castle's first Irish Palladian house, built in 1729. (On Castle, see note 79 below). In the 1830s it was taken down and its materials used to build a now house on the same estate, Ely Lodge. Forty years later Ely Lodge was blown up as part of a birthday celebration to make way for a new house, never built. See Bence-Jones, *Burke's Guide*, p. 119.

76 A deep cave on Station Island in Lough Derg, north of Pettigo, in which the saint fasted and prayed for forty days while freeing the island from evil spirits. It became a place of pilgrimage of European reputation during the middle ages. In the early

eighteenth century Parliament declared the pilgrimage unlawful but failed to stop it.

77 Philip Skelton (1707–1787) was born at Derriaghy in Antrim and educated at Trinity College, Dublin. In 1732 he became curate at Monaghan, and in 1750 received the living of Templecarn in the counties of Donegal and Fermanagh. He published *Ophiomaches, or Deism Revealed* in 1748.

78 Alexander Murray (d. 1777) was so active in his support of the anti-ministerial candidate Sir George Vandeput in 1750 that the House of Commons charged him with encouraging mob violence and committed him to Newgate. When the House was prorogued in June his release from gaol became a triumphal procession. He removed himself to France before Parliament re-assembled, from where George III recalled him in 1771.

79 Richard Castle or Cassel(s) (d. 1751) arrived in Ireland from Germany early in the eighteenth century at the invitation of Sir Gustavus Hume, for whom he built Castle Hume in County Fermanagh. When Lovett Pearce died in 1733 Castle succeeded to his practice. His later designs included Hazlewood, Co. Sligo; Powerscourt, Co. Wicklow; Carton House, Co. Kildare; and Bessborough House, Co. Kilkenny. In Dublin he designed Leinster House in Kildare Street and the Marquis of Waterford's house in Marlborough Street, the Rotunda or Lying-in Hospital and also the music hall in Fishamble Street, where in 1742 Handel's *Messiah* received its first performance. For further information, see *D.N.B.*

80 Hazlewood, County Sligo was built by Richard Castle in 1751; it had three storeys over a basement connected with side wings. For an illustration see Bence-Jones, *Burke's Guide*, p. 150.

81 Erasmus Smith (1611–1691) was a Turkey merchant and London alderman who joined the adventurers in Ireland under Cromwell and received 666 plantation acres plus other territories. After 1657 Smith made over a total of 13,000 acres in various parts of Ireland for the endowment of a number of grammar schools. For further information, see *D.N.B.*

82 Stokes reads 'fire'.

83 Ballina was the first town captured by the French under General Humbert after their landing at Killala Bay in 1798.

84 Pococke has just commented that they call all convents abbeys and monasteries interchangeably in Ireland. Rosserick Abbey is illustrated by Grose in *Antiquities of Ireland* 2, p. 42.

85 Stokes reads 'wastings'.

86 Strade Abbey, County Mayo was a Franciscan friary founded by the MacJordan sept. Later it was transferred to the Dominicans. There are remains of church walls plus some fifteenth- and sixteenth-century carved stonework. See *The National Monuments of Ireland* (Dublin: Published by Bord Fáilte Éireann, 1964), p. 30. Grose illustrates the abbey in *Antiquities of Ireland* 2, p. 75,

87 Stokes reads 'and is without mixture polishing as well'.

88 Stokes reads 'at'.

89 Pray for the soul of David Oge Kelly, who caused me to be [placed] here for himself and his heirs in the year 1623, and of his wife Anabla Barret.

90 Stokes reads 'went'.

91 A stand or frame for holding a cask, or pottery within a furnace.

92 Stokes reads 'when'.

93 Stokes reads 'produced'.

94 Newbrook, County Mayo was built in the later eighteenth century with two storeys over a basement. It was burnt down in 1817. See illustration in Bence-Jones, *Burke's Guide*, pp. 223–4.

95 Stokes reads 'land, the wind'.

96 See 'The County of Mayo' in Petty's *Hiberniae Delineatio*. Pococke's little island 'without a name' has Kildunaf written across it.

97 August 8 1752 was a Saturday, so the Roman Catholics cannot have been fasting from meat. Pococke's action looks like religious discrimination.

98 Burrishoole Friary, County Mayo was founded for the Dominicans in 1469 by Richard Burke. The nave, chancel, tower and south transept remain, along with some domestic ruins. See Harbison, *National Monuments*, p. 42. Grose illustrates it in *Antiquities of Ireland*, 1, 42.

99 Stokes reads 'say there are'.

100 The remains of Grace O'Malley's headquarters, a square keep, may be seen at the south-east corner of Clare Island.

101 The name Connemara or Conamara comes from the Conmaicne Tribe of the Sea.

102 Westport House, County Mayo built by Richard Castle *c.*1730 on the site of an earlier house consisted of two storeys over a basement. Three further sides were added in 1778, making it a square building round an open court, which was later roofed over. Side terraces were added in 1816 and 1819. See illustrations in Bence-Jones, *Burke's Guide*, p. 283.

103 Hollymount House, County Mayo built in the eighteenth century consisted of two storeys over a basement with an extension at the rear. It was refaced in the nineteenth century. It is now ruined. See illustration in Bence-Jones, *Burke's Guide*, p. 154.

104 See note 94 above.

105 Richard, second earl of Pembroke (*c.*1130–76) joined forces with Dermot MacMurrough, the exiled King of Leinster, in Waterford in 1170, married his daughter Eva and was promised the succession to Leinster. When Dermot died in 1171 Strongbow took control of Dublin, offered homage to Henry II of England, and was confirmed in his possession of Leinster. He then split the territory among his supporters.

106 In 1641, when Castlebar had surrendered to the Confederate Catholic forces, safe passage to Galway was promised by Lord Mayo to about 100 persons, who were then slaughtered. Lord Mayo's son was executed for not protecting them.

107 The Navigation Act of 1671, a reinforcement of previous legislation, prohibited the direct importation of colonial produce to Ireland. In 1681 the Act expired, but was renewed in 1685. See J.E. Doherty and D.J. Hickey, *A Chronology of Irish History since 1500* (Dublin: Gill and Macmillan, 1989), p. 58. The elaborate domestic architecture of Galway described by Pococke has long since vanished, but a single carved doorcase—Brown's Doorway—has been set up in Eyre Square as a memorial of past grandeur.

108 'An apologetic and demonstrative argument concerning the right of the kingdom of Ireland on behalf of the Irish Catholics against the heretics': I am grateful to Alan Peacock for help with this note.

109 A request for the visitor's prayers, in garbled Latin.

110 Kilmacduagh round tower is actually 112 feet high, not 82 feet; it leans 2 feet from the perpendicular. The broken top has been restored since Pococke's time.

111 Quin Friary, County Clare was founded for the Franciscans *c.*1400 by Maccon McNamara, and incorporates parts of a thirteenth-century castle. There are extensive

remains. See Harbison, *National Monuments*, p. 3. Grose illustrates the friary in *Antiquities of Ireland* 2, p. 69, quoting Pococke's description.

112 Bunratty Castle, County Clare was built *c.*1460, passed to the O'Brien's (who became the Earls of Thomond) and surrendered to the Cromwellian forces during the Civil War. It is a tall, nearly square building of immense strength with towers rising at each corner. A brick house was built within two towers in the seventeenth century. Thomas Studdert bought and lived in Bunratty in 1720, but it was later abandoned and by the end of the nineteenth century was collapsing. It has now been restored. See illustration in Bence-Jones, *Burke's Guide*, p. 49.

113 See 'The County of Limrick' in Petty's *Hiberniae Delineatio*.

114 Possibly this is Killaliathan in County Limerick, 7 miles from Newcastle on the road to Charleville, which Harbison describes as a small medieval church of unknown origin (*National Monuments*, p. 13). Lewis also mentions the ruins of an ancient church near Bunmore, and, near Springfield, the ruins of Gurnetubber castle, which was held for James II and afterwards dismantled (*Topographical Dictionary*, 2, p. 121).

115 Shannon Grove, County Limerick was built early in the eighteenth century, perhaps to a design of one of the Rothery family of architects. It consists of two storeys over a basement, with dormered attics. See illustrations in Bence-Jones, *Burkes Guide*, pp. 258–9.

116 Grose illustrates Adare Castle in *Antiquities of Ireland* 1, p. 26; a rather pastoral rendering.

117 '31st' has been written in then deleted because of the 1752 calendar change from Old to New Style. See note 129 below.

118 Riverstown House, County Cork was built early in the 18th century and enlarged in the 1730s. It consists of two storeys above a basement with a higher addition at one end, and contains plasterwork which may be the first Irish work of the Francini brothers. The house deteriorated in the present century, but has been restored. See illustration In Bence-Jones, *Burke's Guide*, p. 242,

119 Curraglass, County Cork was a three-storey Georgian house, later abandoned and now vanished.

120 St Cathal, or Cataldus (d. 685?), bishop, was born in Munster and taught at Lismore. He made a pilgrimage to Jerusalem, and later took charge of the see of Taranto in Italy, of which he is patron. See John J. Delaney and James Edward Tobin, *Dictionary of Catholic Biography* (London: Robert Hale, 1962).

121 Robert Boyle (1627–91) was the seventh son of Richard Boyle, first Earl of Cork. He was educated at Eton and on the Continent, then moved to Oxford. He was a founder member of the Royal Society.

122 William Congreve 1670–1729) was born at Bardsey near Leeds but brought up in Ireland, where his father was a military officer. He attended school first at Youghal, then at Kilkenny, and entered Trinity College Dublin in 1686; he left two years later without a degree. Congreve's later life was spent in London.

123 This sentence was added later.

124 Pococke draws here on Charles Smith, *County of Cork*.

125 Knocklofty, County Tipperary was built in the 18th century and consists of three storeys flanked by wings at each end. Additions were made to it in the early 19th century. See illustrations in Bence-Jones, *Burke's Guide*, p. 179.

126 I visited . . . I set out] Pococke has scored through the sentence from 'I visited' to

'with me &'. Stokes ignores this. He connects 'On the 12th' with 'I set out for Cashel', etc. The journal then continues as printed.

127 'I went to see it' The following words, later deleted, originally came at this point: 'where I met the Minister, Mr Walsh, who went with me to the rock, & I met Mr Baxter, the late Archbishop's Chaplain, to whom I had sent, & they both dined with me.'

128 New Park, County Tipperary, later known as Ballyowen, was a three-storey house over a basement built *c*.1750. See illustration in Bence-Jones, *Burke's Guide*, p. 27.

129 In 1752 Britain adopted the New Style or Gregorian Calendar in place of the Old Style or Julian Calendar, which involved omitting eleven days. The day after 2 September, 1752 was named 14 September, 1752.

130 Jeremiah Milles (1714–1784) was the nephew of Thomas Milles, regius professor of Greek at Oxford. He held the treasurership of Lismore Cathedral from 1735 to 1745 and from 1737 to 1744 was precentor of Waterford Cathedral. After 1740 he spent most of his time in England. Milles was Pococke's cousin and had travelled with him throughout Europe from 1735 to 1737. Like Pococke he had antiquarian interests, but took the wrong side in the Chatterton dispute and was mauled by Malone, Thomas Warton, and others.

131 Thomas Milles (1671–1740) was ordained in 1694, became regius professor of Greek at Oxford in 1705 or 1706, travelled to Ireland in 1707 as chaplain to the Earl of Pembroke, and in 1708 became Bishop of Waterford. In Ireland the appointment was not popular; Archbishop King complained that he gave all livings within his power to his close relations.

132 Henry Dodwell (d. 1784) was born at Shottesbrooke, Berkshire and educated at Oxford, where he later studied law. His 1742 pamphlet entitled 'Christianity not founded on Argument', professedly defending the Christian faith, seemed to many an attempt to subvert it.

133 Sea holly or *eryngium maritimum* (*O.E.D.*)

134 I have found no details of the house Pococke viewed. Faithlegg House, County Waterford as it now exists was built in 1783, presumably to replace an earlier dwelling. See illustration in Bence-Jones, *Burke's Guide*, p, 123.

135 A prehistoric chisel-shaped implement made of bronze, stone or iron.

136 A branching figure resembling a tree or moss shape, occurring naturally in stone or mineral.

137 Lake Coumshingaun is a deep tarn positioned 6 miles north-west of Kilmacthomas which forms one of the finest glacial cirques in the British Isles. The surrounding cliffs rise to 1,288 feet, and nearby is Fautscoum, highest peak in the Comeragh Mountains (2,597 feet). Just north of Coumshingaun is Crotty's Lake, hiding place of the 18th century outlaw William Crotty.

138 Pococke draws here on Charles Smith, *The antient and present state of the county and City of Waterford* (Dublin: E. & J. Exshaw, 1746; repr. Cork: Mercier Press, 1969).

139 Declan was a fifth-century Irish bishop. See J. O'Hanlon, *Lives of Irish Saints*, 10 vols. (Dublin: James Duffy & Sons; London: Burns, Oates, and Co.; New York: The Catholic Publishing Co, 1875–1903), 7, pp. 307–54.

140 Cloncoskraine, County Waterford is a two-storey house built in the mid-19th century; Pococke saw its predecessor, said to be incorporated in the present structure. See Bence-Jones, *Burke's Guide*, p. 86.

141 Text unclear.

142 Tube-shaped glass beads.
143 Tintern Abbey is illustrated in Grose, *Antiquities* 1, p. 50, who emphasizes its wooded, romantic setting.
144 An illustration can be seen in Grose, *Antiquities* 1, p. 49, who brings out its rocky character.
145 Loftus Hall, County Wexford was built in the late 17th or early 18th century and consisted of two storeys with a steep roof. Parts of it were incorporated in a new building of 1871. It is now a convent. See illustration in Bence-Jones, *Burke's Guide*, p. 190, who describes the site as one of the most wind-swept in the British Isles.
146 Grose illustrates the bleak Duncannon fort (*Antiquities* 1, p. 45).
147 Stokes reads 'with their short'.
148 Ramsfort, County Wexford was designed and built by George Semple in the 1750s but suffered during the 1798 Rebellion and was replaced by a two-storey house in the early 19th century, which received later additions. It is now a school. Pococke gives some idea of the original building.
149 Ballynastragh, County Wexford was built in the 17th century and enlarged late in the 18th century into a three-storey structure over a basement; there were further 19th century additions. In 1927 the house burnt down and a modern building in the Georgian style replaced it.
150 Altidore Castle, County Wicklow is a late Georgian house in a fortified style with two storeys at the front and three at the sides.
151 Powerscourt, County Wicklow was designed and built in the 1740s by Richard Castle as a three-storey block with two-storey wings at each side. There was much later addition. In 1974 the central block was destroyed by fire. See illustration and further details in Bence-Jones, *Burke's Guide*, pp. 234–5.
152 In the Deer Park Glen, the Dargle river falls over a precipice 300 feet high.
153 Stillorgan House, County Dublin was built in the late 17th century as a two-storey block with side wings. It was pulled down in 1860.
154 In the British Library Add. MSS. 23,001 occurs the following mileage chart of Pococke's 1752 circuit of Ireland. It is printed here for the first time.

A Journey round Ireland in 1752 begun on the 5th of June from Dublin

	Measur'd miles	*Computed*
To Swords	7	7
	6	6
Drogheda	10	10
Dunleer	7	7
Dundalk	10	10
Carlingford	10	8
Rostrevor	3	3
Eight mile bridge	9	6
Tullamore	6	5
Newcastle & back	2	2
Tullamore park & back	4	4
Dundrum	4	4
Mount Panther	1	1
Killogh	7	6
Ardglass	2	1
Down Patrick	7	5
Inch	2	1
Strangford	7	5

	Measur'd miles	*Computed*
Abbay	2	2
Rose mount	8	7
Newtown	6	5
Bangor	4	3
Belfast	10	8
First week	135	
Carrickfergus	8	8
Larne	8	6
To the wells & back	2	2
Glenarme to the park	4	4
Cushendall	10	10
Baley Castle	8	8
Ballintoy	4	3
Don Severik	3	2
Giants Causeway by ye Cliffs	4	4
Bush Mills	2	2
Portrush	6	6
Back to Ballymagarry	2	2
Giants Causeway & back	8	8
by water & on foot	8	8
Second week	77	
First week	135	
In all	212	
omitted in 2 with		
Irish colliery & back		
at Baley: castle	6	
	218	
Mill town Church		
then back a foot	4	
Baly magarry Caves		
& back a foot	3	
Giants Causeway & back	6	
D^o	6	
D^o	6	
To Coleraine	4	
To fishery & back	2	
To Salmon Leap & back	2	
To Solomon's Porch	6	
To New town Limne vaddy	10	7
To Limne vaddy	2	
To Dr Bacon's	2	
To school & L^d.Tyrone's	2	
To Derry	10	
Third Week	70	
Before	218	
make	288	
To Facthan	7	
To Burn Cranner	4	
To Desert Egni	4	
To Clan meny	5	

	Measur'd miles	Computed
To the bridge round	3	
To Malin	5	
to Mr+ Harvey's	2	
To Clandaff	10	9
To Green Castle	10	8
To Red Castle	5	
To White Castle	3	
To Muff	5	
To Mr+ Harts back	1	
To Birte	6	5
To New town Cunningham	6	5
To Manor Cunningham	6	5
To ye school	1	
To Letter kenny	6	
To Kil MaCronnan	6	5
To Falt [?]	5	4
Brought forward	100	
Back to Letter kenny	11	
To Tully	6	
To [ ] Church	3	
To Cranford	4	
To [ ] Chapel	5	
(opposite Rosa penna)		
To Doe Castle	3	
to Dunfanaghy	7	
To Mr Stewarts at Horn Head	2	
Fourth week	146	288
	434	
To Dunfanaghy church & back	4	
To the bay & back	4	
To Mr Wray's at Ards	7	
To Mr Hartleys at Wray	10	
To Mr Orphilts	1	
To Shoar & back	2	
To Mr O Donnels	12	
To Inniskeel	20	15
To Killibegs	15	12
To Donnegall	15	12
To the Pulleins	5	
To Balyshannon	6	
Fifth week	101	
	434	
	535	
Col Foliots & back	3	
To Beleke	4	3
To Sr+ James Calwels	4	3
Back to Baley shannon	8	3
To Sligoe	20	

	Measur'd miles	Computed
To Col. Wyynes & back	4	
To Ballina	30	
To Killalla	8	
To Dunsiny & back	10	
To the Abbies & back	6	
Sixth week	109	535
	644	
To Ballyna	8	
To Foxford	8	8
To Killalla	6	6
To Castle bar	4	3
To New port Pratt	10	8
Within Mullet	36	
To Eastern Head, east & back	8	
To Tarnum hill	8	
To going out of Mullet	8	
To Newport	30	15
Seventh week	126	644
	770	
To The Abby Burisool & Back	4	
Sail to ye Islands & back	12	
To Westport	6	
Ride to severall Hills	3	
To Cave & Balin Tubber	10	
To Ballin robe	6	4
To Lough Mask	3	2
To Hetford	8	
To Galway	12	
Walk out of town & back	2	
Eighth week	66	770
	836	
Ride into Eyre Connaught & back	88 2	
Walk to the East & back	2	
To Gort	16	12
To Kilmaoduagh	3	2
To Crusheen	7	5
To Sixmilebridge	14	9
To Limerick	9	6
To Shannongrove	12	9
To Adair	8	5
Ninth week	73	836
	909	
Kilmallock	12	8
Kilfinan	5	3
Charle ville	9	6
Malloe	13	10
Kingsale	12	10

	Measur'd miles	Computed
Ennishannon	8	6
Bandon	3	2
Iniskarrah	8	6
Cork	6	5
Riverstown	4	3
Middleton	10	8
Castle Martyr	5	4
Tullogh	10	8
Lismore	4	2
Tenth week	138	909
	1047	
Drumanna	3	2
Villers town to ye Park & back	5	
Clonmell	16	12
School & back	2	
Cashel	12	8
Killinau	8	5
Kil corry	8	5
Killaghy	3	2
Kilkenny	8	6
	62	
School & back	2	
Bennets bridge	4	3
Waterford	21	17
Eleventh week	92	1047
	1139	
To Trany More	6	5
walk on in Strand & back	6	
D^o	2	
To Water ford	6	
Twelfth Week	20	1139
	1159	
To Kilmeden & back	10	8
To Green ville & back	6	
To [Philbury?] rock & C & back	2	
To [unreadable] & back	2	
Thirteenth Week	20	1159
	1179	
To Ross	10	8
To school & C & back	2	
To Clamines	12	8
To Tintern	3	2
To Fethard	3	2
To Banow	2	
To Duncormuck	5	3
To Bridgitown	5	3
To Briden of Bargie	3	2
To Ladies Island	6	6

	Measur'd miles	Computed
Round to Carn Head	3	3
To Pollan	8	8
To White house & back	3	3
To Wexford	7	7
To Gory	25	20
To Arklow	10	7
To Dungenstown 10-7	20	14
Fourteenth Week	77	1179
	1256	
To Newry bridge	6	
To Black bull	2	
To Alta dora	5	
To Bray	7	
To Dublin	10	
To Leixlip & back	16	
Fifteenth Week	46	1256
In all	1302	

Tour of 1753

1 Blessington, County Wicklow was built in the late 17th century for Michael Boyle, Archbishop of Armagh, the last ecclesiastical Lord Chancellor of Ireland. It was a two-storey structure built in the shape of an H, with dormered attics. During the 1798 Rebellion the house was burnt down. There is an early illustration of it in Bence-Jones, *Burke's Guide*, p. 44.

2 Ballykilcavan, County Leix was an early 18th century house of two storeys with some later additions. See illustrations in Bence-Jones, *Burke's Guide*, p. 23.

3 County Leix. For a summary of the awkward integration of Irish provinces with the shiring system imposed by the Anglo-Normans, and later modified by the English, see *Encyclopaedia of Ireland* (Dublin: Allen Figgis, 1968). King's County and Queen's County, defined as such in 1556, have resumed the names Offaly and Leix.

4 The present Abbey Leix, County Leix was built in the late 18th century for the second Lord Knapton, son of the Lord Knapton whom Pococke mentions. It received 19th and 20th century additions, including a wing built to replace a conservatory which was blown away in a storm in 1902. In the grounds remain some trees from a primeval oak forest. The house is illustrated in Bence-Jones, *Burke's Guide*, p. 1.

5 Thomas Prior (?1682–1751) was born at Rathdowny in what was then Queen's County and educated at Kilkenny school and Trinity College, Dublin. In 1731, with Samuel Madden and others, he established the Dublin Society whose aim was to promote Irish agriculture, manufacture, arts and sciences. It subsequently become the Dublin Royal Society.

6 Fertagh round tower is actually 100 feet high. It was repaired in 1881.

7 Stokes reads 'his hand'.

8 The Slieve Bloom mountains. Arderin is the highest peak (1733 feet),

9 Barrow found that Ireland's round towers vary from 25 to 35 metres in height but does not offer average width measurements. He notes that Fertagh is 30 by 4.7—a

proportion of 6.38 to 1. See George Lennox Barrow, *The Round Towers of Ireland, A Study and a Gazetteer* (Dublin, The Academy Press, 1979).

10 We went across . . . Tulleagh McJames.] A confused passage which Stokes reads as follows: 'We went across the bog by the pass called Gortahie; X I saw to the right an old Castle call'd if I mistake not Kinslaney X About this place came into the County of Tipperary, and to a large old Castle with two round towers at the corners, and large apartments joyning, to one now in ruins, the enclosure is about half an acre, it is called Tulleach McJames near which there is such a round tower as is seen often in Ireland near churches, which is singular.'

11 Stokes reads 'a market town'.

12 a barrack] Stokes notes that a large section struck out of the copy text at this place belongs to a former letter dated 3 July 1753. The deleted portion runs: 'a mile farther we came to Cahil Castle to the west; & a little beyond saw a very pretty Seat & plantation of Mr. Butler's call'd Newtown. We then passed a Stream which rises from a Holy Well, a little to the west called Tuberboh, & in about a mile & half by a pleasant road between the woods of Castle darrow we came to Darrow a small market town & now a great thoroughfare, the turnpike road from Dublin to Cashel being carryed through it. The Lord Ash brook, who till lately had the title of Castle darrow, has a seat here well situated with a fine park & woods'. Compare the closing section of the preceding letter, actually dated 17 July 1753 (p. 135).

13 Dunsany Castle, County Meath was founded in 1200 by Hugh de Lacy. It was much modernised in the 1780s and again in the 1840s, but retains some of its old character. See illustrations in Bence-Jones, *Burke's Guide*, p. 117.

14 These circles form points in a diagram of Tara, but since the copyist surrounds them with text Stokes has read them as capital letters followed by blanks,

15 Ardbraccan, County Meath was built in the 1730 by Richard Castle for the Bishop of Meath. It first consisted of two-storey wings standing alone; the central block was added in the 1770s. See illustrations in Bence-Jones, *Burke's Guide*, p. 8.

16 These observations make up the next letter.

17 Trimlestown Castle, County Meath as seen by Pococke consisted of a medieval tower to which an 18th century house had been joined. In the 19th century it received further decorative additions: later it fell into ruins.

18 A variety of the citron or lemon tree.

19 At Aughrim, County Galway on 12 July 1691 the Williamite army defeated the Jacobites under St Ruth and settled the Williamite war. It was the last major battle fought in Ireland by professional armies,

20 Jonathan Swift (1667–1745) was instituted in 1699–70 into the livings of Laracor, Agher and Rathbeggan.

21 Dangan Castle, County Meath was built during the early 18th century as a two-storey house, then enlarged at the end of the century by the addition of wings. Afterwards it decayed and fell into ruin.

22 Richard Colley Wellesley (or Wesley) (?1690–1758) represented Trim in Parliament from 1729 to 1746, when he was created a peer of Ireland and took the title of Baron Mornington of Meath. His only son was Garrett Wellesley, whose fourth son was Arthur Wellesley, first Duke of Wellington.

23 Summerhill, County Meath was built in the 1730s, possibly by Richard Lovett Pearce and Richard Castle. It was a two-storey structure with side pavilions joined by curving wings. In 1922 it was burned, then in 1957 pulled down. See illustrations in Bence-Jones, *Burke's Guide*, p. 268.

24 Hugely interesting. John Vanbrugh (1664–1726)'s most famous building was Blenheim Palace with its 'Titanic bridge'. For further details see *D.N.B.*

25 I have found no information on Sir Luke Dowdle.

26 Stokes reads 'over which'.

27 Parts of a moulding.

28 Stackallan House, County Meath was a three-storey mansion built early in the 18th century for Gustavus Hamilton, one of William III's generals. See illustration in Bence-Jones, *Burke's Guide*, p. 264.

29 Slane Castle, County Meath was a medieval castle replaced by the early 18th century house which Pococke saw. This itself was replaced by the present structure, a Gothic Revival effort dating from the 1780s. See illustration in Bence-Jones, *Burke's Guide*, p. 260.

30 Liscarton Castle, County Meath, built in the 15th and 16th centuries, consists of two strong towers, of which one was made into a dwelling.

31 Brittas, County Meath was an early 18th century house which received substantial additions after 1800. See illustration in Bence-Jones, *Burke's Guide*, p. 48.

32 Stokes reads 'half a mile'.

33 Castlemartin, County Kildare was a two-storey house in a U-shape built in the 1720s. It had dormered attics, since lost.

Tour of 1758

1 Ó Maidín reads 'croftyers'.

2 Fethard Abbey was founded in 1306 for the Augustinians, and received additions at a later date. See Harold G. Leask, *Irish Churches and Monastic Buildings*, 3 vols (Dundalk: Dundalgan Press, 1958), 2, p. 129.

3 Pococke had visited Cashel in September 1752. See above, p 104.

4 Timothy Goodwin or Godwin (?1670–1729), archbishop of Cashel, was born at Norwich and graduated from Oxford in 1697. He accompanied the Duke of Shrewsbury to Ireland as domestic chaplain in 1713, when Shrewsbury had been appointed Lord-Lieutenant. In 1714 he was made bishop of Kilmore and Ardagh, and in 1727 archbishop of Cashel.

5 Theophilus Bolton was successively bishop of Clonfert (1722–24), bishop of Elphin 1724–30) and archbishop of Cashel (1724–43). At his death he left 8,000 books to Cashel library. See Walter Alison Phillips, *History of the Church of Ireland from the earliest times to the present day*. 3 vols (London: Oxford University Press, 1933), 3, pp. 221–2.

6 Thomastown Castle, County Tipperary was a two-storey house built in the 1670s and added to in the early 18th century before being refaced in 1812 as a gothic castle. It was later the home of Father Theobald Mathew, the temperance leader. After 1872 the house fell into disrepair and is now a ruin. See Bence-Jones, *Burke's Guide*, p. 272 for illustrations.

7 Twenty years later Damers Court was inhabited by Lord Milton. See Taylor and Skinner, *Maps of the Roads*, p. 113b.

8 In the 1770s there were Masseys living at Paradise Lodge five miles north of Mitchellstown, as Taylor and Skinner show (*Maps of the Roads*, p. 113b). Of New Forest or Massey Dawson I can give no details. But a view of the eighteenth-century

rulers of Ireland from the other side, worth comparing with Pococke's, may be seen in the obituary written on one colonel James Dawson of Aherlow, County Tipperary—possibly a relation of Massey Dawson's—by the Gaelic poet Seán Clárach MacDónaill (1691–1754). See *An Duanaire 1600–1900: Poems of the Dispossessed*, ed. and trans, by Séan O Tuama and Thomas Kinsella (Mountrath, Ireland: The Dolmen Press and St Paul, Minnesota: Irish Books and Media, 1981; repr. 1985), pp. 173–7.

9   Mitchelstown Castle, County Cork was originally the stronghold of a branch of the Geraldines. The house Pococke saw was a two-storey building replaced in 1776 by a new house in which Mary Wollstonecraft worked as governess. This in turn was demolished in 1823 to make way for a palace which became a byword for grand hospitality. It was burnt in 1922 and later demolished. See illustrations in Bence-Jones, *Burke's Guide*, p. 207.

10 Castle Lyons, County Cork was a fortified mansion of the 16th century extended and modernized in the mid-18th century. In 1771 it burnt down and is now a ruin.

11 Pococke's visit to Cork took place in 1752. See above, p. 99.

12 When a new church replaced the old Christ Church in 1720 the steeple settled 3 feet out of true without cracking. The whole church was eventually rebuilt. See Lewis, *Topographical Dictionary* 1, p. 408.

13 Carrigaline Castle, built in the reign of King John, was occupied for two centuries by the Desmond family but under Elizabeth was granted to Anthony St Leger. Later Sir Richard Boyle bought it, who became the Earl of Cork. See Lewis, *Topographical Dictionary,* 1, p. 278.

14 Coolmore, County Cork was built in 1701 , but the house Pococke saw was replaced by a later house built in 1788. See illustration in Bence-Jones, *Burke's Guide*, p. 91.

15 These four small islands in Lake Maggiore, northern Italy, once stretches of bare rock, were adorned during the 17th century with palaces and gardens by the Borromeo family.

16 For further details, see Lewis, *Topograghical Dictionary*, 1, p. 278. The bay in question is now called Drake's pool.

17 Pococke visited Kinsale in 1752; see above, pp. 99-100.

18 Pococke visited Innishannon in 1752. For his description see above, pp.100.

19 Timoleague Friary, County Cork was built in 1370 by William de Barry on the site of an earlier monastery, and further enlarged in 1484. Grose illustrates it in *Antiquities*, p. 30. Extensive ruins remain. See *The National Monuments of Ireland* (Dublin: published by Bord Fáilte Éireann, 1964), p. 4.

20 Ó Maidín reads 'cliffs, Airyes'.

21 Lewis calls this 'the remains of a very extensive heathen temple' (*Topographical Dictionary*, 2, 602).

22 Ó Maidín reads 'share, there being'.

23 Ó Maidín reads 'fretstone'.

24 St Faughnan or Fachanan (d. late 6th century) was probably the first bishop of Ross. He founded the monastic school in Rosscarbery, west Cork, and placed St Brendan there. He is the patron saint of Ross diocese. On Pococke's list of successive bishops and on the church mentioned in the text, see Lewis, *Topographical Dictionary*, 2, p. 535.

25 Coppinger's Court, County Cork was a semi-fortified mid-17th century house now a ruin. Ó Maidín refers to a Victorian description of its dilapidated state in Daniel Donovan, *Sketches in Carbery* (Dublin: McGlashen & Gill, 1876), p. 208.

26 In 1594 Sir Walter Coppinger received the manor and castle of Cloghane plus lands in Carberry confiscated from Donyll McCormuch McCarye. Ó Maidín notes that Coppinger's plans for a market town vanished in the 1641 rising.

27 Ó Maidín suggests the reference is to Kilfinnan Castle, which belonged to the O'Donohoe's.

28 According to Ó Maidín, Léim Uí Dhonnobháin, originally Ceann-mara. Taylor and Skinner mark it clearly as 'The Leap' in *Maps of the Roads*, p. 171a.

29 Samuel Jervais or Jervois lived at Brade House, a three-storey 18th century building situated near Leap, County Cork, Ó Maidín notes that Smith found the place thriving a few years before Pococke, but to Pococke it seems neglected. Later generations further squandered the estate, which by 1850 had passed from the family. See Bence-Jones, *Burke's Guide*, p. 46 for an illustration.

30 Abbeystrewry, a parish in the barony of West Carbery, County Cork, includes the ruins of a religious house situated on the bank of the Ilen west of Skibbereen. No record seems to have survived concerning its origin. See Lewis, *Topographical Dictionary*, 1, p. 5.

31 Richard Levison or Leveson (1570–1605), vice-admiral of England, forced his way into Kinsale in 1601 and according to one story wrecked a Spanish fleet. According to another he was driven off with loss. See Ó Maidín, who gives further details.

32 Francis Derham was rector of Creagh, or Cree, and Tullagh. He put Pococke up on this visit (Ó Maidín).

33 This was the tiny Teampaillín Brighde, or St Brigid's Church; it measured 25c by 12c feet (Ó Maidín).

34 According to Ó Maidín, only a few stones of this castle now remain.

35 Ó Maidín reads 'west'.

36 Not easily identified. Ó Maidín suggests the names may correspond with Tre Head Bay and Sandy Cove.

37 The 1757 potato failure and corn shortage led to a scarcity of bread in Dublin, whereupon Parliament passed an Act grant-aiding the transportation of corn to Dublin. Hence the widespread tillage in 1758 (Ó Maidín).

38 Ó Maidín suggests that this may have been Dunashad Castle, the O'Driscolls' oldest fortress.

39 Now known as Ringaroga (Ó Maidín).

40 A kind of oats (Ó Maidín).

41 Sea urchin.

42 Possibly a spiny thorn (*O.E.D.*)

43 Ó Maidín refers to Smith, *History of Cork*, I , pp. 253–4 and 2, p. 63; see also James Coleman, 'The Sack of Baltimore', *Journal of the Cork Historical and Archaeological Society* I second series (1895), pp. 78–82.

44 According to Ó Maidín, remains of these palaces may still be seen on Cape Clear.

45 Ó Maidín reads 'sell black'.

46 North Cove x,—x] From here onwards the letter has been confused by revision. The passage 'Over which ... with Affadown', originally written after the paragraph ending 'a gallon a day', has been marked for insertion at this point. Ó Maidín transcribes the insertion points as asterisks. He ignores the reorganization of text.

47 Dún an Oir, or in English Dunamore, a 13th century stronghold.

48 Ó Maidín notes that Charles Smith had estimated ten years before that about 400 families lived on Cape Clear.

49 Ó Maidín suggests that Smith contradicts this slur, but of the people of Cape Clear

Smith actually comments that 'brandy-drinking is their only debauch' (Charles Smith, *The Antient and Present State of the County of Kerry* (Dublin: Printed for the Author, 1756; repr. Cork: Mercier Press, 1969) 1, p. 280).

50 The lake is Loch Erul in Ballyicragh (Ó Maidín). Pococke is drawing on Smith.

51 Ó Maidín reads 'saltings'.

52 See 'Tour of 1752', note 30, p. 211 above.

53 This I cannot explain.

54 Arrest or apprehension by judicial process, usually for debt (O.E.D).

55 Ó Maidín reads 'counties'.

56 Ó Maidín reads 'two'.

57 A gall is an excrescence produced on plants by the action of insects.

58 Ó Maidín reads 'lay in'.

59 Ó Maidín reads 'alike'.

60 A kind of mollusc, having a rounded shell with radiating ribs which suggest the tooth of a comb (*O.E.D.*).

61 Ó Maidín reads 'land'.

62 In the 15th century Dermot O'Sullivan Beare erected a Franciscan monastery on the sea shore near Bantry. It has now vanished. See Nicholas Carlisle, *A Topographical Dictionary of Ireland* (London: Printed for William Miller, 1810), 'Bantry' (unpaged).

63 Ó Maidín reads 'dog'.

64 Here in 1602 the Irish after their defeat at Kinsale made a last stand against the English forces. Little of the castle now remains as it was held until its walls were shattered, and to the death.

65 Sir George Carew (1555–1629), who led the English attack against Dunboy, was born at Windsor and educated at Oxford. He entered military service in Ireland and rose quickly to power. On the suppression of Munster Carew retired from Irish affairs.

66 Ó Maidín reads 'skin'.

67 Ó Maidín reads 'Cupes'.

68 A unit of measurement: 'the area capable of being tilled by one plough team of eight oxen in the year' (*O.E.D.*).

69 'Shooleing' may be boolying, described by Edward Ledwich as 'living in extemporary huts of clay and twigs, much the same as the Highland Sheelins or Indian wigwams'; 'Corstuming' may be coshering: 'visitations and progresses made by the Lord and his followers among his tenants'. See Edward Ledwich, *Antiquities of Ireland*, second edition (Dublin: Printed by John Jones, 1803), pp. 376, 317.

70 According to Charles Smith Dr Nathaniel Bland built a summer lodge between two mountain rivers in the parish of Kilcroghan. It seems Bland was no longer there by Pococke's time. See Smith, *County of Kercy*, p. 92.

71 Ballinskelligs Augustinian Monastery was founded by monks from the offshore island of Skellig Michael. The remaining buildings, much eroded by the sea, date probably from the 15th century. See Harbison, *National Monuments*, p. 104; Brian de Breffny and George Mott, *Churches and Abbeys of Ireland* (London: Thames and Hudson, 1976), pp. 14–15.

72 Ó Maidín reads 'meeting'.

73 Cappanacoss or Cappanacush is the chief of a group of islands about 3 miles from Kenmare, County Kerry,

74 Dunkeron Castle, once the chief seat of the O'Sullivan Mores.

75 The Earl of Shelburne received his patent in 1721, having petitioned for it in order to establish in this region of Ireland a system of law and justice which, he declared, had never existed. For further details see Lewis, *Topographical Dictionary*, 2, p. 611.

76 A triton was a sea deity, son of Poseidon and Amphitrite; alternatively, one of a race of see deities, or imaginary sea monsters, of semi-human form (*O.E.D.*).

77 Bishop Kieran (d. *c*.530) was a native of Ossory, and may have been ordained by St Patrick. He reputedly founded the Monastery of Saígir.

78 Ó Maidín reads 'on Avon'.

79 Ó Maidín reads 'in swamps'.

80 Smith comments that gannets nested on the middle Skelig, a league west of Lemon, and nowhere else on the south coast of Ireland; see Smith, *County of Kerry*, p. 111,

81 I cannot explain this term. Pococke seems to bring together something of both 'dolmen'and cromlech', though he is referring to the upright stones only.

82 Ó Maidín reads 'lake'.

83 Gerald of Wales (*c*.1146–1223) studied in Paris, took holy orders and became archdeacon of Brecknock. In 1184 he accompanied Prince John to Ireland and described Ireland in the influential *Topographia Hibernica* (1185).

84 Charles Smith places Agha tubrid Castle in the centre of the Iveragh peninsula north of Ballinskelligs bay, but I have found no further information on it. See Smith, *County of Kerry*, frontispiece map.

85 Bally Carbery Castle was a 15th century stronghold of the MacCarthys subsequently hold by the O'Connells until dismantled in 1652 by Cromwell's troops. There are substantial remains. See Richard Hayward, *In the Kingdom of Kerry* (Dundalk: Dundalgan Press, 1950), p. 177.

86 Cromwell landed at Dublin on 15 August 1649, stormed Drogheda on 10 September, sacked Wexford on 11 October, took Ross on 19 October and besieged Waterford, but on 2 December raised this siege. He captured Cashel and Cahir in February 1750, Kilkenny on 27 March and Clonmel on 18 May. After Clonmel Cromwell returned to England. He did not personally visit Valentia. Lewis comments that he 'caused forts to be erected at each end' of the island to protect it from privateers (*Topograghical Dictionary* 2, p. 672).

87 A name given to various kinds of fish, sometimes used generically for the pike (*O.E.D.*).

88 Bushfield, the house Pococke saw, has long vanished. It was first replaced by a three-storey building known as Kilcoleman Abbey *c*.1800, which received a Tudor facelift twenty years later from William Vitruvius Morrison. In the 1960s this house was allowed to fall into ruins. See illustrations of the later dwelling in Bence-Jones, *Burke's Guide*, p. 165.

89 Sludge or slimy matter (*O.E.D.*).

90 Ó Maidín reads 'washed'.

91 Lewis noted some remains of Kilcolman Abbey, Miltown, built in the reign of Henry III and dedicated to the Blessed Virgin (*Topographical Dictionary* 2, p. 63). In its grounds were the ruins of an older church dating from King John's time (2, p. 63). It is not quite clear which building Pococke refers to.

92 The nearest definition in *O.E.D.* is 'a pool or creek', but Pococke seems to mean a race or artificial canal.

93 Mundic is a term sometimes used as a synonym of pyrite—a lustrous yellowy-bronze mineral which often crystallizes in cubes. It is sometimes mined for the gold

and copper associated with it. See *Glossary of Geology*, ed. by Robert L. Bates and Julia A. Jackson (Falls Church, Virginia: American Geological Institute, 1980), pp. 415, 510.

94 Ó Maidín reads 'north west'.

95 Dingle, Ireland's most westerly town, was taken from the Desmonds after 1641 and made over to the Earls of Ormonde from whom, some time afterwards, Fitzgerald, Knight of Kerry, purchased it.

96 Gallerus Oratory south east of Smerwick harbour is a perfect dry stone chapel some 1200 years old. It measures 26 feet by 16 feet,

97 Ó Maidín reads 'near'.

98 Crotto, County Kerry was a two-storey house built in 1669 and altered in the 'Elizabethan' style of 1819. Kitchener lived there as a boy. The house has now gone. See illustration in Bence-Jones, *Burke's Guide*, p. 96.

99 Lixnaw, County Kerry was an ancient castle of the Fitzmaurices enlarged in the 18th century into a grand residence but allowed to fall into ruins a century later. Some bits of wall are left standing.

100 A castle built in the 15th century by one McGilligan, of which only one half remains. Harbison speculates (*National Monuments*, p. 117) that in its heydey it might have resembled Bunratty. Fitzmaurice destroyed Listowel and took the castle in 1582, but Sir Charles Wilmot recaptured it in 1600.

101 Sir Charles Wilmot (?1570–1644?) was born at Witney, Oxfordshire and educated at Oxford. He joined the Irish wars, serving in 1595 at Newry and Carrickfergus, and later in Munster, where he became an officer under Carew. In 1601 Wilmot was appointed governor of Cork, and in 1602 of Kerry. In 1616 he rose to become President of Connaught, and was made Viscount Wilmot of Athlone in 1620 (*D.N.B.*).

102 Properly, spile: a spill or narrow chip (*O.E.D.*).

103 Smith places this north of the Cashin mouth and opposite Kilcoridon bay in County Clare, in other words behind Pococke as he now travels southwards.

104 Ó Maidín reads 'set out'.

105 Ballyheigue Castle, County Kerry was originally a long thatched house whose enclosed courtyard incorporated an ancient tower, but it made way for a new house —possibly the one Pococke saw—in *c*.1758. This house was battlemented in 1809. In 1921 it burnt down, and is now a ruin. See illustration in Banco-Jones, *Burke's Guide*, p. 23,

106 St Brendan (*c*.489–583) was born on Fenit peninsula, Kerry and founded a number of monasteries, Clonfert being the chief of them. His rule was unusually austere. He is famous for his voyages, one of which is said to have reached America. He is the patron saint of sailors. See *The Book of Saints, A Dictionary of Servants of God Canonized by the Catholic Church, Compiled by the Benedictine Monks of St. Augustine's Abbey, Ramsgate* (London: Adam & Charles Black, 1921; fifth edition 1966), p. 133.

107 Ardfert Abbey, County Kerry was a two-storey late 17th century house with projecting side bays modernized in 1720 by Maurice Crosbie, first Lord Brandon, and again modified in 1830. In the present century it was demolished. See illustrations in Bence-Jones, *Burke's Guide*, P. 8.

108 This may have been a daughter foundation to Mellifont Abbey, established by St Malachy in 1143 on the banks of the Boyne near Drogheda. See de Breffny and Mott, *Churches and Abbeys*, pp. 47–8.

109 A bloomery is the name given to the first forge in an iron-works, through which the metal passes after it has been melted from the ore (*O.E.D.*).

110 Muckruss, County Kerry as it stands today is an Elizabethan-style house built in the 1840s to replace an earlier house. See illustration in Bence-Jones, *Burke's Guide*, p. 220. Of the the building Pococke saw nothing remains.

111 Kenmare House, County Kerry was built in the 1720s as a two-storey dwelling with dormered attics, to which an extra wing and other features were added in the 1770s. In the 1870s this structure was taken away, and a 'Tudor' mansion replaced it which was burnt to the ground in 1913. Stables were then converted into a third house (now called Killarney House). See illustrations in Bence-Jones, *Burke's Guide*, pp. 162–3.

112 Ross Castle was built on the island of Ross in the lower lake of Killarney in the late 14th century by the family of O'Donoghue-Ross. These were succeeded by the M'Carthy Mores, from whom the castle passed in 1588 to Sir Valentine Browne. In 1651 the castle was surrendered to Ludlow after a siege.

113 Ó Maidín reads 'ruines'.

114 Ó Maidín reads 'red ore'.

115 Mangerton rises 2,756 feet above sea level.

116 There is an illustration of this building in Grose, of which he writes: 'Though this is commonly now called Mucrus Abbey, its old appellation was Ivrelagh, or the Building on the lake' (*Antiquities* 2, p. 57).

117 Aghadoe is the site of a 7th century monastery founded by St Finian the Leper. It became part of the diocese of Ardfert and Aghdoe in the 12th century. See Harbison, *National Monuments*, p. 103,

118 Macroom Castle, County Cork was built in the 15th century, restored and modernized in the late 17th century, and in the 19th century reconstructed and redesigned. It was burnt in the present century and is now a ruin.

119 According to Charles Smith, this was a high tower built by the MacSwineys. See his *County of Cork*, 2 vols. New edition (Cork: printed by John Connor, 1815), 1, pp. 177–8.

120 Kinneigh round tower, County Cork, is 68 feet high with six storeys. It is unique in being hexagonal for its first 18 feet.

121 Ó Maidín reads 'and some houses',

122 Sir William Coxe founded a linen manufacture in Dunmanway in the reign of William III, when he was Lord Chancellor of Ireland. On Sir Richard Cox's improvements, see Gill, *Irish Linen Industry*, pp. 83–5. Cox's own account of the work is given in his Letter to Thomas Prior (1749).

123 Ballyna Carriga Castle, County Cork, though dated 1585 in a top floor window, is said to be older. It was built by Randal Hurley. The top floor was used as a church until 1815. See Harbison, *National Monuments*, p. 51.

124 Palace Anne, County Cork was built in 1714 as a three-storey house over a basement, with side wings. It suffered from neglect in the 19th century and is now a ruin. See illustrations in Banco-Jones, *Burke's Guide*, p. 230.

125 Charles Smith describes this former seat of the Earls of Clancarty, situated south of the river Bride, as a strong building with a dark marble staircase 70 feet high. See Smith, *County of Cork*, 1, pp. 200–201.

126 Kilcrea Franciscan Friary was founded by Cormac Laidír MacCarthy in 1465. On suppression, it was granted on lease to Sir Cormock MacCarthy in 1577. Cromwell's soldiers occupied it in 1650. Charles II granted it to Donough, first Lord Clancarty.

127 Castle Blarney was built from the 15th century onwards as a M'Carthy stronghold.

It was part of the estate confiscated and sold after the Williamite wars. See C.L. Adams, *Castles of Ireland* (London: Elliot Stock, 1904), pp. 57–62.

128 That is, a hanging ground. See 1752 tour, note 32 above.

129 Edmund Spenser (?1552–1599) was granted 3,000 acres of land after the crushing of the Desmonds in 1586. He spent eight years at Kilcolman Castle, and while there wrote three books of *The Faerie Queene*.

130 Marlfield, County Tipperary was an 18th century house of three-storeys joined to long, single-storey wings. The centre block was burnt but rebuilt in the 1920s. See illustration in Bence-Jones, *Burke's Guide*, p. 203.

131 Carlisle noted the remains of three ancient castles at Callan in 1810; it is not clear which one Pococke refers to. See Carlisle, *Topographical Dictionary*, 'Callan' (unpaged).

Tour of 1760

1 Woods omits the volume's title and the salutation, place and date of the letter.

2 See note 35 in 'Notes to Tour of 1752', p. 211 above.

3 Banbridge,

4 Woods reads 'houses fronted'.

5 Woods reads 'rock'.

6 Woods reads 'small town'.

7 Woods notes that twenty years earlier Walter Harris had observed (*County of Down*, p. 43) a thriving linen and bleaching manufacture in Banbridge.

8 Woods reads 'country'.

9 Moira Castle, County Down was a three-storey house built in the eighteenth century; it had single-storey wings at each end. It was demolished in the nineteenth century. See Bence-Jones, *Burke's Guide*, p. 208; Taylor and Skinner, *Maps of the Roads*, p. 282a.

10 See Taylor and Skinner, *Maps of the Roads*, p, 56.

11 Woods reads 'tithe'.

12 Woods notes that no coal deposits were found in County Down during the eighteenth century and suggests that Pococke may have mistaken the lead mine at Clonligg for a coal mine.

13 Woods reads 'tenure being'.

Bibliography

1. *Works by Richard Pococke*

Manuscript sources

Pococke, R., 'Copy of Dr. Pococke's Irish Tour 1752' (Trinity College Library, Dublin: MS 887)

———, 'A Copy of Bp. Pococke's tour in South and South-West Ireland, in a series of twenty letters, in July-Sept., 1758'(Bodleian Library, Oxford, Ms Top. Ireland d. 1 (30,722)).

———, 'Journal of Bishop Pococke's tours in Ireland, 1747 and 1752' (British Library, London. Add. Mss 23,001).

———, 'Journey round Scotland to the Orkneys, and through parts of England and Ireland, by R. Pococke, Bp of Ossory, in 1760. Notes of other tours by Pococke in England and from Ireland to Oxford, in 1736' (British Library, London: Add. Mss. 14,256-9).

Published sources

Pococke, R., 'An Account of the Giant's Causeway in Ireland, in a Letter to the President from the Rev. Richard Pococke, LL.D. Archdeacon of Dublin, and F.R.S.', *Philosophical Transactions of the Royal Society* 45 (1748), pp. 124–7.

———, 'A farther Account of the Giants Causeway in the County of Antrim in Ireland, by the Rev. Richard Pococke, LL.D. Archdeacon of Dublin, and F.R.S.', *Philosophical Transactions of the Royal Society* 48 (1753), pp. 226–37.

'Pococke's Journey through County Down in 1760', ed. by C.J. Woods, *Ulster Journal of Archaeology* 48 (1985), pp. 113–15.

'Pococke's Tour of South and South-West Ireland in 1758', ed. by Pádraig Ó Maidín, *Journal of the Cork Historical and Archaeological Society* 63 (1958), pp. 73–94; 64 (1959), pp. 35–56, 109–130; 65 (1960), pp. 130–141.

The Travels through England of Dr. Richard Pococke . . . 1750, 1751, and later, ed. by J.J. Cartwright (London: Camden Society, New Series volume XLII, 1888).

Tours in Scotland, 1747, 1750, 1760, by Richard Pococke, ed. by Daniel William Kemp (Edinburgh: Publications of the Scottish History Society, vol. 1, 1887).

Pococke's tour in Ireland in 1752, ed. by George T. Stokes (Dublin: Hodges, Figgis, and Co., and London: Simpkin, Marshall, Hamilton, Kent, and Co., 1892).

2. *Irish topographical writings: a selection*

Carlyle, Thomas, *Reminiscences of My Irish Journey in 1849* (London: Sampson, Low, Marston, Searle & Rivington, 1882).

Davies, Sir John, *A Discoverie of the true causes why Irlande was never entirely subdued* (London: Printed for John Jaggard, 1612, repr. Shannon: Irish University Press, 1969).

Dineley, Thomas, 'Extracts from the Journal of Thomas Dinely, giving some Account of his Visit to Ireland in the Reign of Charles II', ed. by E.P. Shirley, *Journal of the Royal Society of Antiquaries of Ireland* 4 (1856–57), pp. 143–6, 170–88; 5 (1858), pp. 22–32, 55–6; 7 (1862–3), pp. 38–52, 103–9, 320–38; 8 (1864–6), pp. 40–48, 268–90, 425–46; 9 (1867), pp. 73–91, 176–202; ed. by F.E. Ball, 43 (1913), pp. 275–309.

Dunton, John, *Teague Land, or a merry ramble to the Wild Irish*, ed. by E. MacLysaght (Dublin: Irish Academic Press, 1982).

Dodd, James Solas, *The Travellers' Director through Ireland* (Dublin: Printed by J. Stockdole, 1801).

Gerald of Wales (Giraldus Cambrensis), *The History and Topography of Ireland*, trans. by J.J. O'Meara (Harmondsworth: Penguin, 1982).

Harris, Walter, *A Topographical and Chorographical Survey of the County of Down* (Dublin pr., and repr. London: Tho. Boreman, 1740).

Harris, Walter, and Charles Smith, *The antient and present state of the County of Down* (Dublin: Edward Exshaw, 1744; repr. Ballynehinch: Arthur Davidson, 1977).

Luckombe, Philip, *A Tour through Ireland in 1779* (London: T. Lowndes, 1780).

Petty, William, *Hiberniae Delineatio, Atlas of Ireland* (London: 1685; repr. Newcastle: Frank Graham, 1968).

Petty, Sir William, *The Political Anatomy of Ireland*, ed. by John O'Donovan (Shannon: Irish University Press, 1970).

Smith, Charles, *The ancient and present state of the County and City of Cork* (Dublin: published by A. Reilly for the Author, and sold by J. Exshaw, Bookseller, on Cork Hill, 1750).

Smith, Charles, *The antient and present state of the county of Kerry* (Dublin: Printed for the author, 1756; repr. Cork: Mercier Press, 1969).

Smith, Charles, *The antient and present state of the county and City of Waterford* (Dublin: E. & J. Exshaw, 1746; repr. Cork: Mercier Press, 1969).

Spenser, Edmund, *A View of the Present State of Ireland*, ed. by W.L. Renwick (Oxford: Clarendon Press, 1935; repr. 1970).

Taylor, George, and Andrew Skinner, *Maps of the Roads of Ireland* (London: Published for the authors, 1778; introduced by Dr J.H. Andrews, Shannon: Irish University Press, 1969).

Twiss, Richard, *A Tour in Ireland in 1775* (London: Printed for the author, 1776).

Wesley, John, *The Journal of the Rev. John Wesley, A.M.*, ed. by Nehemiah Curnock, 8 vols (London: Culley, 1909–16).

Wilson, William, *The Post Chaise Companions; or, Traveller's Directory, through Ireland, containing a new & accurate description, etc.* (Dublin: Printed for the author, 1786).

Young, Arthur, *A Tour in Ireland: with general observations on the present state of that Kingdom: made in the years 1776, 1777 and 1778, and brought down to the end of 1779*, 2 vols. (London: T. Cadell and J. Dodsley, 1780).

3.   *Secondary works: a selection*

Adams, C.L., *Castles of Ireland* (London: Elliot Stock, 1904).

Bartlett, W.H., *The Scenery and Antiquities of Ireland, Illustrated in One Hundred and*

Twenty Engravings, from Drawings by W.H. Bartlett, 2 vols (London: James Virtue, [1842]).

Barrow, George Lennox, *The Round Towers of Ireland. A Study and a Gazetteer* (Dublin: The Academy Press, 1979).

Bence-Jones, Mark, *Burke's Guide to Country Houses, Volume 1. Ireland* (London: Burke's Peerage Ltd., 1978).

Book of Saints, The. A Dictionary of Servants of God Canonized by the Catholic Church, Compiled by the Benedictine Monks of St. Augustine's Abbey, Ramsgate (London: Adam & Charles Black, 1921; fifth edition 1966).

Brewer, J.N., *The Beauties of Ireland: Being Original Delineations, Topograghical, Historical, and Biographical, of each county* (London: Printed for Sherwood, Jones & Co., 1825).

Carlisle, Nicholas, *A Topographical Dictionary of Ireland* (London: Printed for William Miller, 1810).

de Breffny, Brien, and George Mott, *The Churches and Abbeys of Ireland* (London: Thames and Hudson, 1976).

de Paor, Liam, *The Peoples of Ireland from prehistory to modern times* (Notre Dame, Indiana: Hutchinson and University of Notre Dame Press, 1986).

Doherty, J.E., and D.J. Hickey, *A Chronology of Irish History since 1500* (Dublin: Gill and Macmillan, 1989).

Encyclopaedia of Ireland (Dublin: Allen Figgis, 1968).

Fackler, H.V., 'Wordsworth in Ireland 1829: a survey of his tour', *Éire-Ireland* 6 (1971), pp. 53–64.

Fisher, Jonathan, *A Picturesque tour of Killarney, describing, in twenty views, the most pleasing scenes of that celebrated lake, accompanied by some general observations* (London: O.G.J. and J. Robinson, 1789).

Frantz, Ray W., *The English Traveller and the Movement of Ideas, 1660–1732* (Lincoln, NE: University Studies of the University of Nebraska volumes 32, 33, 1934).

Freeman, T.W., 'John Wesley in Ireland', *Irish Geography* 8 (1975), pp. 86–96.

Gill, Conrad, *The Rise of the Irish Linen Industry* (Oxford: Clarendon Press, 1925).

Grose, Francis, *Antiquities of Ireland*, 2 vols (London: Printed for S. Cooper, 1791).

Hadfield, Andrew, and John McVeagh (eds.), *Strangers to that Land: British Perceptions of Ireland from the Reformation to the Famine* (Gerrards Cross, Bucks.: Colin Smythe Ltd., 1994).

Harbison, Peter, *Guide to the National Monuments of Ireland* (Dublin: Gill and Macmillan, 1970; repr. 1977).

Harrington, John P., *The English Traveller in Ireland: Accounts of Ireland and the Irish through five centuries* (Dublin: Wolfhound Press, 1991)

Hastings, James, *Encyclopaedia of Religion and Ethics*, ad. by James Hastings with the assistance of John A. Selbie and Louis H. Gray, 12 vols. plus Index (Edinburgh: T. & T. Clark and New York: Charles Scribner &Sons, 1918; repr, 1963).

Hayward, Richard, *In the Kingdom of Kerry* (Dundalk: Dundalgan Press, 1950).

Joyce, P.W., *Irish Names of Places* (Dublin: Cork, Belfast, Phoenix Publishing Co., 1913).

Leask, Harold G., *Irish Churches and Monastic Buildings*, 3 vols. (Dundalk: Dundalgan Press, 1958),

Ledwich, Edward, *Antiquities of Ireland*, second edition (Dublin: Printed by John Jones, 1803).

Lewis, Samuel, *A Topographical Dictionary of Ireland*, 2 vols. (London: S. Lewis & Co., 1837).

Moody, T.W., F.X. Martin and F.J. Byrne (eds.), *A New History of Ireland, IX Maps, Genealogies, Lists. A Companion to Irish History Part I* (Oxford: Clarendon Press, 1984).

National Monuments of Ireland, The (Dublin: published by Bord Fáilte Éireann, 1964).

Neale, John P., *View of the Seats of nobleman and gentlemen in England, Wales, Scotland and Ireland* 6 vols. (London: W.H. Reid, 1818–23).

O'Henlon, J., *Lives of Irish Saints*, 10 vols. (Dublin: James Duffy & Sons, London: Burns, Oates, and Co. and Yew York: The Catholic Publishing Co. 1875–1903).

Parks, G.B., 'The Turn to the Romantic in the Travel Literature of the Eighteenth Century', *Modern Language Quarterly* 25 (1964), pp. 22–33.

Patterson, Edward M., *The Ballycastle Railway. A History of the Narrow-Gauge Railways of North East Ireland: Part One* (Dawlish: David and Charles, 1965).

Petrie, George, *Picturesque Sketches of some of the finest landscapes and coast sconecy of Ireland, from the drawings of G. Petrie* (Dublin: A. Nicholl, and H, O'Neill, 1835).

Phillips, Walter Alison, *History of the Church of Ireland from the earliest times to the present day*, 3 vols. (London: Oxford University Press, 1933).

Quane, Michael, 'Pococke School, Kilkenny', *Journal of the Royal Society of Antiquaries of Ireland* 80 (1950), pp. 36–72,

Richardson, John, *The Local Historian's Encyclopaedia* (New Barnet: Historical Publications Ltd., 1974; repr. 1985).

Room, Adrian, *A Dictionary of Irish Place Names* (Belfast: Appletree P ress, 1986).

Stafford, Barbara Maria, 'Toward Romantic Landscape Perception: Illustrated Travel Accounts and the Rise of "Singularity" as an Aesthetic Category', *Art Quarterly*, new series I (1977), pp, 89–124,

Van Dusson, D. Gregory, 'Methodism and Cultural Imperialism in Eighteenth-Century Ireland', *Éire-Ireland* 23 (1988), pp. 19–37.

Index

Some placenames will also be found under
the entries for Castle, Charter School and Church.